Polemics

Polemics

ALAIN BADIOU
Part Two, Chapter 8 by Cécile Winter

Translated and with an Introduction
by
Steve Corcoran

VERSO
London • New York

Liberté • Égalité • Fraternité
RÉPUBLIQUE FRANÇAISE

This book is supported by the French Ministry of Foreign Affairs as part of the Burgess programme run by the Cultural Department of the French Embassy in London. (www.frenchbooknews.com)

This edition published by Verso 2006
© Verso 2006
Translation © Steve Corcoran 2006
'Part One' first published as *Circonstances 1* in 2003 © Editions Léo Scheer: Lignes et Manifestes 2003 and *Circonstances 2* in 2004 © Editions Léo Scheer: Lignes et Manifestes 2004; 'Part Two' first published as *Circonstances 3* in 2005 © Editions Léo Scheer: Lignes et Manifestes 2005; 'Part Three' first published as 'La commune de Paris' and 'La revolution culturelle' in 2003 © Les Conferences du Rouge-Gorge, Paris 2003

1 3 5 7 9 10 8 6 4 2

Verso
UK: 6 Meard Street, London W1F 0EG
USA: 180 Varick Street, New York, NY 10014-4606
www.versobooks.com

Verso is the imprint of New Left Books

ISBN-13: 978-1-84467-089-5
ISBN-10: 1-84467-089-9

British Library Cataloguing in Publication Data
A catalogue record for this book is available from the British Library

Library of Congress Cataloging-in-Publication Data
A catalog record for this book is available from the Library of Congress

Typeset in Baskerville by Hewer Text UK Ltd, Edinburgh
Printed in Colombia by Quebecor World

Contents

Part Two: Uses of the Word 'Jew'

Part Three: Historicity of Politics:
Lessons of Two Revolutions

Translator's Introduction

Steve Corcoran

This collection of Badiou's political essays brings together some of his pointed contributions to the resistance to today's general ideology, and to the preparation of the ground for future political invention. What general ideology? The rampant promotion of neo-liberal economics and the ethics of human rights, to be sure. The double discourse on democracy that says democracy is bad when it allows itself to be corrupted by demands for the equality of all and good when it rallies individuals to the war chant to spread itself across the globe, of course.[1] But also the ideology that says a political movement cannot be grounded in any reference to metaphysical truths or *a priori* universals, that philosophy cannot have a *bearing on* politics. The notion that the experience of our century, having proven that such references lead to totalitarian social consequences, that the Enlightenment results in the Gulag, requires that we accept, humbly, that in our complex 'risk societies' the only appropriate politics is one of the dialogue of interests, strategic judgement and expert management, precluding all notion of politics as the application of cognitive insight. On the contrary, Badiou maintains, it is fully possible, 'even' in today's conditions of global contingency, to revive a politics of universal truth.

As the name suggests, *Polemics* is not so much a general reflection on principles as it is an engagement with these forms of reaction as they have surfaced during a number of recent events.[2] Badiou launches a vigorous polemic against the forms of leftist melancholia, guarded reformism and right-wing offensive that all accept, in one way or another, the inevitability of the end of transformative revolutionary politics. As is necessary when past progressive sequences have been year in year out buried under masses of Thermidorian propaganda, the assertion of the existence of something whose visibility is altogether obscured will require a relentless critique of what passes for normality. And Badiou's work, as Peter Hallward remarks, is nothing if not polemical. But what distinguishes his thinking from that of other voices who today call into question the prevailing consensus is his insistence – against mere pragmatic assertions of what is or nostalgia for what once was – that the novelty of universal forms of affirmation can only ever take place as a rigorous *break* from the situation, a break with the norms governing everyday political existence.

Part One consists of a number of essays originally published in French as the first two volumes of a series called *Circonstances*.[3] Fittingly, then, we begin with an essay – originally the preface to the second volume – in which Badiou explains how he understands the relation between philosophy and circumstances, or the notion of a philosophical situation. This very accessible essay emphasizes that, for Badiou, philosophy is not just a discipline of general reflection on any phenomenon whatsoever. What imports is that philosophy can *produce* an encounter, one that sheds light on the irreducible distance between thought and power, that marks the value of the exception and seeks to know whether or not an event bears a rupture. The first terrain of investigation concerns the encounter between philosophy and war today. Essays on the September 11 2001 terrorist attacks in the US, on the American war against Iraq and on the NATO intervention against Serbia, all explore the nature of war and power in the world today. Following these come three articles dealing with parliamentary 'democracy' and racism, in which the question is to know whether or not the figures of racism and intolerance that (French) parliamentary democracy projects as external to it really are so. Is Le Pen really external to the French parliamentary scene? His very presence in the second round of France's presidential elections of 2002 suggests otherwise. Does the recent French law banning the wearing of headscarves in schools really reflect a concern that 'communitarianism' is encroaching upon the egalitarian ideals of the Republic? That the real effects of this law may result in the exclusion of young (Muslim) women from school suggests not. What then is really at stake? The third article is a shorter, more personal piece, originally published in *Le Monde* after the riots in the Parisian *banlieues* and throughout France in November 2005. In it Badiou recounts the daily humiliation that his own adopted son, who happens to be black, is forced to endure at the hands of that same Republic. The last section in Part One contains two essays that will not surprise those already familiar with the programmatic side of Badiou's philosophizing. The first essay articulates his bold plea for a political fusion of Germany and France, and the second comprises the latest version of his *Manifesto of Affirmationist Art*.

Part Two of *Polemics* was published in French as the third, and to date last, volume of the series: *Circonstances 3: Portées du mot 'juif'.*[4] It has been reproduced here in its entirety. The theme of this volume concentrates more specifically on questions of the political circulation of communal predicates, that is, the question of the status to be accorded to communal predicates in public intellectual discussion in general and on the current uses and appropriations of the word 'Jew' in particular. These texts, as Badiou underscores, are not texts 'on the Jewish question' – a question that would evoke a 'solution'. Instead, what is at issue is to know 'whether or not the "word" Jew constitutes an exceptional signifier in the general field of public intellectual discussion, exceptional to the point that it would be licit to have it play the role of a destinal, or even sacred, signifier'. The texts themselves come from a variety of sources – short essays, interviews, excerpts from literary and philosophical texts – published over a period of twenty-three years. Two more essays round off Part Two; one that is not by Badiou himself but by Cécile Winter, which originally comprised the annex of *Circonstances 3*. In this essay, Winter undertakes a provocative unravelling of the tortured history of the word 'Jew' in order that it might once more be restored to the infinite variability of its past. The other, entitled 'The Word "Jew" and the Sycophant', warrants a little explanation. This article was not part of the original volume, but was written by Badiou in response to the violent polemic provoked by the publication of *Circonstances 3*. Articles in *Le Monde* by Frédéric Nef and Roger-Pol Droit appeared shortly after the book's publication, acting to disqualify its main proposition by asserting that anything contrary to the Zionist promotion of 'Jews' as belonging to an essentially religious ahistorical substance is tantamount to racial anti-Semitism. An article in *Le Monde* by Daniel Bensaïd, defending Badiou's general thrust, put the context of the debate back into focus: it is indeed hard to deny the fact that the predicate 'Jew' has become 'marked by the usage the Nazis made of it; that Hitler indeed invested the name Jew, and that the genocide irreversibly branded it, to the point that its identity glorification can today appear as the inversion of this stigmata and the reproduction of this branding'.[5] So much so that it is of the utmost intellectual dishonesty to suggest that by so doing Badiou identifies, as his detractors make out, today's Israeli Jews with the Nazis! The censuring effects of such intellectual dishonesty are well-known and the reactions provoked by the book's publication merely confirm Badiou's above-mentioned reason for publishing it in the first place. Nonetheless, Bensaïd's intervention did not have the effect of warding off an improbable attack published in *Les Temps Modernes* by Eric Marty, in which Badiou stands accused of harbouring hidden intentions. 'The Word "Jew" and the Sycophant' is Badiou's response to this twenty-page trial.[6]

From critique to the Truth-Event

In Part Three we move on to two essays originally published as part of the Rouge-Gorge conferences, where what is at stake is not a critique of the conjuncture, but an attempt to construct a philosophical fidelity to two great sequences of political innovation: the Paris Commune and the Great Proletarian Cultural Revolution. Badiou's work has become well-enough known in English-speaking countries not to warrant making any detailed introduction to his thought.[7] Nevertheless, I shall make a few brief remarks here in order to situate these essays within Badiou's general project.

Very schematically, the fundamental distinction in Badiou's work is between Being and Event. The realm of Being is figured as the positive ontological order accessible to knowledge – as the infinite set of what presents itself to our experience, categorized in terms of species and genus. A situation is defined as a consistent multiplicity ('Paris after the Franco-German War in 1871'). It is a structured presentation but, Badiou argues, the *stuff* of what is so structured is nothing other than pure multiplicity *per se*. Nothing – or void – then, is the proper name of Being *qua* Being. Badiou's operational assumption then, is that inconsistent multiplicity lies always at the heart of consistency. It is quite simply the void of the situation, which from the standpoint of knowledge simply appears as nothing. Further, a situation is structured but it does not have the capacity to count its own structure; its being counted as one necessarily implies the metastructure that designates it as one, that re-presents it in the symbolic order. Such that, as Žižek puts it, 'when a situation is thus "counted as one", identified by its symbolic structure, we have the "state of the situation". (Badiou plays here on the ambiguity of the term state – "state of things" versus "State" in the political sense; there is no "state of society" without a "State" in which the structure of society is re-presented/ redoubled.)'[8] The knowledge of the situation provides the means for grouping its elements into parts, but it is the state of the situation that orders these elements into parts to which it gives a global organization. (The state is what organizes the multiplicity of elements into various tax-paying brackets, gives them a legal status, etc.) The state of the situation is what counts the count, as it were, through sanctioning a series of knowledges that serve to name, identify and index bodies to places. Because there are always more parts than elements, re-presentation is always in excess of pre-sentation, and it is this excess that, as Žižek again reminds us, accounts for why the liberal idea of a state reduced to the service of civil society will always remain a dream: it misses the fact that 're-presentation always act as a violent *intervention* into what it repre-sents'.[9]

In order to maintain this structure in dominance, certain elements must remain uncounted or excluded, elements that inhabit what Badiou calls the edge of the situation's void. The void cannot, of course, be localized or presented in the situation, it is scattered throughout it (the capitalist situation, for example, is structurally incapable of recognizing the capacity for proletarian innovation which inhabits everyone). But those on the *edge* of the void, those with 'nothing to lose but their chains', *are* situated in it, but as a sort of negative magnitude, the living lack of positive qualities that define the way the situation is re-presented. In Badiou's terms, then, they are presented in, and hence belong to, the situation, but are not re-presented in it. So long as the elements of a situation do not radically deviate from their assigned places, or lack thereof, this gap will normally not show. To the always total structure of knowledge, which knows neither void nor excess, this element will simply appear as a non-essential or contingent disturbance to the situation, not as a symptom of the structural 'lie' of the situation itself. From the standpoint of the state of the situation, this inconsistent multiplicity simply appears as nothing, as non-being. It is, of course, much more convenient, if your aim is to keep the dominant structure intact, simply to construe this inconsistency as the locus of 'evil' external to the situation. The theme of evil is the best way to avoid having to think the situation *from the standpoint of its void*, which is the only way, Badiou argues, to grasp the specificity of the situation. (The systematic recourse to evil among today's ideologues is just as disastrous as the refusal to think Nazism politically by positing it instead as an inexplicable evil.)

Grasping this specificity thus remains inaccessible to the totalizing structure of knowledge. What it knows of individuals in any given situation is the criteria they fulfil that helps to locate them in the situation: their scholastic aptitude, their social status, their tax bracket, their efficiency, and so on. But, what remains unknown, what is void for the situation, are those capacities which can appear in the situation only as unauthorized or unqualified, those qualities that can be presented but not re-presented with the terms structuring the situation.

Then, every so often, in a completely unpredictable fashion, a Truth-Event comes to pierce a hole in the totalizing, static structure of knowledge. An Event for Badiou is a properly contingent and unaccountable occurrence, exceeding everything that can be known in the situation – its identity conflicts, ideological struggles, fluxes of people and money, etc. An event cannot, Badiou argues, be generated nor deduced from the situation; but that it exceeds the terms of the situation does not mean that it arrives from some beyond or outside. There is no transcendence here; the Event attaches itself precisely to the void of the situation, revealing its inherent inconsistency.[10] To be sure, inherent inconsistency can never be presented or counted *as such* since it is properly meta-situational. But what can come to be counted, and what links each specific situation to this inconsistency, are those that inhabit the edge of the void. Politics, in so far as it is universal and democratic, is for Badiou a process that comes to count those who are uncounted. Stigmatizing the uncounted as backward, dangerous, etc., then, is the best way to ward off a more profound 'evil': the emergence of a popular subjective force that would be capable of opposing the sterility of comfortable self-perpetuation, capable of developing the latent possibilities for democratic action that are *immanent to the situation;* a subjective force that, as subtracted from all sociological categories and classifications ('illegal immigrants', 'citizens'), is grounded in the simple norm of belonging to the situation.

Badiou separates out from the always particular structure of Being an 'exceptional' realm of singular events that do not have any objective foothold in the situation, but which persist only through those individuals who constitute themselves *as* the *Subjects* of a Truth. The passage from the realm of Being to that of Truth demands a Subject which, in taking a wager on the Event ('the Revolution has begun', 'Workers are political beings too'), develops ways of maintaining a 'fidelity' to it. The Subject here is the collective agent which, as it were, serves the Truth of that situation by intervening in the particular historical multiple, identifying signs of the Truth-Event and drawing out its consequences. It demonstrates the Truth of what the previous situation simply dismissed with collectively sanctioned labels (social difficulties caused by 'communist infiltrators', 'illegal immigrants'). And by so doing it demonstrates the lie that sustained the preceding situation ('Capitalism i.e. the logic of profit, is simply an objective basis for progress').

In so far as, for Badiou, the power of the state is precisely the power of the count, the power of the truth-procedure that follows an Event lies in its capacity to construct a set of elements – this is its goal – that challenges the hierarchical structure of the situation, a set whose sole norm is the pure belonging of the elements to the situation. In times when the count of the state is unchallenged, the effective ontological closure means that the sphere of politics will always *consensually* appear to be localized in the State, as a matter of looking after the affairs of the 'political community'. With exceptional rigour, Badiou shows that, on the contrary, *democratic* politics, properly speaking, is never simply about managing collections of specified individuals or groups. Nor is it about a state of the social as if there were such a thing as democratic 'society'. It is about the presentation of the collective itself as *indivisible*. And this presentation, since the general interest always opposes dominant, particular interests, is inevitably *divisive*.[11]

Both the Paris Commune and Cultural Revolution represent events of this kind. In these essays, Badiou's concern is to grasp the *historicity* specific to the invention of egalitarian political forms, and the lessons that they have bequeathed to future political invention. Why discuss these events now? Of the reasons for focussing on these events in the present conjuncture I shall mention two.

The first concerns the historicity of truth-events themselves; the question of how we are placed with respect to the lessons of past truths, and, in particular, with respect to the vexing question of the status of the political organization. The second reason has to do with the fact that the Paris Commune is an especially vivid example of the organization of a proletarian political capacity that did not allow itself to be appropriated by representative forms. For this reason, it provides Badiou with the perfect material for his most recent work, which concerns not so much the way the Truth-event punctures a hole in the knowledge of the existing situation, but the way that the onto-logy of situations transforms, that is, the way the elements of the situation transform in the intensity of their *appearing*.

The historicity of truth-events

The historicity of political sequences is not to be understood in the historicist sense, i.e. as something that can be explained by the indwelling relations of power and knowledge comprising the situation. We know that one of the chief characteristics of ideology is precisely that it involves dissolving the punctuality of the event in the *longue durée* of mechanist change, on the one hand; and on the other of compacting its advent and its corruption together into a single inevitable disaster, as though Lenin always leads to Stalin.

François Furet's work on the French Revolution is exemplary in this regard. In contrast to historicism, historicity proper is the time proper to the always unpredictable, incalculable event, the time spanning the event's beginning and its ultimate end. It is the time that begins with a wager, proceeds, by drawing the consequences of that decision, through a series of chance-ridden investigations and ends when it is finally exhausted, betrayed or overturned.

If the historicity of an event is the time that an event genuinely opens or founds, then what can be the present justification for returning to the Commune? In the 'classical interpretation' of the Commune, that initiated by Marx, homage is paid to it but its failure is seen as ensuing from the weakness of its political forms, from its incapacity to take over the more centralized functions of state. Marx, Engels, Lenin, Stalin, Brecht and Mao, are all in agreement on this point. Indeed, it was in response to the perceived weaknesses of the Commune that Lenin would propose the solution of a more enduring party instance that would 'dominate the way to non-domination'.

Instead of lauding the Commune for its innovation of political forms and social issues, for its principled stances, but deploring its failure as a failure to take over more centralized operations of state, Badiou sees in *this* failure its real import: the radicality of a structural gap between political invention and the state. If the history of revolutionary movements (1830, 1848, 1870, 1968) in France has been one of rupture and then quick reabsorption and betrayal by state representatives, then the Commune is what for the first and, to this day, only time succeeded in breaking with this apparent destiny: the idea that the social movements must be represented by a parliamentary 'Left'. The contemporary interest of the Paris Commune, then, lies for Badiou not only in the way its subjective force presented itself or separated itself out from the ordinary rules according to which things are distinguished in a given situation, but also from the way it refused to be incorporated within the existing institutions of state.

What about the Cultural Revolution, then? Has it not long ago been discredited as simply a violent struggle for power within the top echelons of the party? A struggle that Mao, after the failure of economic voluntarism and his loss of influence in the party, was unable to win without a chaotic and violent recourse to popular forces? Badiou argues that for all its violence and radicality, and the cruel failure of the Great Leap Forward, the Cultural Revolution is the political sequence that takes the radical ambiguity of the classical interpretation and solution of the unresolved problems of the Paris Commune to its extreme. As the instance that is supposed to lead the way to a non-state society (the theme of revolution) but that is also devoted to taking over centralized functions of state, the party apparatus, in the last analysis, is never able to maintain the gap between political innovation and functions of state – never able to free itself from the state. The Cultural Revolution clearly shows that of the two it is, in the last instance, always the latter that ends up imposing itself on the former. Badiou seeks to show that the Cultural Revolution is the last significant political sequence that is internal to the party-state. What it demonstrates is nothing other than the point of saturation of the classic Marxist–Leninist interpretation of the Commune – a saturation that it accomplished, if you will, for politics to be thinkable today outside of the party-state.

The onto-logy of the situation

In the terms of *Being and Event,* what the Paris Commune succeeded in doing was making pure presentation, i.e. pure and simple belonging to a situation irrespective of all cultural predicates, the principle of its politics. It succeeded in rupturing with all relation and creating a new set that was *subtracted* from the existing classifications and nominations structuring the preceding situation. Badiou's more recent work does not go back over this point, but sets out to grasp the way that an event comes to transform the *logic* of the situation, that is, the way that its elements *appear* in it or the intensity with which they are endowed. For not having any objective foothold in the situation, a truth will succeed in imposing itself on the situation only in so far as it manages to transvaluate the intensity of its elements – or come to impose a different regime for their *appearing*. So, a truth proceeds as a subtraction from the classifications and distributions of the state, but it does so by altering the appearing, or the intensity, of the elements constituting the situation. As Peter Hallward says, 'the key point of reference remains the anarchic disorder of inconsistent multiplicity';[12] but because the *being* of the situation must also be made to be *there* (i.e. experienced as connected, related) it must always be made subject to the logical constraints of a particular situation. As Badiou figures it, these logical constraints mean that there will always be, in any situation, elements that exist *maximally* (politically speaking, those whose voices are sanctioned, whose speech leads to action), elements that are less intense, and elements that, like those on the edge of the void, are effectively invisible (whose speech registers as pure noise, and who as such constitute the 'non-existent' element of this situation).

This distinction between maximally and minimally existing members enables us to account, amongst other things, for the stakes of public discussion about communal predicates. The maximally existing members of this situation appear to embody the (economic, educational, linguistic, etc.) criteria that structure the situation to greater perfection than others. In France in 1871, for example, it is clear that some things – industrialists, bourgeois politicians, the Vendôme Column – appear incontestably more French than others, which nonetheless also belong to the situation: worker organizations, internationalist elements, disaffected literati, etc. At a given point in time, what it means for a situation to be French will involve the degree to which certain things appear in the situation: the degree to which, for example, religion should be included as an integral part of state declarations and educational institutions, the extent to which workers are seen as being able to participate in decisions affecting the community, the allowance made for women's demands for equal rights, the adherence of a country to the principles of international law, to the principle of fraternity, and so on.

In his recent work, Badiou figures the truth-event not just as the eruption of being in the situation but as an emergence that transforms in a revolutionary manner the logic structuring the appearing of bodies in the situation. When Terry Eagleton calls the Paris Commune 'that most *political* of revolutions' he touches upon something essential. The way Eagleton sees it, this peculiarly political quality arises from the fact that the Commune's 'seizing of the streets was not about using the streets as a front-line of defence of the seizure of capital, as about the streets themselves; it was not so much a revolt within the means of production, rooted in factory soviets and a revolutionary proletarian party, but a trans-formation of the means of everyday life itself'.[13] For what is of key interest in the Paris Commune is something it shows all the more clearly for *not* attempting to take over the operations of the state: that it is not, in a sense, the taking hold of the reins of state in the name of the proletariat that is most revolutionary, but rather, the way a truth process imposes a revolutionary change on the logic structuring the situation. Badiou's work on the onto-logy of the situation is an attempt precisely to give us the formal means[14] to understand the nature of such revolutions of everyday life and why, in a way that is not determined in advance by any preformed party apparatus, they open onto the sort of investigations they do.

Prior to the Paris Commune, for example, the situation is one of a country at the end of a long war: a visibly divided world with, on the one hand a set of maximally existing elements, i.e., everything appearing in the sphere of consecrated political power – the Prussian occupiers, the Assembly of traditionalist Rurals, Theirs' *capitulard* Republican regime, and a regular army spoiling for a fight with the mainly working-class National Guard. The other half of this divided world is what appears outside this sphere – a chaotic mix of Parisian worker organizations, the Federation of trade unions, local military committees, the Central Committee of the National Guard, and so on.

This world is split, but there is one thing holding it together, one thing that *both* sides share or consent to, namely, the assumption of the political *incapacity* of the workers. On the side of established power, there is fear, and so visibility, of the workers and people as an unruly, irrational mass. But within the terms structuring the situation, there can be no recognition of their *political significance*. By contrast, Badiou demonstrates that when, on the side of the workers, a decision is taken to end betrayal, to take matters into their own hands and to follow through on the proclamation of the Commune by creating, out of this inconsistent grouping internal to the situation, properly political forms of proletarian discipline and organization, these previously politically non-existent workers come to exist *absolutely*, in their own right. In a process that takes place independent of the norms of state, they are called upon to proceed to elections and occupy government. It is from then on that the new non-existent term of the situation becomes, on the contrary, the political *incapacity* of workers. In its apparent failure, what the Commune bequeathed to the future was an 'unheard-of transcendental evaluation of the political scene'. That is why the Paris Commune would, starting with Marx and Lenin, come to inspire a century of political innovation.

If the Commune made exemplarily clear the structural gap between political innovation and state representation, it can be said that the Commune is *still* present, still with us to the extent that it is liable to furnish us with inspiration for the creation of new political alternatives right here and now.[15] Its example makes explicitly clear how a true political event today would necessarily attach itself to those whose political capacity constitutes the non-existent term of our consensual 'democratic' states. As measured against the Paris Commune, our prevailing consensus looks less like an exchange between partners rationally discussing their interests, than the intolerable arrogance of an oligarchy whose main aim is to ward off the possibility that, according to the norms of radical equality, anyone at all might appear in the place of politics.

It is more important than ever to emphasize this gap today, when the sole criterion of democracy is usually taken to be the representative system. The amalgam 'representative democracy' is not a form of government necessary to our socially, economically and technologically complex societies – this is historicism at its most conservative. 'Representative democracy' is the political form that has come to prevail more or less unimpeded thanks to the weakening of egalitarian inventiveness and a general submission to the blind power of the economy. There is no necessary link between political forms and states of society. Instead, there are situations: situations which must be thought of with respect to that which is in radical exception, that is, in relation to events that are singular in their occurrence but universally addressed. Only a thinking of the *political* specificity of situations is capable of undoing the suffocating identification of democracy with the representative system, by working to reveal the double movement of separation and appropriation (and betrayal) that more often than not befalls egalitarian innovation. Against this closure, against the chorus of voices that fashionably dismiss the 'essentialism of the proletariat', it is necessary to reaffirm one of Marx's key ideas: that of a force of a subjective intervention adequate to a process – the logic of Capital – that puts an end to all 'feudal, patriarchal, and idyllic' relations, an intervention that goes on to formalize 'above and beyond the merely negative force of Capital', a collective power that operates at an irreducible distance from the limitless movement of wealth.

Badiou's philosophical system and the diagnoses stemming from it that you are about to read are very compelling. They represent, perhaps, one of the forms of affirmative thinking that is most resistant, most heterogeneous to the consensus that reigns – though

 9 Žižek, 'Psychoanalysis and Post-Marxism'.
10 And it is precisely because an Event cannot arrive from the exterior of a situation that, for example, neither the 'democratic' military intervention in Iraq, nor the destruction of the Twin Towers can qualify as events.
11 For elaborations of his conception of politics post *Being and Event* see Badiou's *Metapolitics*. For the implications that Badiou's conception of politics has for thinking ethics see his *Ethics: An Essay on the Understanding of Evil*, Verso, 2001 [1998].
12 See his introduction to *Think Again: Alain Badiou and the Future of Philosophy*, Continuum, 2004, p. 10.
13 See his preface to Kristin Ross's *The Emergence of Social Space: Rimbaud and the Paris Commune*, University of Minnesota Press, 1988, p. ix.
14 For a more complete discussion of these formal means, the reader should consult Badiou's *Logiques des Mondes*, Le Seuil, 2006.
15 This implies an account of *inter-evental* causality to rival Walter Benjamin's more redemptive account.

Acknowledgements

I would like to thank all those who helped with the project: Jasmin Mersmann for her ever ebullient and supportive discussions; Brian Corcoran, Gene Ray, Sarah Rice and Andrew Watts for their very helpful comments on various sections of the translation, and Sebastian Budgen for his fastidious editorial work. Last but not least, I would like to thank Alain Badiou himself for his ongoing support and encouragement.

Part One:
Philosophy and Circumstances

Introduction

This text is extracted from the transcription of the beginning of a seminar held at the Alliance française in Buenos Aires at the invitation of Gerardo Yoel. The overall theme of the seminar was 'cinema and philosophy'. In it I tried to show in what sense cinema can present a philosophical situation. An earlier version of the text was given as part of an amicable encounter with Slavoj Žižek at the invitation of the Institut français in Vienna.

What is a philosophical situation? What do circumstances propose to us that is relevant to philosophical examination? Certainly not just anything at all. Certainly not – as Guy Lardreau maintains – any discourse, any assertion, excepting those of 'grand politics'. I propose the following abstract definition: a situation is philosophical, or 'for' philosophy, when it forces the existence of a relation between terms that, in general, or in common opinion, can have no relation to each other. A philosophical situation is an encounter. It is an encounter between essentially foreign terms.

I shall give three examples.

The first example is already, I might say, philosophically formatted. It may be found in Plato's dialogue, *Gorgias*. This dialogue presents an extremely forceful encounter between Socrates and Callicles. A philosophical situation is created by this encounter, which is, besides, arranged in a totally theatrical fashion. Why? Because the thought of Socrates and that of Callicles have no common denominator. They are two types of thought that are totally foreign to one another. The discussion between Callicles and Socrates is presented by Plato in such a way as to make us understand what it is to have two different kinds of thought that, like the diagonal and the side of a square, remain incommensurable. The discussion consists in a relation between two terms without any relation. Callicles maintains that right is force, that the happy man is a tyrant – he who wins others over with cunning and violence. Socrates maintains that the true man, identified with the happy man, is just, in the philosophical sense of the term. Now, between justice as violence and justice as thought, there is no simple opposition, i.e. one that can be dealt with by means of arguments submitted to a common norm. Any real relation is lacking. As it so happens, then, the discussion is not a discussion. It is a confrontation. And what becomes clear to everyone while reading the text is not that one will convince the other, but that there will be a winner and a loser. This further explains why Socrates' methods in this dialogue are hardly fairer than Callicles'. Where there is a will there is a way; what is at stake is to win, and especially to win over the minds of the youths who witness the scene.

Callicles is eventually defeated. He doesn't acknowledge defeat, but becomes mute and remains in his corner. Note that he is the loser in a theatrical dialogue by Plato. Here we have probably one of the rare occurrences where someone like Callicles is defeated. Such are the joys of theatre.

As regards this situation, what does philosophy consist in? The unique task of philosophy here is to show us that we must choose, that we must choose between these two forms of thought. We must choose either to be with Socrates or to be with Callicles. In this example, philosophy confronts thinking as choice, thinking as decision. Its proper task is to make the choice clear. Hence, we can say: a philosophical situation involves the moment in which a choice is proclaimed – a choice of existence, or a choice of thinking.

Second example: the death of a mathematician, Archimedes. Archimedes is one of the greatest minds ever known to humanity. To this day, his mathematical texts amaze. He is someone who had already reflected upon the infinite; he practically invented infinitesimal calculus twenty centuries before Newton. He was an exceptional genius.

Archimedes was a Sicilian Greek when Sicily was invaded and occupied by the Romans. He participated in the resistance and invented new war machines, but the Romans finally won out. Once the Roman occupation began, Archimedes took up his activities again. He was in the habit of drawing geometrical figures in the sand. One day, as he was thinking on the beach, using complicated figures traced on the shore, a Roman soldier arrived, a sort of liaison officer, telling him that the Roman General Marcellus wanted to see him. The Romans were very curious about the Greek thinkers, a little like the CEO of a cosmetics multinational might be curious about a philosopher of renown. So General Marcellus wanted to see Archimedes. Between us, I don't think that it could be said that General Marcellus was proficient in mathematics. Simply, and it is an honour to his curiosity, he wanted to see what a *résistant* such as Archimedes was like. Hence the liaison officer on the beach. But Archimedes didn't budge. The soldier repeated: 'General Marcellus wants to see you.' Archimedes still did not respond. The Roman soldier, who can't have been terribly conversant with mathematics either, couldn't comprehend that someone might disregard an order from the General Marcellus. 'Archimedes! The General wants to see you!' Archimedes looked up slightly and said to the soldier: 'Let me finish my demonstration.' The soldier responded: 'What, are you going on with "your demonstration"? Marcellus wants to see you!' Without responding, Archimedes resumed his calculations. After a certain time, the soldier, by now absolutely furious, drew his sword and struck him. Archimedes fell dead, his body effacing the geometrical figure in the sand.

Why is that a philosophical situation? Because it expresses the following: that between the right of state and creative thought, especially the pure ontological thought embodied in mathematics, there is no common denominator, no real discussion. In the end, power is violence, whereas creative thought knows no constraint other than its own immanent rules. In the law of his thought, Archimedes remains outside of the action of power. The time proper to mathematical demonstrations is unable to integrate into its process the urgencies and the summons of military victors. This is why violence was ultimately used – proof of the fact that there is no common denominator, and no common chronology, between power, on the one hand, and truths, on the other: truths as creation.

Let's recall in passing that at the end of the Second World War when the American Army was occupying the suburbs of Vienna, a GI killed, seemingly without recognizing him or being aware of who he was, the greatest musical genius of the time, the composer Anton Webern. An accident. An accidentally philosophical situation. Let's say that between truths and power there is a distance, which is the distance between Marcellus and Archimedes. It is a distance that the liaison officer, no doubt an obtuse but disciplined soldier, did not succeed in crossing. Philosophy, in this instance, has a mission to shed light on this distance. It must reflect upon and think the distance without measure, or the distance whose measure philosophy itself must invent.

First definition of the philosophical situation: clarify the choice, the decision. Second definition of the philosophical situation: clarify the distance between power and truths.

My third example is a film, an astonishing film by the Japanese director Mizoguchi called *The Crucified Lovers*. It is without a doubt one of the most beautiful films about love ever made.

The nature of the film's story is extremely commonplace. It is set in classical Japan, whose plastic qualities, especially in black and white, seem inexhaustible. A young woman is married to the proprietor of a small workshop, an honest man who lives in affluence. He is a bit of a drunkard, and a bit of a womanizer, not in a nasty way, but she doesn't love him, doesn't desire him. Enter a young man, an employee, with whom she falls in love. Obviously, in these classical times, whose women Mizoguchi exalted for their endurance and misfortune, adultery is punished by death: the guilty must be crucified. The two lovers end up fleeing into the countryside. This sequence, which depicts their flight into the forest, into the world of paths, of cabins, of lakes and of boats, is absolutely extraordinary. Love, itself tormented by its own power over this hunted and harassed couple, is enveloped in a nature as opaque as it is poetic. All the while, the honest husband tries to protect the runaways. Husbands are obliged to denounce adulterers, otherwise they come to rue being held a party to it. Nevertheless, the husband, and this is proof that he loves his wife deeply, tries to gain time. He pretends that his wife has left for her parents' place in the provinces . . . He really is a good husband. He is a very beautiful character in the film, of a dense mediocrity. But all the same the lovers are denounced and captured. They are taken to be tortured.

Finally, we come to the film's last images, which constitute a new instance of a philosophical situation. The two lovers are tied back to back on a mule. The shot frames the two bound lovers going to their atrocious deaths; both of them are as if rapt, but without pathos: on their faces is simply the hint of a smile, a kind of fortification in the smile. The word 'smile' here is only an approximation. What their faces reveal is that they are totally in their love. But the film's thought here, embedded in the infinitely nuanced black and white of the faces, is not at all the romantic idea of a fusion of love and death. These 'crucified lovers' never desired to die. The shot says, on the contrary: love is that which resists death.

At a conference at the Femis,[1] Deleuze, citing Malraux, said that art is something that resists death. Well, precisely, in those magnificent shots, the art of Mizoguchi not only resists death but gives us to understand that love also resists death. In doing this, he creates a tacit agreement between love and art, which is something that we know has existed for a long time.

What I refer to here as the 'smile' of the lovers, for lack of a better word, is a philosophical situation. Why? Because once more we come across the incommensurable, the relation without relation. That is, we see that between the event of love – the turning upside-down of existence – and the ordinary rules of life – the laws of the city and the laws of marriage – there is no common denominator. What will philosophy say to us? It will say: 'We must think the event.' We must think the exception. We must know what we have to say about that which is not ordinary. We must think change in life.

So, we can sum up the tasks of philosophy in relation to situations as follows:

1. Clarify the fundamental choices of thought. And such choice is 'in the last instance' (as Althusser would say) always a choice between that which is interested and that which is disinterested.
2. Clarify the distance between thought and power, that is, the distance between the state and truths. Measure this distance. Know if it can or cannot be crossed.
3. Clarify the value of the exception, of the event, of rupture. Moreover, do so against the continuity of life and against social conservatism.

Such are the three great tasks of philosophy: deal with choices, distances and exceptions. Or we should say, such are the tasks of philosophy as soon as it counts for something in life, for something other than an academic discipline. Further, and more profoundly, philosophy, confronted with such circumstances, seeks the link between the three types of situations: it seeks the link between a choice, a distance and an exception. A philosophical concept, in Deleuze's sense, that is as a creation, is, I maintain, always that which knots together a problem of choice (or of decision), a problem of distance (or of gap), and a problem of exception (or of event).

The most profound philosophical concepts say something like: 'If you want your life to have meaning, it is imperative that you accept the event, that you remain at a distance from power, and that you hold resolutely to your decision.' This is the story that philosophy is forever telling us, in all kinds of ways: be in the exception, in the sense of event; keep a distance from power; and accept the consequences of a decision, however remote and difficult they may be.

Understood in this way, and only in this way, philosophy really is something that helps to change existence.

Following Rimbaud, it is often said that 'true life is elsewhere'. Philosophy is not worth an hour's effort if it is not committed to the fact that the true life be present. As regards circumstances, true life is presented in choices, in distances and in events.

Yet, on the side of circumstances, one should not lose sight of the fact that a choice is forced upon us to arrive at the thought of the true life; and this choice, as I have said, is grounded in the sole criterion of incommensurability.

Uniting our three examples, then, is the fact that they are founded on a relation between heterogeneous terms: Callicles and Socrates; the Roman soldier and Archimedes; and the lovers and society.

Any philosophical rapport with a situation will thus involve staging an impossible relation; it is like a story we are told. We are told about the discussion between Callicles and Socrates, about the murder of Archimedes, about the story of the crucified lovers.

Hence, we are told about a relation between two elements. But at the same time the narrative establishes that this relation is not a relation, that it is a negation of all relations. So much so that what we are ultimately told about is a rupture: a rupture with natural and socially established relations. Of course, in order to relate a rupture it is necessary to relate a relation. Yet, ultimately, such a story is about rupture. A choice must be made between Callicles and Socrates. It is imperative to break absolutely with one of the two. Similarly, if you side with Archimedes, you cannot side with Marcellus. Or again, if you voyage with the lovers right until the end, then you will never again side with the rule of conjugality.

So it can be said that philosophy, which is thought, not about what is, but about what is not – thought, not about contracts but about ruptures of contracts – is exclusively interested in relations that are not relations.

Long ago, Plato said that philosophy implies an awakening. And he knew perfectly well that awakening implies a difficult rupture with sleep. As it was for Plato, and will always be, philosophy is what consists in the seizure by thought of what breaks with the sleep of thought.

So it is legitimate to think that each time there is a paradoxical relation, that is, a relation that is not a relation, or a situation of rupture, then philosophizing is possible.

I insist on this point: it is not because there is 'something' that philosophy exists. Philosophy does not simply involve reflecting upon anything at all. Philosophy is possible because there are paradoxical relations, or because there are ruptures, or because there are decisions, distances and events.

Regarding the following essays, the reader might well wonder whether I am justified in philosophizing on the basis of the circumstances they depict. Is the American attack on Iraq paradoxical? Does it contain a violent rupture? And what can we say about the historical couple, more spiritual than material, formed by Germany and France? A speculative paradox? And between the affirmative value of art and certain contemporary aestheticizing sophists, who deconstruct affirmation for the sake of exclusively critical profit, is there not something subtracted from all measure?

And as for the 'law on the Islamic headscarf', does it not indicate that a number of France's intellectuals have lost all sense of the world in which they profess to live?

On these various points, let the reader examine my arguments.

Philosophy and the
Question of War Today

1

On September 11 2001: Philosophy and the 'War against Terrorism'

Method

The destruction of New York's Twin Towers by planes whose passengers and neo-pilots – those assassinating impostors – were transformed into incendiary projectiles brought about everywhere a particular affect. Even for those who more or less secretly celebrated – an extremely numerous crowd, some hundreds of millions of enemies of the lugubrious and solitary American superpower – it nonetheless amounted to an unbelievable mass crime. 'Attack' is an inappropriate word; it evokes the nihilist bombings of the Tsar's coaches, or the attack of Sarajevo. It has a *fin de siècle* ring to it, but is of another century. At the beginning of this millennium, the self-evidence of that affect registers the extraordinary combination of violence, calm, quiet relentlessness, organization, indifference to destruction, agony and fire that is required in today's technologically sophisticated conditions to bring about the death of many thousands of everyday people and workers deep in the heart of a great metropolis. It was an enormous murder, lengthily premeditated, and yet silent. No one claimed responsibility for it. For these reasons, we can say that formally speaking this mass crime, which aimed indiscriminately, and with the most perfect cruelty, to destabilize blindly a 'normal' situation, conjures up the fascist concept of action. Consequently, throughout the world, and regardless of the immediate condition – devastated or complicit – of one's soul, there was a numbing stupefaction, a kind of paroxysmally denied disbelief: the affect signalling a disaster.

Philosophy must certainly register this prime evidence of affect. Yet it has a duty never to be satisfied with it. Religion might proclaim to have faith in the self-evidences of the heart, while art, as Gilles Deleuze says, gives form to percepts and affects. Philosophy, for its part, must – this is its arid objective – come to the concept, no matter how traumatic the affect being opened up to investigation or placed under construction might be.

So, suggesting itself to philosophical labour is a second kind of self-evidence, not that pertaining to the affect, but that pertaining to a name: 'terrorism'. This nominal self-evidence (that the mass crime of New York, signalled by the affect of the disaster, is a terrorist action) has played a decisive role. In fixing the designated enemy, it has cemented a world coalition, authorized the UN to declare that the US is in a state of 'self-defence', and enabled the programming of the targets of vengeance. More significantly, the word 'terrorism' here has had a threefold function:

First, it has determined a subject; that is, the one targeted by the terrorist act, the one who has been struck, is full of bereavement, and must lead a vengeful riposte. This subject has been referred to, depending upon the preference, as 'our societies', 'the West', 'the democracies', or even as 'America' – but the last only at the price, paid for quickly by the editorialists, that 'we' are 'all American'.[2]

Second, it supports predicates. On this occasion, the terrorism will be 'Islamic'.

And third it has determined the sequence under way in its entirety, henceforth called that of the 'war against terrorism'. We've been informed that it will be a long war. An entire era. In short, the 'war against Islamic terrorism' replaces the Cold (and Hot: Korea, Vietnam, Cuba . . .) War against communism.

Here, once again, philosophy, when it registers as important a symptom as the widespread self-evidence of the word 'terrorism', has the duty to examine its origin and its impact.

Simply, there are two rules to the method. First, philosophy must not be transitive to affect, no matter how widely accepted it might be. A crime is a crime, agreed. But the consequences of a crime, even one that is formally fascistic, should not mechanically lead to other crimes. And this designation ('crime') should equally be applied to state crimes, including those – innumerable – committed by 'democratic' states. For, ever since Aeschylus' *Oresteia*, so for a long time, we've known that the question is to know how to replace violence with justice.

Second, philosophy does not accept dominant names without critical examination, irrespective of how commonly held they are. We know that these designations are under the control of the established powers and their propaganda.

Hence we shall undertake a meticulous examination of labels. Our point of departure is the central label, 'terrorism'. Then, on the basis of this, we will engage in a critique of the triplet of the predicate ('Islamic'), the subject ('the West') and the sequence ('the war against terrorism').

Terrorism?

Originally, a 'terrorist' was one who legitimated and practised Terror (*la Terreur*). It was an objective designation, defamatory only for political adversaries. Hence, the great Jacobins of the Committee for Public Safety during the French Revolution declared themselves to be 'terrorists' pure and simple. They placed Terror officially 'on the agenda'. They designated therewith a comprehensive and provisional unity of political and judicial power, as justified by exceptional circumstances (civil war and war); the repressive deployment of expeditious measures without appeal;

and widespread recourse to the death penalty. Terror was explicitly thought of as a contingent necessity (Robespierre was known for his categorical and principled opposition to the death penalty) when the political virtue – that is, the republican conviction – was still too precarious to ensure victory over the enormous coalition of foreign and national counter-revolutionaries. As Saint-Just asked: 'What do those who want neither terror nor virtue really want?' The Thermidorians gave the response: the end of the revolution, the reign of corruption, and suffrage only for the wealthy.

It is remarkable that the word 'terrorism', which clearly qualified a particular figure of the exercise of state power, has succeeded, little by little, in coming to signify exactly the contrary. Indeed, for a long time now the word 'terrorist' has been used by states to designate all violent and/or armed political adversaries precisely in view of their non-state character. We may list as examples: the Russian terrorists of Narodnaia y volia at the end of the nineteenth century; the anarchist tradition, including the Bande à Bonnot in France; and the character of Chen, in *Man's Fate*, who personifies the decision of the suicide mission, to which Malraux accords, although without justifying it politically, a terrible grandeur. The word has finally come – and it's here that it takes on a negative connotation – to designate, from the viewpoint of the dominant, anyone who, using whatever means available, commits to a combat against the prevailing order that the latter judges to be unacceptable. For Pétain and his militia anti-Nazi resistors were 'terrorists'; for every French government without exception between 1954 and 1962 the Algerian patriots of the National Liberation Front were 'terrorists', just as the Palestinian fighters are for the State of Israel, and the Chechens for Putin and his clique; and lastly, just as the nebulous (or at least extremely opaque) group of those who take the goods and lives of Americans are 'terrorists' for Bush and his servile, opinionated, patriotic following.

It must be said that today, at the end of its semantic evolution, the word 'terrorist' is an intrinsically propagandistic term. It has no neutral currency. It dispenses with all reasoned examination of political situations, their causes and their consequences.

In fact it has become an essentially formal term. 'Terrorist' no longer designates either a political orientation or the possibilities inherent to such and such a situation; rather, it exclusively designates the form of action. And it does so according to three criteria: such action is, for public opinion and those concerned with shaping it, first and foremost a spectacular, non-state action that emerges from clandestine networks, whether in reality or in myth; secondly, it is a violent action aiming to kill and/or destroy; lastly, it is an action in which no distinction is made between civilians and non-civilians.

This formalism goes hand in hand with Kant's moral formalism. That is the reason why a 'moral philosophy' specialist such as Monique Canto-Sperber believed she could declare that the absolute condemnation of 'terrorist' actions and the symmetrical approval of reprisals, including those of Sharon in Palestine, could and should precede any critical examination of the situation, and be abstracted from general political consideration.[3] In matters of 'terrorism', this new breed of iron lady declares, to explain is already to justify. One ought to punish without delay and without further examination. The term 'terrorism', then, qualifies an act as the formal figure of Evil. And right from the start that is exactly how Bush comprehended the vengeance to be reaped: Good (factually speaking, state terrorism against villages and ancient cities of Central Asia) against Evil (non-state terrorism against 'Western' buildings).

At this crucial point, where all rationality risks crumbling beneath the immensity of propagandistic self-evidence, one must be careful to be sure of the details and, in particular, to examine the effects of the nominal chain induced by the passage from the adjective 'terrorist' – as the formal qualification of an act – to the substantive 'terrorism'. For this is the moment when, insidiously, form becomes substance. This process gives rise to three kinds of effect: a subject-effect (facing 'terrorism' is a 'we' avenging itself); an alterity-effect (this 'terrorism' is the other of Civilization, barbarous Islam); and finally, a periodization-effect (now begins the long 'war against terrorism').

Who is this 'we' facing Terrorism?

It is clear that 'terrorism' is a non-existent substance, an empty name. But this void is precious since it can be filled. And, as always happens, it is in the first instance filled (as with 'the Boche' or 'the Jew') by what is allegedly in opposition to it (the 'Frenchman' or the 'Aryan'). On any such occasion, opposite 'terrorism' there will always be a 'we' defending itself. In the present case, outside 'America' – a name sufficient for American imperialist patriotism but hardly so for the anti-terrorist coalition, except if 'we are all American', which even committed anti-terrorists balk at declaring – the following three names have been found for this 'we' face to face with the beast: 'the West', a perilous but weighty name; 'our societies', a neutral name; and 'the Democracies', a legitimizing name.

Of the first of these names, it is to be regretted that philosophy has often been compromisingly involved with it, as for example in *The Decline of the West* – Spengler's bestseller at the beginning of the twentieth century – in the contemporary theme of 'the end of Western metaphysics', and with the opposition between the West (Christian? Jewish?) and 'Islamic terrorism' – in which one hears resounding a 'Western' appropriation of thought, that is, nothing but the intellectual trace of four centuries of imperialism. Besides, let's recall for the sake of the younger among us that for many decades the political deployment of the term 'Occidental' was confined to the extreme, racist right wing, to the point of being a name of one of its most violent small groups.[4] Moreover, it seems to me that the litany of colonial atrocities committed throughout the entire world, the savagery of global slaughters, the wars of national liberation in Asia, the Middle East and Africa, the armed revolts in Latin America, the universal value of the Chinese revolution, and the febrile sterility of the world we live in today, are sufficient for those who see that what is being applied is an opposition between 'terrorism' and the 'values of the West' to conclude that 'terrorism' is a hollow word.

When one refers to 'our societies', and declares that 'terrorism' tried to 'strike at the heart of them' and 'destabilize them', we can agree that either one may still refer to the 'West', but in a more muted fashion, or else that one designates only a material paradigm, that is, a certain state of objective wealth, which, as such, can have no kind of value for the philosopher and could not constitute a basis for any kind of consistent solidarity. And if that is not the case, then why does the crime of New York so affect our societies, when neither the millions of AIDS victims in Africa nor the genocidal disasters in Rwanda touch them in the least? 'Our societies' simply designates, in a thoughtlessly obscene way, the wholly relative well-being of some of the wealthiest (minority) groups on the planet, which hardly makes for an acceptable opposition to the supposed substance of terrorism. This is so, even if Monique Canto-Sperber – once again! – deems it philosophically superior and indispensable in the circumstances to remind us that being rich is not a moral fault. That point we would grant her, going against the grain of her formalist zeal, only after a meticulous and concrete examination of the origins of the wealth in question. For it could well be that all really considerable wealth today is, by necessity, entirely implicated in certain indubitable crimes.

That leaves us with the fundamental propagandistic name: what 'terrorism' targets are the 'democracies', at the centre of which lies – as we all know – that exemplary democracy, the United States of America. As any old patriot from over there will tell you, 'It's a free

country', and that's why the Saudi fanatics wanted to destroy it. So
the consensus in the last analysis is: 'terrorism against democracy'.
Well, I want to say the following to the overwhelming majority of
my contemporaries: here, in this jaded democracy we call France,
the political space of that formula is the space of inscription of the
mass crime of New York. It is this formula that has neutralized
reactions and won the ever-so-slightly-plaintive general support for
the American war. For, inevitably, it is in any case admitted that if
our 'democracies' are attacked by terrorism, then, in view of their
excellence, they have the right to avenge themselves. All that
remains to be known is against whom these legitimate reprisals are
to be carried out.

Terrorism: substance and predicates

At this point, I'd like to put forward a precise philosophical
proposition: every substantialization of a formal adjective requires
a dominant predicate. If you go from the adjective 'terrorist',
which qualifies an act by its form, to 'terrorism', which is an empty
substantive, you cannot hope to fill the void by its opposite alone
(i.e. the West, democracy, etc.). You must endow it with a
predicate, precisely in the way that around 1914 the Boche –
contrary to the reflective and Cartesian Frenchman – was ultimately marked out as being bestial and subject to dark instincts,
and that around 1933 the Jew was branded as being cosmopolitan
and abstract – contrary to the Aryans, who were bonded by blood
and soil. Today, the supposed substantial support one refers to as
'terrorism' only has being so that it can take on the predicate
'Islamic'.

What, exactly, is the value of this predicate? One might be
justified in noting that it has already been corrupted by its function,
which aims to give 'terrorism' a semblance of historical colour.
Taken by itself, this boils down to the observation that there is at

work here a political instrumentalization of religion, which, by the way, is also a long 'Western' tradition: the wily alliances between State and Church do not date from today. The conjunction of religion and all kinds of political processes, some extremely violent, is not, in any case, a particularity of Islam. Recall that wherever religion – for example, Catholicism in Poland – played an important role in the resistance to communism, 'democratic' states were very pleased about it.

In the case at hand, that of Bin Laden (if it really has to do with him, something that nobody has been able to prove to date), we know with certainty that our point of departure concerns some extraordinarily complex manoeuvring in relation to Saudi Arabia's manna of oil fields, and that, when all is said and done, this figure is a good American, someone for whom what is important is wealth and power, little matter the means employed; someone exactly like his rivals and accomplices for power in the region. We know that the sovereigns of Saudi Arabia have never desisted from imposing terror in the name of hard-line Islamic fundamentalism. Yet, to my knowledge, not a single notable democrat has ever asked for an armada of B-52s to go and wipe them out.

We must strongly suspect, then, that for these democrats there is 'Islamic terrorism' and 'Islamic terrorism'. The first, supported by the Americans and, as a consequence, considered a friend of 'our societies', is to be if not admired then at least tolerated. Turn a blind eye to the facts and pretend that nothing happened! The second, which with its devious calculations succeeded in hitting us: well, stigmatize it and crush it with bombs! In the final analysis, it comes down to knowing where one is situated as regards access to oil.

In passing, let's underscore Wagner's prophetic virtue when, in his *Tetralogy*, he staged the curse put on the Rhine's gold. Indeed, it is one of the great modern curses to have the equivalent of that gold in one's subsoil. South Africa's diamonds, Bolivia's tin-metal, the precious stones of the Congo and Sierra Leone, the oil in the

Middle East and the Congo – so many regions or countries that have been put to fire and to sword because, as the stakes of rapacious and cynical calculations, the global administration of their mineral resources must necessarily escape their grasp. It does not seem as if 'our societies', 'our paradigmatic democracies', in so far as they are involved, have drawn the least conclusion from these atrocious disasters. In any case, even if, like the god Wotan, Bin Laden speaks at length, and somewhat confusedly, about destiny and religion, it rather seems that his business is to know how to seize (more) black gold and take over the Nibelungen collection that is the petroleum monarchies of the Gulf.

It is worth noting that the political instrumentalization of religion has been persistently performed by the United States itself. That has been one of the great constants of its politics for decades. Fearing Soviet influence, it fought everything that even mildly resembled secular politics in the Arab world. Whether Nasser in Egypt, or the Ba'ath Party in Iraq and Syria, it got involved only to create ever more serious problems; on the other hand, however, it has unfailingly supported the retrograde fanatics of Saudi Arabia, Kuwait and Pakistan. In Indonesia, it lent a helping hand to the eradication of a progressive pro-Third World regime, bringing about the death of five thousand people by promoting an alleged Saint Bartholomew of communists. In Palestine, everyone knows that the development of Hamas was always considered by the Israeli services to be an excellent thing, because they were against the hegemony of Fatah, whose watchword, you will recall, expresses the demand for a secular and democratic Palestine, and which includes Christians in its ranks. Finally, the Taliban themselves are the conjoint creation of the Americans and the Pakistanis, both of whom were against the coming to power in the region of any potential Russian, Chinese or Iranian allies. The ensemble of these manoeuvres makes the predicate 'Islamic' totally irrelevant in the matter of designating the United States' 'terrorist' enemies.

Note the singular status of what we might call the instrumentalization of an instrumentalization. In the Middle East and elsewhere, certain cliques of politicians instrumentalize religion with the aim of serving their projects (in fact: in order to take over power from other ageing or discredited cliques of politicians). Then, American governments regularly attempt to instrumentalize that instrumentalization, with a view to taking control of this or that situation. But the instrumentalization of an instrumentalization is a delicate mechanism. It is exposed to brutal *dérives*. As a case in point, the United States (and the French, who were very active at the time) instrumentalized Saddam Hussein, who had instrumentalized the opposition between the Sunnis and the Shi'ites against his Iranian neighbour. The 'West's' goal was to put the brakes on the Iranian revolution, while Saddam Hussein's goal was to set himself up as the greatest power in the region. The result: a terrifying war on the scale of 1914–18, with hundreds of thousands dead; the consolidation of the Iranian regime; and the turning of Saddam Hussein into an uncontrollable monster, and later a 'terrorist' enemy. As this scenario has once again been reproduced with the Taliban, we propose the following maxim to all states: 'Take care when you're instrumentalizing an instrumentalization', especially one involving religion – a subjective commodity that won't be easily manipulated by cruel and sly politicians.

In truth, what becomes hidden behind the predicate 'Islamic' – and other such 'cultural' categories, whose subjective resources can be activated at leisure – are generally unappetizing (state) political operations that must be kept from public attention. For a plethora of reasons, it is very easy to awaken an anti-Arab zeal in France, whether in the vulgar and post-colonialist form it takes on the extreme right, or the 'ethical' and historiographical form it takes with Zionist or feminist petit-bourgeois intellectuals. Hence, while some will be rejoicing that Kabul is being bombed in order to 'liberate the women', others will be saying to themselves that Israel can always procure some benefits from the situation; while the extreme right will be thinking that a massacre of 'bougnoules'[5] is good for the cause. None of that has anything to do with the crime of New York, either in relation to its causes, its form, or its real effects. Yet all these groups have joined together to rally behind the flag of the vengeful crusade of various political colours and innumerable apathies to validate the syntagm 'Islamic terrorism'.

So the philosophical lesson is the following: when a predicate is attributed to a formal substance (as is the case with every derivation of a substantive from a formal adjective), it has no other function than to give an ostensible content to that form. Thus, in 'Islamic terrorism', the predicate 'Islamic' has no function except to give apparent content to the word 'terrorism', itself devoid of all content (in this instance, political). It is a matter of an artificial historicization which leaves what really happened (the crime of New York) unthought. This does not prohibit thought, but rather determines that what emerges from that unthought – that is, in the name of the inconsistent term designating it ('Islamic terrorism') – is a sort of history in *trompe l'oeil* of the period that is beginning.

What 'war' against terrorism?

What has come about, so our leaders tell us, is the 'war against Islamic terrorism'. A long and difficult period. But why a 'war'? Just like 'terrorism' and 'Islamic', this word is extremely problematic with regard to the situation. Here, I shall maintain that 'war', also entirely formal, is the symmetrical term to the very vague term 'terrorism'. It is important to be aware that the usage of the term 'war' (which was immediate in the declaration of American officials, then in those of their servants, i.e. their opinionated public support and foreign governments) is something new. Previously when governments declared that their duty was 'to eradicate terrorism', they were careful not to speak about war. Indeed, how can war be declared on a few delinquent civilians, on some fanatical bombers, or on a group of anarchists? The term 'war' was considered far too dignified for such a phenomenon, and had therefore been reserved for altercations between states. Even during the interminable and very violent colonial war against the Algerian patriots, which mobilized hundreds of thousands of soldiers, French governments from De Gaulle to Mitterrand always spoke of 'maintaining order' and of 'pacification'. And still today, in settling accounts with the Chechen nationalists using the same methods (systematic torture, internment camps, destroying villages, raping women) that the French used in Algeria forty years ago, Putin is careful not to say that there is, strictly speaking, a war. Instead, it's an immense police operation, wherein, to employ his own expression, 'we will go looking for the terrorists right into the sewers', and so on. In sum, governments have opposed repression to terrorism, generally using the most violent and abject means, but always in the symbolic register of the police.

Why, then, in the case at issue, has it to do with war, and especially in the symbolic register? The crime of New York, like all crimes, calls for a mobilizing of police to track and to judge its perpetrators and financial backers. In so doing, without doubt the feared and extremely unethical methods of the modern 'services' will be used. But war?

My thesis is that, in the formal representation it makes of itself, the American imperial power privileges the form of war as an attestation – the only one – of its existence. Moreover, one observes today that the powerful subjective unity that carries (away) the Americans in their desire for vengeance and war is constructed immediately around the flag and the army.

The United States has become a hegemonic power in and through war: first, in the Civil War, called the War of Secession (the first modern war by its industrial means and the number of deaths); then, in the two world wars; and lastly, in the uninterrupted succession of all kinds of local wars and military interventions extending from the Korean War to the present ransacking of

Afghanistan, via Lebanon, the Bay of Pigs, Vietnam, Libya, Panama, Barbados, the Gulf and Serbia, not to mention its persistent support for Israel in its endless war against the Palestinians. Of course, we might also add that the USA won the day in the Cold War against the USSR on the terrain of military rivalry (Reagan's Star Wars project pushing the Russians to throw in the towel) and are understood to be doing the same against the Chinese through the imposition of an exhausting arms race (that is the only possible sense of the pharaonic anti-missile shield project) that hopes to discourage any sizeable project.

Even in these times of economic obsession, this should remind us that, in the last resort, power continues to be military. Even the USSR, dilapidated as it was, in so far as it was considered to be a significant military power (and above all by the Americans), continued to co-direct the world. Today, the USA has a monopoly on aggressive projections of enormous forces of destruction, and does not hesitate to use them. The consequences can be seen, and include (notably) the idea the American people has of itself and of what must be done. Let's hope that the Europeans – and the Chinese – draw the imperative lesson from the situation: servitude is promised to those who do not watch carefully over their armed forces.

Thus forged from the continual barbarity of war – leaving quite aside the genocide of the Indians and the importation of tens of millions of black slaves – the USA quite naturally considers that the only reprisal worthy of itself is a spectacular staging of power. The particular adversary chosen matters little, actually, and may be entirely disconnected from the initial crime. The sheer power of destruction will do the job, even if what is left at the end is a few thousand miserable devils and a phantom 'government'. Any war will do, in short, so long as the appearance of victory is overwhelming.

We have (and will have, too, if the USA continues in Somalia and in Iraq, etc.) war as an abstract form of the theatrical capture of an adversary ('terrorism'), which is in its essence vague and elusive. The war against nothing: itself subtracted from the very idea of war.

Parenthesis on 'anti-Americanism'

Certain 'intellectuals' have judged the moment ripe to stigmatize the compulsive anti-Americanism to which French 'intellectuals' are would-be slaves. We know that in such polemics, those that the journalist–intellectuals call 'French intellectuals' are other journalist–intellectuals who are not of the same mind. As a result, the more the word 'intellectual' is emphasized, the more all intellectuality is absent. This debate requires that each camp proclaim itself to be in a persecuted minority, especially if it is made up of battle-weary veterans who appear on the television every day, and whose demeanour and eloquence are splashed all over the pages of glossy magazines.

Thus, two particularly copious editorialists, Jacques Juillard and Bernard-Henri Lévy,[6] have treated us to a spectacle in which they present themselves as the solitary dispensers of justice, exhausted with fatigue from their good fight for liberty and modernity against the enslaving, archaic and repulsive horde of French 'intellectuals'.

The central argument of these brothers in heroic alliance with the American bombers amounts to this: that to be against the USA in this affair, as in many others, is to be against freedom. It is as simple as that. Bernard Henri-Lévy, who never bothers with niceties, states that to be anti-American is fascistic. As for Julliard, truly in the twilight by dint of having been right all along, his axiom is that 'French intellectuals' do not like freedom. We could be justified in saying that orientations of thought, for the sole reason that Bernard-Henri Lévy declares them fascist, deserve to be considered with attention. To this we could add that if 'freedom' means being like Jacques Juillard politically and intellectually, it is assuredly better not to be free.

But what should be said is this: if there exists a sole great imperial power that is always convinced that its most brutal interests coincide with the Good; if it is true that every year the USA spends more on its military budget than Russia, China, France, England and Germany put together; and if that nation-state, bowing to military excess, has no public idol other than wealth, no allies other than servants, and no view of other peoples except an indifferent, commercial and cynical one, then, for the basic freedom of states, peoples and individuals, everything must be done and thought, so as to escape as much as possible from the commandments, interventions and interference of that imperial power.

'Anti-Americanism' is a meaningless term. The American people have brought humanity admirable inventions in all registers of experience. But today there cannot be the least political liberty, the least independence of mind, without a constant and unrelenting struggle against the *imperium* of the USA.

Of course, one might have as one's sole ambition to be considered by the masters in Washington as their most zealous servant. It seems sometimes as if Tony Blair dreams of obtaining posthumous repose for his Old England by becoming the 51st state of the Union. His attitude is reminiscent of those vassal 'Kings' of Rome, whose pusillanimity is depicted in certain of Corneille's tragedies: 'Ah! Don't put me on bad terms with the [Roman] Republic!' says Prusias (Bithynie's Pétain) to the potential resistance fighter, Nicomedes. Let us take the liberty of siding with Nicomedes in thinking that the inevitable condition of our freedom is to be at odds, seriously at odds, with American 'democracy', just like the Corneillian hero was against the Roman 'Republic'. At odds, one might say, 'until death'. For the American superpower is nothing but the deadly guarantor of the obscene accumulation of wealth, and the American Army the key instrument in the race of 'Western' masters against all the unfortunates of the earth.

The disjunctive synthesis of two nihilisms

Let's return to our point of departure: philosophy faced with the event. We have come to the critical stage, that of the critique of terms. Of our consensual statement 'the war of the democracies against Islamic terrorism' little intelligibility remains.

What, then, is our own formula? Joyfully borrowing a concept from Gilles Deleuze, we say: what the crime of New York and the wars following it attest is a 'disjunctive synthesis of two nihilisms'.

Let's clarify this phrase.

There is *synthesis* because, in my view, the principal actors are of the same kind. Yes, both Bin Laden (or whoever financed the crime), on one side, and the foundations of the American super-power, on the other, belong to the same world – nihilistic – of money, blind power and cynical rivalry, of the 'hidden gold' of primary resources, of total scorn for the everyday lives of people, and of the arrogance of self-certitude based on the void. And slapped onto all that are moral and religious platitudes: on both sides, Good, Evil and God serve as rhetorical ornaments in jousts of financial ferocity and schemes for hegemonic power.

There is *disjunction* because it is inevitably through crime that these actors seek and find each other: irrespective of whether what is at issue is the private, secretly machinated and suicidal crime of New York, or crimes of state – Kabul, Kandahar and elsewhere – reinforced with anaesthetized machines bringing death to others and zero death to oneself.

This mass crime is the exact obverse of imperial brutality. It was stitched to the latter like an inner lining and its, real or loaned, personnel (Bin Laden, the Taliban etc.) come directly from the scullery of that American hegemony, were educated and financed by it, and only desire a place of choice in the American system. Religion in relation to this is nothing but demagogic vocabulary, worth neither more nor less than the populist 'anti-capitalism' of fascists in the thirties. One speaks about 'disinherited' Muslims, but really wants to become a Saudi Arabian billionaire, that is to say, an American; just as one had 'German worker' on the lips in order to become the table companion of cannon merchants. On Bush's side, one has God, the Good, Democracy, and also America (it's the same thing) to track down Evil – but in reality it boils down to reminding all those disobedient imperial creatures that they will be reduced to ashes if they even think of biting the master. And if they are not reduced to ashes, it'll be their parents. It's the aerial vendetta, damn it! And if not their parents, then the accursed with whom they live. And if not them, then their hosts. In fact, any unfortunates vaguely resembling them will do. As the Defense Secretary, Rumsfeld, declared with the frank speech of an imperialist in chase, it is a matter of killing as many people as possible. It must be said that he was lent a helping hand by some of those suave American professors who asked whether or not, in view of the circumstances, it might not be useful to use torture. To which some even more refined American professors objected that it would be in any case preferable to expedite the suspects to allied countries where torture is an official method. The latest news is that these suspects are being rounded up, drugged, and chained for transportation to the thousands of hastily constructed cells at a base at Guantanamo Bay, Cuba. Savour the irony!

Just like the crime of New York itself, America's war is not linked to any law and is indifferent to every project. On both sides, the point is to strike blindly to demonstrate the power of that strike. At stake are purposeless and truthless bloodthirsty and nihilistic games of power.

The formal traits of the crime of New York all point to its nihilistic character: the sacralization of death; the absolute indifference to the victims; the transformation of oneself and others into instruments . . . But there is nothing that speaks louder than the silence, the terrible silence of the authors behind the crime, since with affirmative, liberating, non-nihilistic political violence, responsibility is not only always claimed, but finds its essence in being claimed. In 1941, whenever the resistance fighters killed a German officer or blew up a pylon, it was only ever to say 'It's us, the Resistance! Resistance exists and will continue to strike back!' The leaflet (*tract*), saying who did what, however perilous that may be, must accompany the act (*acte*). Violence is, to forge a neologism, a *tract(e)*. There is none of any of that today. The act remains unnamed and anonymous, just like the culprits. We see in that the infallible sign of a sort of fascist nihilism.

And on the other side of this we have the nihilism proper to the old name of 'capital'. *Das Kapital.* We have it in its extensive form, the market now being worldwide: in its fetishization of the formalism of communication; and in its extreme political poverty, i.e. in the absence of any project other than its self-perpetuation, the perpetuation of hegemony for Americans and vassalage, as comfortable as possible, for the others.

In its structural aspect, this nihilism might be called the nihilism of virtual equality. On the one hand, the governments serving it organize monstrous inequalities, even in basic life. If you are born in Africa your life expectancy is perhaps 30 years of age, whereas it is 80 if you are born in France. Such is the contemporary 'democratic' world. But at the same time (and this is what sustains the 'democratic' fiction in the soul) there is an egalitarian dogmatism, that of equality *vis-à-vis* the commodity. The same products are on offer everywhere. Armed with that universal offer, this abstract equality is used by contemporary 'democracy' to forge a subject: every consumer in his or her virtuality in relation to the commodity is ostensibly identical to all the others from the standpoint of abstract buying power. Market Man. As Man (or Woman) he (she) is the same as everybody else in so far as he (she) looks at the same displays of commodities. That he may have less money than others, and thus has unequal buying power, is a matter of secondary contingence and, anyhow, is no one's fault (except his own, upon closer examination?). In principle, anybody and everybody is posited as being equal to everybody else, as being able to buy whatever is being sold as a matter of right.

Nevertheless, we know that this equality is nothing but frustration and resentment. It is the only equality that both 'Western' governments and billionaire 'terrorists' can conjointly claim.

In its circumstantial aspect, capitalist nihilism has reached the stage of the non-existence of any world. Yes, today there is no world as such, only some singular and disjointed situations. No world exists simply because the majority of the planet's inhabitants today do not even have a label, a simple label. When there was class society, (supposedly) proletarian parties, the USSR, the national wars of liberation, etc., any farmer of any region, or any worker of any town, could receive a political denomination. That is not to say that their material situation was better (it certainly was not), nor that that world was excellent. But the symbolic positions existed and that world was a world. Today, outside of the grand and petty bourgeoisie of imperial cities who proclaim to be 'civilization', there is only the anonymous excluded. 'Excluded' is the name for those who have no name, just as 'market' is the name for a world that is not a world. In fact, apart from certain singular situations – that is, apart from the unremitting efforts of those who make thought, including political thought, live – there is nothing apart from the American Army.

To conclude: philosophy?

If the situation is as we say it is – the disjunctive synthesis of two nihilisms – then, as we see it, it is a frightening one. It announces the repetition of disasters.

As such, it is incumbent upon philosophy to welcome into thought everything that distances itself from that synthesis. Philosophy must make the condition of its own existence everything that affirmatively seizes something real and raises it to the level of the symbol.

But to do that, it must break with whatever leads it through nihilistic detours, that is, with everything that restrains and obliterates affirmative power. It must push beyond the nihilistic motif of the 'end of Western metaphysics'. And more generally, it must de-link itself from the Kantian heritage, from the perpetual examination of limits, from the obsession with critique, and from narrow forms of judgement. For a single thought is far greater than any judgement.

In a word: it is essential to break with the motif, omnipresent today, of finitude. With origins in the critical as well as hermeneutical traditions, as well regarded by phenomenologists as by positivists, the motif of finitude is the discrete form by which thought crumbles in advance, by which thought is forced to play the modest part of conserving, in all circumstances, the fierce contemporary nihilism.

So philosophy's duty is clear: to reconstitute rationally the infinite reserve of the affirmative that every liberating project requires. Philosophy is not, and has never been, that which disposes by itself of the effective figures of emancipation. Such is the primordial task of what concentrates on making thinking political. Instead, philosophy is like the attic where, in difficult times, one accumulates resources, lines up tools and sharpens knives. Philosophy is exactly that which proposes an ample reserve of means to other forms of thought. Right now it is on the side of the affirmative and the infinite that philosophy must select and accumulate its resources, its tools and its knives.

2

Fragments of a Public Journal on the American War against Iraq

Paris–VII Jussieu, lecture theatre 44
(February 26 2003)

War and time

'A present is lacking', Mallarmé said. This is our problem in a nutshell: how are we to identify, inside and beyond ourselves, the infinity of a present? For what we are given by way of a present is only a perpetual instant of absence, of purchasable enjoyment measured out in millimetres.

For some time, war has been what historically attests to the present. And this has been the case for at least three reasons.

First, the order of time: we've always spoken about the 'pre-war' period and the 'post-war' period, as if the moment of war, a pure present, fixed the long forms of the before and the after.

Second, the decision: in forms that are, it is true, sometimes dubious, war is what decides, and in this sense what determines, the present of politics. As Clausewitz conceived it, battle, fought under the authority of someone firmly decisive, is the passing into the present of war. Carl Schmitt generalized this vision of things.

Third, the exception: war, especially in the distribution of images, is a fraternal sharing of the exception. It localizes the community outside the normal rules. To share danger is to share the present itself.

Now, I would like to propose that the characteristic of the American ('Western'?) wars following the collapse of the USSR, from the Gulf War to the planned invasion of Iraq, via the attacks against Serbia and Afghanistan, is precisely that they do not constitute any kind of present. The aim of these wars is to protect, to endure, and for this reason to destroy anything that is not homogeneous with this duration, and this protection – protection of 'Western' comfort, of measured enjoyment. They are wars that are totally sterile with respect to the order of time.

Let's begin by situating them. At what point in the general history of wars are we? The post-war period (the world war of 1939–45) is over with; we are now living in the post-post-war period.

The post-war period was referred to in various ways, all of which are now obsolete. We used to say that there was a Cold War between two superpowers, the USA and the USSR. The lifeless collapse of the USSR (which elsewhere I've called an 'obscure disaster'[7]) brought this arrangement to an end. We used to refer to China's revolutionary isolation, which is also its distant *aura*. Of that, Teng Hsiao Ping's pragmatism has retained nothing, leaving only commercial frenzy and corruption. We used to refer to the struggles of national liberation – Vietnam, Algeria, Palestine . . . – struggles that set the world's youth alight. Today, all nationalist violence lacks universality. Above all, we were able to refer to the powerful dialectic of war and revolution at work among those inclined to political action. That is what the present was, precisely: a point of condensation of the 'present-creating' [*présentifiante*] force of war and the emancipatory force of revolution. Lenin, and then Mao, were the great names of this condensation. 'Insurrection is an art.' 'Power grows out the barrel of a gun.' 'Either the war will provoke revolution, or revolution will prevent war.' Great maxims of nearly a century's history of political emancipation.

Further to our customary references, let's mention here – in the margins of this vast current of thought – the practice and theory of guerrilla war: Che Guevara and Fidel Castro. We should mention this if only to distinguish ourselves from the scoundrels who today clamour for some 'humanitarian' expedition to be led against the Cuban regime, and who thus wish that the island would revert to what it was before the members of the Resistance of the Sierra Maestra took power, the thing these scoundrels passionately desire that it revert to: the brothel of the US.

Whatever the case, from 1917 to 1976 (Mao's death), war and revolution constituted the transcendental regime of the present.

Of this present, which bound together the localized force of war and the remote becoming of emancipation, nothing remains that might be activated at the moment. The post-war period is over; in any case, undeniably so from the beginning of the 1980s.

Yet this ending does not by itself constitute any kind of present. No revolution, no political invention, no creation of anything at all has taken place. Rather, everywhere there is collapse, restoration, imitation, incorporation. And as for 'democracy', it has become a kind of generally unpopular spiritual supplement for dealers and predatory politicians, for sellers and the sold.

Of course, the Gulf War was the war that began the era of wars in the post-post-war period. This beginning, however, does not constitute a present for the era it begins. No present put an end to the post-war period, which died saturated, bloated, impotent.

We are now in a limbo world, suspended between an old, inactive dialectical figure (war and/or revolution), and a false commercial and military present that seeks to protect its future by dispensing with the present, and by erasing everything of the past that was, in the past, in the present.

War and peace

If the American war is incapable of creating the sign of a present, it is because the very category of 'war' has become considerably obscured. There was, there is, and there will be war. George W. Bush has characterized the whole period that began with the mass crimes of September 11 as the period of 'the war against terrorism'. But what kind of war is this?

To begin with, and this is very important, these wars are never *declared*. Ancient capitals are massively bombed (Baghdad, Kabul, Belgrade . . .) without serving notice to anyone of the fact that war has been declared on them.

Such *mores* previously incriminated those who confessed to them. In the first section of a poem by Victor Hugo, 'Ratbert' ('Fair and independent counsellors' ['Les conseillers probes et libres'], a title that's absolutely relevant today), there is a string of sycophantic speeches addressed by various courtiers to the powerful of the day. You'd think you were hearing today's assembly of Glucksmann, Kouchner, Goupil and Bruckner,[8] all responsible for finding noble reasons, sublime moral ornaments, and intensely democratic motivations for the diverse crimes of American power. One of the courtiers, the priest Afranus, is particularly mawkish. This is because he is a 'great and very learned casuist', very 'pious, charitable, alms-giving', and because 'he invokes the divine spirit, then tackles the questions'. A perfect New Philosopher, in sum. Now, from among the ethical legitimizations with which he showers Ratbert's imperial violence, I'll read this one:

> *The Ottomans being outside the common law,*
> *They can be attacked without declaring war.*

Let's translate: 'Muslims not being democrats', or, 'totalitarians not being humanists', and the conclusion follows as a matter of course.

From the moment, indeed, that we begin to live indistinctly in the war of democracies against Islamic terrorism, or, simply put, in the war of (democratic) Good versus (dictatorial) Evil, operations of war – expeditions, bombings – need no more solemn announcement than do police raids on thieves. Likewise, the assassinations of heads of state, their wives, children and infants, or the setting of bounties on their heads, as in a western, no longer surprises anyone. As such, the continuity of war is slowly established, whereas in the past declaring war would, to the contrary, have expressed the present of a discontinuity. Already, this continuity has rendered war and peace indistinguishable.

As a result, the question of the protagonists of the state of war becomes increasingly evasive. 'Terrorists', 'rogue states', 'dictatorships', 'Islamicists': what exactly are these ideological entities? Who identifies them? Who proclaims them?

Classically, there were two kinds of war: on the one hand, symmetrical wars between comparable imperial powers, like the two world wars of the twentieth century, or the 'Cold' War between the USA and the USSR; on the other hand, asymmetrical wars between an imperial power and popular forces technically vastly inferior in terms of military power, like the wars of colonial conquest (the conquest of Algeria, the Rif War, or the extermination of the North American Indians . . .) and the wars of national liberation (Vietnam, Algeria, etc.).

Today, we can speak about asymmetrical war, but without being quite able to identify the political identity of the asymmetry. The proof of this lies in the fact that the operations of invasion and occupation (Afghanistan, Kosovo, soon Iraq?) are explicitly presented as liberations, despite the patent fact that the local populations do not see things in this way at all. In fact, the concept of war designates only the use of violence, organized in variable asymmetries. That is, asymmetry is the unique invariable trait: only the weak are bombed, and as soon as the shadow of a power shows itself (the atomic bomb of the North Koreans, Russia's savage exactions in Chechnya, the heavy-handedness of the Chinese in

Tibet . . .) a conflict – one that would really risk turning into a war rather than police-like peace, or the peace/war ('la péguerre après l'après-guerre')[9] – is not on the agenda.

In the end, if these American wars do not constitute any kind of present, it is because, not being linked to any dialectic, whether inter-imperialist or modelled on the war/revolution schema, they are not really distinguishable from the continuity of 'peace', understood as American or 'Western' peace, the democratic peace/war, which consists entirely in securing the comfort of the aforementioned 'democrats' against the barbarous aggressiveness of the poor.

Pacifism and parliamentarism: the UN

This merging without a present of war and peace renders the pacifist impulse – the slogan 'No to war!' – even more laughable. But, in all honesty, the slogan 'No to pacifism!' fares no better. Chirac, who likes to be a bit provocative, especially if the consequences are only rhetorical, declared, unlike the German Greens, that France 'was not a pacifist country'. Alas, this is because it is more often prepared to capitulate than it should be, and is without doubt about to be once more, when its last-ditch stand in the Security Council is over.

For weaker even than pacifism is the idea that attacking Iraq would be excellent were it only to be endorsed by the UN.

What is the UN? For forty-five years, it was the body responsible for moderating the Cold War between the USA and the USSR, a body responsible, in general, for examining the conditions under which that war might remain cold rather than hot. To achieve this, the UN never hesitated for one second to transform itself into the arbitrator of local wars, and especially of American or European wars, for example in Korea or in the ex-Belgian Congo. Since the collapse of the USSR, the UN has been put in charge of embodying the very strange concept of the 'international community'. This term in effect designates the supposed subject of democratic comfort in the post-post-war period. The UN is the parliament where, by a count of votes, the fiction of this supposed subject is brought into being. The armed wing of this fiction, itself very real, is the American Army and its various incidental satellites.

The present situation is that of an elusive regulation between American power games (the financial and military reality of the 'international community') and the parliamentary game of the UN (the subjective fiction of the former). With power comes the decision (the American government and its British poodle decided to invade Iraq), but the fiction requires a parliamentary vote at the Security Council or the UN General Assembly. Decided without a vote, deprived of a majority or parliamentary support, the attack in preparation inflicts damage on the supposed subject, that is, the consensus of the post-post-war period around 'values': human rights, humanism, humanitarianism, democratic intervention and other silly jokes.

But what is it that constitutes the essence of the parliamentary fiction, of politics as representative delegation and counting of votes? It is obviously the existence of an opposition. Today at the UN, Chirac is making France play the saving role of the opposition. His mission is less to prevent attack (the French government accepts the fairytale of the 'weapons of mass destruction', keeps up the ridiculous suspense of the 'inspections', considers the departure of Saddam Hussein to be an excellent notion, etc.) than to act as the harbinger of parliamentary legitimacy. In short: it is to rescue, from the naked real, the do-gooder moral fiction of the 'international community', which Chirac has renamed 'multilateralism'.

Let's just say that France works towards 'parliamentarizing' American power, a power which, by the way, it otherwise recognizes as being the only one fit to decide and to handle successfully a war of aggression. Although such a war is by its very nature abject, the only thing being disputed is its procedure of legitimization: not only must it be decided by those about to wage it, but it must also be voted for by those without the means to do so.

For that is just what parliamentarism – 'modern democracy' – is: the replacement of political principles by which situations might be judged with the juridical fetishism of the numerical majority. It is consensual impotence busying itself with the propaganda of naked power.

The nature of American power

American power, which derived to some extent from the long conflict with the USSR – a conflict that established the norms of its exercise – has three particularly striking characteristics.

The first is the way it has, for quite some time now (in fact, since Reagan's 'Star Wars' programme), implanted itself in a representation of *absolute* military superiority. Although its visible hegemony is total and uncontested, the USA's military build-up has known no let-up. The defence budget of the USA is higher than that of all the other 'great' powers combined. It's as if each successive government (and here Bush is doing no more than managing an inheritance) has worked towards obtaining a qualitative superiority, a state of things in which it would be simply impossible for anyone to compare themselves to American power, or hope to catch up with it some day. There is here an impressive autonomy of the military factor, constituted around the motif of an irreversible *disproportion* between the USA and the rest of the world.

Second, one should consider the self-centration of the USA, its total screening out of everything that is of concern in the rest of the world through the very particular system of its interests. For Americans, the world has no objective existence. It is only the stage of their interests, a disparate assortment of situations scrutinized according to the threats or prospects they present to American comfort (long referred to as the 'American way of life' or the 'American dream', i.e. what is presented to the whole world as the supreme goal that everyone must strive to realize). The extraordinary ignorance of the majority of Americans concerning the most elementary facts of other peoples' lives – and one can give endless and staggering examples – is in reality only a consequence of the fact that America is, for Americans, the finality of the world. This is an acceptable consequence for an Aristotelian: if the USA is the supreme unmoved mover of the rest of the world's activity, then turning oneself towards the USA is what fulfils thought completely. This is exactly what is proclaimed by the hired-gun Europeans, and especially the French, for whom America is the 'great democracy', defender of our liberties, or, as the Americans have always maintained (all of them, even indisputable progressives), the very example of what we might call 'a free country'.

Last, we must consider the nature of American interventionism. It is not, in fact, of a classically imperial type. An empire looks after the regions it occupies, settles problems of territorial administration, examines questions about the diversity of customs, builds infrastructure, determines with accuracy the rapport to the metropole, etc. There is nothing of the kind in American interventions: they make the best of frightful and protracted disorder (in Palestine, in Afghanistan, in Africa, tomorrow in Iraq), so long as whatever motivated the bombings and invasions is, as they say, 'secure'.

Does this mean that the USA is only a secondary, or in any case non-central, piece of a systemic transnational apparatus such as the one Negri designates as 'Empire'? I believe this construction to be totally unfounded; it is, as usual, solely destined to conjure up, as the inverse of that systemic power, the radiant promises of the constitutive 'multitude'. As is well known, for Negri, the Spinozist, there is only one historic substance, so that the capitalist empire is also the scene of an unprecedented communist deployment. This surely has the advantage of authorizing the belief that the worse it gets, the better it gets; or of getting you to (mis)take those demonstrations – fruitlessly convened to meet wherever the power-ful reunite – for the 'creation' and the 'multiform invention' of new petit-bourgeois proletarians.

In truth, the USA is an imperialist power without empire, a hegemonic power without territoriality or front line. To designate its relationship to the world, I propose the term 'zoning': any part of the world may be considered by the American government to be a zone of vital interest or a zone of total disinterest, subject to their shifting judgements about what comprises their 'democratic' comfort. Death may occur *en masse* without America raising an eyebrow (as has been going on for years with the African AIDS crisis), or, on the contrary, you may be subjected to being piled up in the middle of a desert by a colossal army (Iraq today). This system of zoning makes the American military interventions more like the razzia type than the colonial type. They are no more than massive blows that are particularly brutal but as brief as possible. Kill people *en masse*, strike them into a stupor, crush them with the latest technology, then return home to enjoy some of the comforts so ably defended in a provisionally 'strategic' zone: such is the idea that the USA has formed of its power and about how to use it.

We will certainly have the occasion to raise this observation to the level of the concept: the metaphysics of American power is a metaphysics of the unlimited. The great imperial theories of the nineteenth century were theories of division, of dividing up the world, of fixing borders. But for the USA, there are no limits. This is what Nixon's advisers, whom Chomsky analysed, announced with the expression 'a politics of madness': the USA must attempt to impose the idea that it is, precisely, *capable of anything*, and especially of things that are neither rational nor foreseeable. The disproportionate brutality of the interventions has as its aim to make the adversary realize that an American riposte might be totally unrelated to the initial stakes. The adversary in question will therefore judge it preferable to concede management of the disputed zone, for a time, to the 'mad' power.

The invasion of Iraq in preparation is a figure of that madness. It testifies to the fact that, for American governments, there are neither countries, nor states, nor peoples. There are only zones in which anything may be destroyed for however little the (at any rate empty) idea of American comfort may be at issue in these zones.

Paris–VII Jussieu, lecture theatre 44
(March 26 2003)

Imagery of war

In thinking about war, it is useful to reflect on what is shown of it, on what images of the war are circulating. For what is not shown is also part of war. Controlling images is a military function, half-way between intelligence, disinformation and propaganda. This time it has been announced that, as a technique to enhance 'transparency', journalists will be embedded with the American combative units. We should have serious misgivings about this 'embeddedness'.

Suffice it to say that, in any case, images provide the most limited way of entering into an understanding of war. Recall that the famous photos of the last world war, like the photo of the Soviets atop the Reichstag, resulted from staged poses.

In times of war, it is possible to distinguish three types of image-representations based on how they are put into circulation.

1. Images shown by both camps, images 'available to all'.
2. Images shown by only one of the camps.
3. Images not shown by anyone.

Let's take, for example, the images of the first bombing of Baghdad. These are of the first type, at least when a general shot is shown, because they serve only to mark the fact that the war has begun – a beginning both camps acknowledge. The pillars of smoke, the darkened horizons, the deafening explosions: all of this summons everyone to the imminent battle.

Other images are shared by both sides simply because they are open to two contradictory interpretations. Thus, most especially, the horrible images of the dead strewn across the earth, or of chained-up, hooded, humiliated prisoners. Such images may speak of victory and serve as a warning to the camp of the apparent losers. Or they may express the barbarity, the ferocity, of the ostensible victors, and serve as humanitarian propaganda for the opposite camp.

In the case of images that are available to all, such images are there only because their meaning is evasive, either because it is deficient (the image, at once vague and pregnant with meaning, only says what everyone already knows, i.e. that the war has begun, that the bombing has started, etc.), or because it is ambiguous (the image is amphibological, as is in essence the theme of victims).

Images of the second type are only of interest and, in fact, only attain 'visibility' because they are obviously constructed to serve one of the camps. Take, for example, the image of the ruins of a civil building in Baghdad. Even the realization that we are in Baghdad does not depend directly on the image, but on its protocol of demonstration (as it so happens, by the services of the Ba'ath regime). This fact alone determines the image's supposed meaning: Americans are blindly destroying residential areas. Here again, any meaning the image might have, properly speaking, separated from its context of circulation, evaporates. This also goes for images in which you see a small group of alleged Iraqis saluting an American tank. Who are those people? Are they free to do what they are doing? And what do they represent? It's a mystery. The only certainty is that the image works in the service of the American claim not to be an army of invasion and occupation, but an army of liberation.

As for the third type of image, we do not see them, or else see them only by chance. One suspects they exist, but they do not have an adequate protocol of demonstration in either of the two camps. In fact, there is complicity, agreement between both camps, who maintain that these representations are useless, if not harmful. This is the case for the images of destruction of the Iraqi Army fleeing into the desert during the first Gulf War, which were not initially shown by anyone. The Iraqis did not want to display the magnitude of their defeat. But the images of bodies blown up by cluster bombs or carbonized by firebombs were so hideous that the Americans also insisted they remain out of circulation. In truth these images – and it was the same with those images, this time with too little horror, of fraternization between French and German soldiers during the war of 1914–18, which generals of both camps equally regretted – attest to a shared reality of war, to that which affects both camps or opinions alike: death, the absurd, the shared exception . . . That is why, within the logic of war, they remain invisible.

So, you might say, images do not give thought any access to situations of war. When, from the fact that we saw nothing of the Gulf War, Baudrillard concludes as to its non-existence in the world – since he presumes that this is a world of the virtual and the image – he posits as a criterion of modernity a simple truism: because what is publicly transmitted of the war is a part of the war itself, it cannot constitute a point of departure for thinking the war's reality. From this point of view, there is no difference in principle between the images of the Gulf War, or their absence, and Pericles' speech justifying the Peloponnesian war; there is no new boundary between the real and the actual. This is certainly not to say that these wars do not exist.

We must start out courageously from the idea that we do not see anything of wars, and that, as a consequence, the existence of war, just as much as the positions we take on its existence, derives from abstract decisions, from political axioms. If we see nothing, we must think without seeing, thereby enabling ourselves to see things, from time to time, by surprise, or through that which is not shown.

Indeed, it can happen that in type-one or type-two images – images that are either a-signifying or propagandistic – an element escapes the official protocols of image circulation. There is an immanent excess of the image over its own function.

Take, for example, the image showing the planting of an American flag in a small Iraqi port after several days of combat. This image has two characteristics. First, it signifies the taking of the port by the invading army, although the port was still largely held by the Iraqis at the time of its diffusion. This is typical of the lies of the type-two image. But more important than this journal-istic blunder is what it conceals: in fact, the image is politically aberrant, since it shows that this is a war of conquest and occupation, and not the war of liberation allegedly being fought. In general, we can say this: this image is real inasmuch as it is an error internal to its propagandistic destination. In excess of its protocol of demonstration, the image possesses an unintended fragment of truth.

Another example: the broad diffusion of Saddam Hussein's first speech, just after the outbreak of conflict. The universal reception of this discourse makes it typical of a type-one image. Nevertheless, it gives the immediate impression of a worn-out power, and of a leader who, in the face of foreign invasion, is completely incapable of mustering any real patriotic energy.

If, in the first example, the act (planting the American flag in an Iraqi town) is in immanent excess of the function of a type-two image, in the second, the inertia of the image (and of the speech delivered in a gloomy, defeated tone) does not fulfil its type-one function: that is, to establish the determination of the war's protagonists for the public. So much so that, oddly, you might think it was a type-two image fabricated by the Americans. Uncertainty as to its type creates a truth effect.

You can see that once a position regarding the war has been

axiomatically determined, the protocol for reading images should not be carried out in accordance with their function (type one, two or three), but in accordance with what is legible of the image – in excess or in default of its function – *against* the protocol of demonstration by which the images are produced.

The paradoxical result is that often a fabricated image is more real than a realistic one. This is because the value of an image of war in no way lies in its representative virtues. Its value lies in that aspect of the image that gives the lie to or exhibits its circulation protocol. This is what ultimately enables us to relate the images to the various political axioms within which the war is thought and practised.

American solitude

It is imperative to understand that in the USA's history of diplomacy and war there is no contradiction between isolationism and interventionism. We might say that isolationism is internal to interventionism so long as the domestic principle of interest (of comfort) prevails over every other consideration. The USA really is a solitary power, and that is what renders the Americans incapable of creating an empire. That is also why their way of relating to situations, filtered through bitter solitude and incomprehension as to what exists elsewhere or differently, very quickly heads toward a violent abstraction.

That the USA unhesitatingly dropped an atomic bomb on Hiroshima remains an inaugural event. War for the Americans (who are nearly always at war) no longer has anything feudal or chivalrous about it, not even by inference. It is not even a dialectical confrontation, a head-to-head combat with an identified and vaguely respected adversary. On the contrary, war is – and the dropping of the atomic bomb on tens of thousands of Japanese civilians is the frightening symbol of it – the moment when incommensurability exists, when naked power brings devastation to anonymous inferiors.

The place where the UN should be sending inspectors in great numbers is the USA. For not only do the Americans dispose of prodigious quantities of weapons of mass destruction, but to this day they are the only ones who have dared use them on a large scale, and who periodically threaten to re-offend.

This is because the figure of unlimited power, or of power disproportionate to any other, has a key drawback: every obstacle, even every patent exteriority, that tends to set a limit must be wiped out, and that includes its very claim to exist. For the invaders, the duty of the Iraqis was in a certain sense to assume their military and political non-being. Indeed, it would have been ideal if, terrified by the power's unlimitedness, the Iraqis had simply awaited their liberators as an apathetic mass waving lots of striped and starry flags. Instead, limited as it is, the resistance from Ba'ath militia in the south has dumbfounded not only the Americans, but also all the commentators whose servility to tutelary 'democracy' has become second nature.

Hegel would have been interested in this figure, because it is different from the dialectic of the master and slave. This is not a combat in which the one who yields, so becoming the other's slave, is the one who fears death. A power governed by a representation of its unlimited character relates to the other under a predicate of non-existence. Theology is a great back-up here: demonized, compared once and for all to the historical figures of Evil (Saddam Hussein, like Milosevic, is Hitler, is Stalin, in short the Devil), the adversary fades into Nothingness, which priests habitually maintain is the essence of Evil. War can destroy everything, because those it destroys need not be acknowledged; they have no more right to exist (for the good power) than Evil has for God.

This is how war may be replaced by assassination, why in the end war becomes nothing but a collection of dark murders. Indeed, the bombing aimed right from the outset to kill Saddam Hussein and his family, and, before him, Osama bin Laden and his clan, and Milosevic and his wife, just as in some ancient vendetta. We know that the Israelis, who are always in accord with their American masters (and disciples), long ago adapted the practice of vulgarly murdering every Palestinian who displeases them – and many Palestinians displease them – under the cynical name of 'targeted assassination'. The universalization of targeted killing: that is what, under the name of 'war', we are promised by the theology enveloping the American doctrine of power.

The USA invented the violence of the relation to the one whose non-existence it posits. Plato might have devoted a subtle dialogue to it: how to think the dialectic of the One and the non-existent. In fact, we may already refer to *The Parmenides*. The USA is the One that has no other. And the mode of being of that One is the destruction of the other, which is not destruction but liberation, since the other does not exist. Liberate the Iraqis from their claim to exist; bring them back down to the comforts of their non-existence: this is the spiritual essence of American war.

Before Aeschylus' *Oresteia*

The Americans, at bottom, consider that their senseless attacks (Afghanistan, Iraq, Somalia, perhaps Iran . . .) are legitimated by their right – that they, and only they, possess – to avenge themselves. It follows, then, that even the UN would recognize this right in declaring, after the mass crime of September 11, that the USA was in a 'state of self-defence'.

Historically, the USA has harboured a culture of vengeance. It has applied without interruption a very singular dialectic of law and vengeance, which might be put as follows: the law organizes vengeance, so should the law become weakened, vengeance, being the true essence of the law, must override it.

It is this dialectic that is at the basis of the maintenance, or the return, of the death penalty in that country, just as it supports the gigantic spread of its own infernal prison system.

At the cinema, the western is the formal organization of this dialectic of vengeance. On the one hand, the crime is to be punished in the name of the law, so there must be a trial, an oath taken on the Bible, and so on. But, on the other hand, in relation to crimes that are this odious, villains that are this perverted (of the Saddam Hussein or Milosevic variety) the law is always insufficient, so a solitary righter of wrongs (the figure of the One without other) must intervene to restore the law, just like the Americans and their British poodle must intervene to do the job for the impotent UN. This righter of wrongs, just like American warriors, will kill more unfortunates during the course of the film than the villain himself, before he at last comes to the final duel where, with his infallible Colt, he will blow the latter away. But this destruction, in which the path of vengeance resides, restores the law in its essence, which is precisely that vengeance be wreaked *at any cost*.

The type of man – and problem – engendered by this vision of things has been brilliantly composed, analysed and sublimated in the American novel. To understand its basic motivations it is essential, for example, to read Melville's *Billy Budd*, Faulkner's *The Bear* or Russell Banks' *Cloudsplitter*.

In America, law is subordinate to a reparative vision of order ('Law and Order' should be read: 'Law as Order'), which demands above all that the price be paid. So vengeance founds the law through the mediation of order. Yet, from Aeschylus' *Oresteia* we know that law (justice and trials that are public and fair) *replaces* vengeance in order that the order be one of civil peace and not one of war.

But American order *is* an order of war, both civil (competition of all against all) and external (interventionist zoning of the world to consolidate the isolation of its power). There is, then, in the most intimate subjective essence of the USA, something anterior to Aeschylus, *something non-Greek*.

A Protestant Bible unfiltered by Greek philosophy: such is the American conception of the law. Today, America imposes upon us its planetary vendetta. We shall oppose to it, inevitably, the combination advanced by Saint Paul, which says this: certainly, law without subjective determination is nothing, but vengeance devoid of thought, a retributive victimized subjectivity, is even less.

What exists for us is politics, which is a process of justice without law or vengeance, that is, a politics finally freed from moral imperialism, or from any morality at all, whether objective (the law) or subjective (the price demanded by the victims). A rational, intellectual politics, creative of possibilites – 'communist', in the generic sense of the term.

Marseilles, General Council Room (April 3 2003)

Void and infinity

There is a striking contrast between the representation of unlimited power and its increasingly obvious lack of content. Now that the destruction of Iraq – as state, as country, and as people – is under way, it is useful to ask oneself: What for? All the more so as, slowly, insidiously, shamefully, journalistic propaganda in France, momentarily taken in by Chirac's cock-a-doodle-doo (they voted for him in May 2002, lest we forget it), is rallying to the *fait accompli* of the war, to the stupid Yankee 'victory'.

Yes, what for? What is the USA proposing to the world? Its inability to create new values, or to transevaluate old ones (as Nietzsche would have said), is patent. Bush's Good designates the violent emptiness of conservatism. Even the Islamist 'proposition', which I have said elsewhere is obviously in complicity with American vacuity, is nonetheless articulated on a semblance of transcendence, and on rules comprehensible to those that the leaders of the Iranian revolution called the 'disinherited'. In comparison with this, Western 'liberty' is nothing but the illusion of intolerable luxury.

This is the disaster of the unlimited under way: it is like a false infinity of which only an envelope of power exists.

Power as the emptiness of the Idea: that is the principle of the devastation that's brewing.

Enlightenment and discipline

From this point on, what is the principal task of thought and action? Let's simply say that it is to *produce some separation from unlimited power.*

This marks a major difference with the preceding, post-war, period. In the post-war period, there existed in general something 'pre-separated', i.e. a separation that had been constituted in the form of socialism, that is, by the socialist camp, by Marxism, by the revolution, by the working class . . . You might have opposed the USSR, Stalinism, or Leninism, you might have preached the 'recasting' of Marxism, sociologized the 'mutations' of the working class, or called for a 'new type of party', but you did so in the space of this preconstituted separation from imperial power. The fact was that on a world scale the existence of another political, and moreover statist, possibility was not in doubt.

Today, however, a political possible must prove its possibility. Instead of differing over the conditions of realizing a possible, what is at stake now is the very *creation of a possible.* This can only be created, it must be admitted, with the resources of that which is generally not admitted into the realm of the possible.

That is why separation with the pretension of unlimited power takes the form of a pure creation.

There is a historical example of such a creation: in the eight-eenth century, French, English and then German philosophers had to create the conditions of a radical separation of thought from the infinite pretension of religion. This is the example, in short, of the Enlightenment.

Let's say that in order to support a new idea of politics in its experimentation, philosophy is beholden to invent the Enlightenment we now lack. An Enlightenment, that is, that works to separate thought from the 'democratic' limitlessness of power; an Enlightenment that claims for itself – against the negative infinite of state power and its international parliamentarization, which only envelop the emptiness of the Idea in the form of Western comfort – an affirmation that is itself infinite, but positive, of the totally autonomous deployment of politics *qua* practice/thought. Such a politics, it goes without saying, is Enlightened to the extent that it is subtracted from the evil spells of number and representation. And, in this sense, such a politics is basically un-'democratic', or non-party, and so universally practicable by all people, here and now. This would be a politics accountable only to itself, one solely attentive to its own process.

One principal lesson of the two episodes of which Chirac was the unwitting hero (the imposture of his election by a defeated Left on May 5 2002, and the last-ditch oppositional stand at the UN before the outbreak of war) is that the parliamentary model of democracy – to which I personally have ascribed no value since May 1968 ('Elections, arsehole trap'[10]) – has proven itself to be objectively threadbare, unable to give form to any principle at all. Let's say that state democracy is no more than a sort of platform argument against all even mildly serious attempts at emancipation.

But it is true that the Bolshevik model of authority, if is understood by that the 'iron discipline' of the Party, has also outlived itself. It was consumed by a state terrorism which, in the USSR, exhausted even those who were in charge of it.

The Enlightenment, whose elements we are slowly assembling, illuminates the invention of a path that is neither state democracy (parliamentarism, parties in the plural) nor state bureaucracy (socialism, party in the singular).

The difficult question is that of discipline. If it is neither that of parties, nor of the party, nor the defensive consensus of comfort, how or where shall it be constituted? Let's just say that it is about a *discipline of the real*. That is, we must maintain that those who, militarily and financially, have nothing can have no other strength than their total discipline of action and of thought, which – as in mathematics – is identical to total liberty, to absolute creation. It matters only that a rule of discipline is established, not in relation to a form of apparatus (since then one remains within state discipline, that is to say, today, within the disaster of the unlimited), but in relation to the solving of real problems (once again, as in mathematics). Such is the real content of every experience linked to the speculative advance of the Enlightenment. As restrained as it may be, action here is infinitized by the detour through thought that solves, in an organized way, a precise political problem, where an unexpected possible is extracted from matter outside the realm of the possible. On this point, too, the mathematical paradigm can be of use: the emergence of an entirely new, far-reaching theory comes about when thought concentrates on a problem whose formulation may seem entirely singular, or even extraordinarily narrow.

Any premature enlarging of perspectives dilutes the discipline of thought, its power of separation, in a 'democratic' gloss.

A tooth-and-nail fight to resolve a problem and to organize, on the basis of the principles that throw light on the solution to this problem, a united popular force (and even, dare we rediscover the term, a proletarian force), is the sole course of infinite affirmation, the sole course against the negative limitlessness of nihilistic comfort and of its vain and cruel power. Such is the only discipline that goes beyond the boundary the 'democratic' dogma wishes to lay down for us. This dogma, with its airs of liberal morality, consists only in the corrupting of spirit, nihilistic renunciation, and defeatist consent to millimetred enjoyment.

Hugo expressed it well. Addressing himself to the destructive capacity of power, about which he subtly says that it is really 'only the fury of black impotence' ('que la fureur de l'impuissance noire'), and calling 'life' all thinking that endures as far as 'where the real begins', he said: 'Incorruptible life is beyond your boundary.'

That 'incorruptible life' is simply another name for what we will soon no longer be lacking: the present.

Appendix

What are we to say now that some months have passed? Were I to continue this journal, it would simply become a chronicle of the tearing asunder, the dismembering, the suffering of Iraq. That the occupying powers had no real concern for any order, for the effective subsistence of a people and a state, has been totally borne out by the events.

The sole axiom of the 'war against terrorism' is this: better to have a bloody and costly anarchy than a state situated in a strategic zone that would not, would no longer, be vassalized.

A military, imported type of 'democracy' does not exist and never will. At best, it seems we will wind up with some kind of Shi'ite communitarian regression, which will not be able to force itself permanently on either the Kurds or whatever remains in Baghdad of the long-secularized Iraqi bourgeoisie.

We are slowly learning about the extent of the irrational violence during the military action, including the entry into Baghdad: a 'liberation' paid for by blind shooting at anything that moved. Civil deaths by the thousands, it seems.

Now, in response to this violence, there are attacks without norm, massacres without precedent, and the blowing to pieces of bodies by suicide bombers: an obscure milieu of plots and weapons.

But there are also some guerrilla actions against the occupying troops that are both organized and easy to read. They are obviously legitimate actions. The American war was not a riposte against any threat, nor did it even vaguely resemble a counter-offensive, so it can only be thought of as aggression and invasion. From then on, it is in accordance with the natural right of every people that they be able to declare a state of resistance against the occupation. The rightly named 'puppet government', that is, the authority put in place by the occupier, is also illegitimate, and so it is quite right that all the Iraqis who put themselves at the disposal of the reign of Western military, or put their pens and their programmes in its servile service, bear the infamy of being called 'collaborators'.

Further, there has been a great deal of propaganda proclaiming that 'foreigners' are involved in the resistance, etc. It is shameful to see it being taken up again with no mention of the fact that it is exactly the same as the propaganda the Nazi and Pétain govern-ments used against the Polish, the Italians and the Spanish. It was precisely the internationalist conviction of the last that led them to play a crucial military role in the Resistance in France. Does that mean that we can expect great things of the resistance in Iraq? Or that we are required to support it militantly, as we did the wars of liberation in Algeria and Vietnam? Alas, probably not. The reasons for this little hope are, to tell the truth, larger than the Iraqi situation itself. They concern the transformation of politics of emancipation in the post-Leninist and post-Maoist sequence. This transformation – which is everywhere in an experimental phase, and practically invisible in the Middle East – is also shown by the fact that it is so difficult to go, beyond principles, into any really effective action for the positive destiny of Palestine.

The question of universal significance that is forced upon us by the chaos in Iraq is not principally that of American power, of the control of oil, of Israeli villainy, or of capitalist globalization, even if, apart from principles, having really detailed analyses of these latter is of great use. The question is that of politics. I referred to the Enlightenment thinkers, and to the requirement of inventing a new Enlightenment that would counter the unlimited and advance the real infinite. What global concept of politics is appropriate to that invention? Therein lies the difficulty.

In the preceding sequence, we were able to respond to imperialism by saying 'internationalism', and to 'democracy' by saying the 'dictatorship of the proletariat'.

Neither the project of an International, nor one for a new form of state dictatorially imposing a decisive transition, has any consistency today; the former, since we are under the condition of a politics without party and the Internationals were all centralized federations of parties; and the latter, since the states of the dictatorship of the proletariat in no way advanced what they were theoretically supposed to: the withering away of the state as such. On the contrary, before collapsing, they all became terrorist states.

Consequently, the framework for effective international action – in relation to Iraq, for example – has not been constituted. This much was revealed by the fact that after massive anti-war demonstrations, the war won out, and succeeded in separating those who struggled against it from any public power.

It is a properly political task to invent, in the wake of localized experiences and their grasping in thought, new conceptions in which a radical critique of electoral democracy, on the interior, and of the 'international community', on the exterior, will find their power. There would be conceptions in which, situation by situation, a new internationalism (certainly not the reformist unrest of the anti-globalization movement) might be deployed, and in which an unexpected conception of political places and their decentring – that is, a new concept of democracy (certainly not the 'social movement', that hopeless inversion of electoral 'democracy') – might unfold.

Can philosophy accompany that invention? Without any doubt. And I believe it can do so in two ways.

The first way is ontological. It is necessary both to think the long-term stability of oppressive regimes (states and economies), and that which cuts into them, that which leads to the possibility of different forms of practice and thought. This can be referred to as: being and event.

The second way is logical. It is necessary to think the significance and reach of local experiences, of that which appears in the world, at a point, in such a way that a new instance of the universal (relative to the world considered) can be identified in that appearing. This can be referred to as: logics of worlds.

As abstract as the programme may appear, it really is in situating anew the correlation between being, or appearing, and 'that-which-comes', that philosophy can accomplish its task of welcoming, and of mentally facilitating, the operations of politics.

3

On the War against Serbia:
Who Strikes Whom
in the World Today?

We can pose the question that I've used as a title in relation to NATO's war against Serbia. It is just as pertinent in relation to the sanctions and air strikes against Iraq; the mass murders in Africa; the methods the Israeli state uses against the Palestinians; in the matter of Russia's colonial war against the Chechens; or the repressive operations of the Chinese state in the margins of its territory, in Tibet, in Sinkiang. It's the question of war in the world today after the Cold War. Yet, in what has been called the 'conflict of Kosovo', the notion of war has been avoided, as has that of *who* is at war. For example, was France, whose planes bombed Belgrade, at war with Serbia? The government would have sworn it wasn't. This is evidence that in this affair we must observe very carefully the language employed.

To start with, let's review the consensual vision of the war against Serbia in magazines of all persuasions; or rather, the general notions that support this vision, of which the NATO intervention is the only example (besides, it is because it is the only case, the only type, that, for those it bewitches, this war is not a war).

Totalitarian systems, dictators thirsty for power, new Hitlers, brutishly strike defenceless victims, infringing their human rights. Although Western powers, the only ones that are in essence democratic and humanitarian, are daily horror-struck by these atrocities via newspaper reports, they still suffer from the inertia entailed by reason of state and hesitate to do anything. Happily, public opinion is exerting an ever more insistent pressure, represented in France by philosopher-journalists who are entitled to speak out about rights. Yielding to that irresistible moral pressure, allied democratic and humanitarian armies tirelessly bomb the Brute. Moral war wrenches the hearts of the spectator crowds, but justice must be done. There are some immoral blunders. According to the generals' communiqués (as usual in war, there are no others), these blunders remain minimal. Some tens of unfortunate deaths here and there. Practically nothing. Finally, troops of human rights occupy the disputed territory, wherever it is. They appoint a proconsul whose morality is unquestionable. The troops will be there for perhaps thirty or fifty years, but little matter: public opinion has no longer anything to worry about, the humanitarian storm is over.

I would like to use a semantic method to evaluate this montage. I would like to examine the names that, for years, have been used to structure the situation in the former Yugoslavia, and that have structured it around the trilogy of the criminal, the victim and the humanitarian intervention, that is, the liberator straight from the beautiful West. These names are used to make people believe, people who have not even the remotest interest in these lateral regions, that the process of decomposition of the federal State of Yugoslavia boiled down this 'moral' trilogy. And that it is in terms of this trilogy, this nominal structure, that everyone must understand the situation, and call for intervention in it.

How did this chain of names function, and what did it signify?

First, let's look at things from the side of the criminal and his crime. The criminal cannot be a democrat, since – especially in France, where the intellectual counter-revolution has been constructed around these terms since the end of the 1970s – the whole drama is played out in a display of opposition between democracy and totalitarianism, between liberty and dictatorship. Thus Milosevic is presented as the last tyrant of the Balkans in the usual folklore inherited from Tintin (*King Ottokar's Sceptre*): there is the villainous Madame Milosevic pulling the strings behind the scenes, the gold stocked up in Switzerland, the cruel stupidity of the potentate, the secret service, the hesitant plot of the colonels, and so forth.

Obviously, it is in no way a fact that Milosevic is essentially different from the Croat, Franco Tudjmann, from the Bosnian, Izetbegovic, or the Russian, Boris Yeltsin. Nor, ultimately, from any head of state at all. He was legally elected, as is also the case for all his colleagues ever since the European 'socialist' party-states collapsed; like them he only confers with his immediate entourage (like every head of state) and particularly with his family (as was true of Mitterrand, Nixon, the ageing Mao, and has been with Clinton and Chirac); like them, he is tightening the screws on the media; and like them, having renounced all internal political goals and having been caught in the middle of the collapse of the former state system, he has at least sought to make a good show of nationalism. But he is (a little) more powerful than his Croatian, Bosnian, Montenegrin, Macedonian and Albanian neighbours and rivals . . . So he will make do as, contrary to the others who acted in the same way when the occasion presented itself, the designated criminal.

That crime is inherent to dictatorships is a major thesis of politics today, which does not prevent it from being totally false. To stick to the case of France, we could not say that either the governments of the Fourth Republic under De Gaulle or those of the beginning of the Fifth were totalitarian dictatorships. But all the same they accumulated abominable crimes in Algeria – systematic torture, rape, deportation and the burning of villages, etc. There is as much reason to make the generals and politicians of this period appear before the so-called court of human rights as there is to drag Pinochet or the mercenaries of the Yugoslav civil war before it. Not to mention the American leaders and military who destroyed Vietnam.

We'd do better to distinguish between situations than between regimes. Wars are always cruel, and colonial wars are particularly hideous. It is not clear that they were any less so when led by parliaments than when led by 'dictators'. The Yugoslav problem is one of the collapse of a state and the bloody dividing up of a country on the basis of ethnicity, language and religion, not one of the crimes of totalitarianism.

After the criminal comes the crime. Today, in the custom of 'civilized' Western populations, there is no true crime that merits immediate military punishment other than one that is commensurable with the essential Crime, with the unconditioned Crime: the destruction of the European Jews by the Nazis. Just as the bureaucratic upstart Milosevic must be Hitler (as, before him, Saddam Hussein, and in more distant imperial memory, Nasser, for the French and English of the miserable Suez expedition), so the ordinary and frightful massacring of civilians that occurs in every civil and territorial war (Vietnam, Bosnia), and in every colonial war (Algeria, Chechnya, Kosovo), must be racist genocide.

What served as the pivotal point for this syntactical conversion (which is also an abject desingularization of the destruction of the Jews by the Nazis) was the expression 'ethnic cleansing', under whose banner, and almost innocently, the killers of various 'national' militia of former Yugoslavia cleared their enemies out of the territories they coveted. We know that, in such cases (the techniques have been masterfully utilized by the Israelis in Palestine since 1947), in order to chase people away, terror and destruction must be announced and visible. This is what Croats, Bosnians and Serbs were all well aware of and executed perfectly, each according to their means: the Serbs, largely victorious in the beginning, did it as much as possible; the Croats quite a lot; the small Bosnians in the small regions where it was possible. This is also what, despite the occupation of the province and despite the usual moral declarations of the proconsul Kouchner, the Albanian militia of the KLA is doing today against the remaining Serbs and gypsies. As it happened, there were hardly any gypsies remaining in 'pacified' Kosovo. A few savage massacres, a few ransacked houses, a few roughly treated women, and you scarper. There was no such luck for the gypsies. Hitler had really decided to 'cleanse' Europe of them.

All that is assuredly barbarous; it pertains to the old story of the bloody rapine of armed bands that is often played out when a decomposing state falls into the hands of temporary adventurers. In former Yugoslavia during this time, vast areas of land, goods, houses, women, were – once the rules of state had come undone and the new ones were still uncertain – offered up to the militia troops and their state majors, those dull nationalist politicians. They were the spoils. Fiefdoms were carved out and people shot on sight; then, others established themselves in the abandoned properties and reaped the spoils. What does that have to do with the genocidal politics of the Nazis? Which nation has not had dark episodes of this nature, or worse, in its national history, and in the not too distant past? What is this Western moral conscience that believes it sees here the incomprehensible return of Evil?

It is extraordinary that those who forged their power by burning and bloodletting the entire planet – the English did it in an Ireland depopulated by famine and by means of an imperial order forged with convicts; the French and Americans by the slave trade and wars in Indochina and Algeria; the Spanish by committing genocide of entire peoples (real genocides those ones: not one remaining survivor of the original population of the Antilles); without counting the butchery of 1914–18 and 1939–45 – now, having attained an arrogant prosperity, act like beautiful souls who are completely astonished and indignant at seeing some small nations ever so often take the same path of violence and conquest that their own history often took. Must we conclude that, having prospered from war and empire, these imperialists must thereafter thwart anybody else's slightest aspiration to power? That is what I see lying beneath the amphigouri of moral interventions.

In the propaganda, it was repeatedly said that this 'totalitarian dictator' was a 'born liar', which I don't doubt. But what to say about the people from NATO? It is really interesting to read the reports on the situation, including the military ones, now that we have precise, or more precise, information. Precision bombing? The British air force tells us today that if 40 per cent of the bombs that were dropped on Kosovo and Serbia hit their target, then that's not bad going. Can somebody please tell us on what or on whom the rest of the bombs fell? Was there a genocide of the Kosovar Albanians? Impossible-to-find mass graves are sought everywhere, and the report of the OSCE puts the figure at some thousands of dead, which means, as if it were in doubt: massacres (even more so as the KLA engaged in guerrilla warfare), but nothing that resembles an 'ethnic cleansing'. And what about the famous 'liquidation plan' triumphantly discovered by the Germans in order to calm the pacificism of their public opinion? Nothing, false news. The OSCE inquiry shows that nothing was centralized or planned. The truth is that the Serbian troops were left largely to themselves (on account of the fact that the humanitarian allies had seriously damaged their communications systems) and committed random massacres for petty pleasure, hunting people for sport. Now we come to the biggest lie, comparable to the brainwashing of the war of 1914: all of the above occurred after the NATO air strikes began, which are thus directly responsible for this catastrophe. Beforehand, there existed a kind of bloody civil war, as in many parts of the world. There is simply no doubting it: the set of reasons given to justify the interminable and violent bombing of Serbia and Kosovo were a bunch of enormous lies.

NATO's three publicity statements were:

1. Democracies strike at totalitarian dictatorships.
2. In memory of the Shoah, ethnic cleansers will be attacked.
3. The troops of Truth strike at propagandistic lies.

All three were only pieces of fallacious rhetoric, badly cut clothes made to fit concealed aims, aims of a completely different nature.

Further, it was the very *identity* of those that struck that was indefensibly constructed. Who indeed are these allies whose principal characteristic is the Right to bomb? Let's study the invented names once more. It was claimed that NATO made up the armed wing, first, of democracies, second, of the opinion of the entire world (the 'international community'), third, of a legitimate judicial power – one whose norms are established by the 'philosophy' of human rights and whose policemen, always ready to seize the culprits, are the (American) military – and, finally, that the court of justice of this judicial power was the International Criminal Court.

All of that is only a scandalous pretence.

First of all, the decision to bomb Serbia was anything but democratic. The bombing was decided by a secret conclave, even though Milosevic had agreed to the Rambouillet Accords, bar one clause that any nation would find unacceptable (to be occupied by NATO!), and which was only there to bring the situation to a war. The Americans and the British wanted the intervention at any price, just as they want to bomb Iraq indefinitely, without any sort of mandate. One has to acknowledge that they are consistent imperialists. Whoever does not totally subjugate themselves will be punished, and that's that. Democracy has nothing to do with it. Even less so as this politically committed coalition, i.e. NATO, is in principle a purely defensive military alliance, so to make it into an instrument of aggression is to care precious little about the rules. Finally, there is no 'democracy' anywhere to be seen in the obscene parade of the powerful over the weak that is implied by the doctrine of 'zero [Western] deaths' – zero deaths, that is, for as many deaths as were necessary, and well beyond, on the Serbian side. This aspect of things was confirmed when no 'democrat' even raised a little finger for the Chechens. That's because, were Moscow to be bombed, then it is doubtful there would be 'zero deaths'. In this expedition, democracy boils down to saying that the weak who jib will be crushed, and that there'll be a pat on the back for the powerful, who can sink further into villainy.

Second, we know that this expedition was not the result of the entire world's wishes. The expression 'international community' is one of the most striking examples of the powerful of the day presenting themselves as the incarnation of what exists. As it is, the UN does not represent much, but even the strike on Serbia couldn't have been pushed through it! This 'international community' in fact designates the Americans and their various servants. Duly surveyed, public opinion was massively against the war. Both the Russians and the Chinese were, as also the Latin Americans and a good part of Europeans, and especially the Italians and the Greeks. Even the Germans were, so that the sordid rallying of the Greens and repeated ministerial lies were necessary to sway their hostile inertia a little. It is an outrage to designate NATO, its military leaders and its governments, as being in any way 'representative' of a supposed 'international community'.

Third, the judicial power represented by the quaternion at The Hague is a pure servant to imperial military intentions. We all saw this when, during the bombing, whose only fault was to have lasted longer than announced, this 'court' thought it wise (just to speed things up and give fodder to the moralists) to charge Milosevic. This decision was entirely determined by the propaganda concerns of NATO's military leaders. How is it that until now this same 'impartial' court has never dreamed, for example, of charging Putin? It would be hard to find a more opportunistic, servile court of justice.

In truth, as regards justice, the only authentic thing to do would be to demand both the dissolution of NATO – which we've clearly seen is an irresponsible international armed band that is very threatening to the rights of peoples and nations – and the dispersion of the ICC – whose autonomy of judgement is evidently non-existent, and which charges and sentences people only when the Americans deem it useful to their particular interests for them to be charged and sentenced. This will soon mean, we can be sure, everyone who proposes that the established order be transformed in a revolutionary manner. For be in no doubt that it won't be difficult to pin a 'human rights' tragedy on them. Then, the American marines could seize them, though not without striking some surrounding populations, and the court could sentence them. Democracy *oblige*.

In truth, we must advance the materialist hypothesis that no state has ever committed its army for the sake of the grand ideals of morality and rights. To have this believed is the obligation of the propagandist, and of the propagandist alone. Admittedly there are people who believe that the Allies engaged in war against Hitler to stop the genocide of the Jews, even though it has been established that the Allies weren't in the slightest concerned about it either strategically (they tried to block German expansionism, not Nazism) or tactically (they didn't take any action against the concentration camps, of whose existence they were aware). So there might also be people who believe that Belgrade was bombed for weeks to enforce respect for human rights.

We do not count ourselves among them.

The war against Serbia served as a medium-scale test of the relationship of forces in the world after the collapse of the Soviet system and the end of the Cold War. The Americans wanted this war to humiliate the Russians, but without any direct confrontation, and to address a severe warning to the Chinese (who still believes that the US air force bombed the Chinese Embassy 'by mistake'? Not the Chinese, in any case). The war also demonstrated, right after the launching of the Euro, that the Europeans were incapable, even within their own perimeter, of any independent military action of scale. As a result, the war made NATO into the principal military apparatus on the planet, the world's policeman in the service of the existing imperial order. Note that since this war, no one has taken the risk of doing anything, in any domain, that might displease the Americans. For the whole world *saw* the impotence of the Russians, saw confirmed the vassalic commitments of the Europeans, and witnessed the extreme (temporary?) caution of the Chinese.

For France, the chief importance of its presence in the ranks of the bombers was its visible reintegration into NATO. One can now see how Gaullist 'independence' contributed to the world's division into two blocs and to the Cold War. Average and small powers were able to enjoy a relative margin of manoeuvre. Today, it seems, servility is *de rigueur*. Yet what a response France's refusal to associate itself with American police operations might have elicited around the world! It seems then that Spain and Italy would have felt released from their obligations, and Greece would have been able to materialize its hostility. The Germans would have thought twice about it. We could have, and we should have, referred the Americans to their endless *tête-à-tête* with the English. But don't hold your breath. It appears that France has need of the protection the American military offers for its far-off enterprises and capital, and that it will sink more and more comfortably into servility to NATO. We obviously cannot expect anything worthwhile from the Atlanticist tradition of the Parti Socialiste, nor from Chirac's renunciation of everything that made for a semblance of pride in Gaullism.

The only conclusion to be drawn is that despite all the talk about the all-powerful economy, to have a strong military apparatus at one's disposal remains the alpha and omega of having international pretensions and national independence. Europe will amount to nothing if it does not equip itself (but this would require a state that is much more unified and constituted) with military resources, and aero-naval resources in particular, that are totally independent of American control. To this the Americans have already served notice that they'll oppose a *de facto* veto.

The war in Serbia was a test of power. For it worked both to configure the states of existing power, and it manifested (as it did formerly to Khomeini, then to Saddam Hussein) the absolute will of the current imperialists to prevent new regional powers being established, something that since the dawn of time has implied the possibility or the reality of war. The intervention in Serbia showed that, except in remote corners of the earth where people can craftily kill each other for decades without 'morality' being at all moved, the imperial powers, led by the USA and organized by NATO, with the UN as a scorned cover, dispose of the monopoly of war in the following form: *we will let no one win a war*. To counter Iran, Iraq was armed. To counter Iraq, the UN was armed. To counter Serbia, NATO was sent. In all cases, what matters is that the ambitious do not succeed. It might be objected that Westerners, and especially the USA, forged their planetary power by winning wars. Quite right. All that says is that the lesson has been learned: *we shall let no one become powerful*.

That lesson entails another. The logic of power has never been the consequence of noble principles, even if power likes to have it believed. What is not obligatory is to make philosophy subservient to this kind of propaganda.

The worst thing is not that philosophy is linked to bloody and daring undertakings. For in this case it remains, even when in extreme error, on the side of invention, on the side of the genius of the weak, on the side of a power *to come*. The worst thing is to link it, purely and simply, to the arrogance and the self-satisfaction of the master in place.

There has always been an imperial triad: first, the military that conquers; second, the commerce that opens the markets; and third, the proselytizing missionary. Irrespective of whether it involves converting people to Christ the King or preaching 'human rights', it does not befit the philosopher to occupy this third position.

The 'Democratic' Fetish
and Racism

4

On Parliamentary 'Democracy': the French Presidential Elections of 2002

The moment is no doubt propitious for examining, being careful to keep an ethnological distance, the custom of voting: the last sacred cow of our comfortable and pleasantly nihilistic countries. Leading the way is the United States, where half of the people, and a majority of youth and popular classes, have begun to stop conforming to this custom. Savage disbelief in the democratic religion, in its joint cult of numbers and the secretive conviction of souls, grows. And as we have recently witnessed on several occasions, voting has become increasingly unstable and irrational. Finally it calls for philosophical critique!

Here I will focus on the French presidential elections of 2002, in fact, on the sequence from April 21 to May 5. The details of this sequence are as follows: the socialist candidate, incumbent Prime Minister and poll favourite, Jospin, is eliminated in the first round. Instead, it's the extreme right-wing candidate, Le Pen, who progresses to the second round to challenge the incumbent President, Chirac, who, with less than 20 per cent of the votes, has himself not shone in all his glory. This situation provokes considerable unrest between the rounds throughout the country. The left-wing parties (the Socialist Party, the Communist Party, the Greens [ecologists] and even the Trotskyist Revolutionary Communist League) call for people to vote for Chirac, their intimate enemy, so as to block the road to Le Pen and 'save democracy'. High-school students take to the streets. On May 1, a demonstration of five hundred thousand people proclaims the duty to say 'no' to Le Pen, and calls for everyone to vote for Chirac as a means of doing so. On May 5 Chirac is elected with a soviet-style score, Le Pen's score stagnates, and the emotion dissipates into the air like mist.

Method

How might we conceive of a philosophical method in relation to such a short and singular sequence? And why give to this surprising turn of events in French parliamentary history the honour of a philosophical reflection?

On the second point, I'd say that what matters is the powerful manifestation of a public affect, what in the language of the eighteenth century was referred to as an 'emotion'. Indeed, Le Pen's presence in the second round of a French presidential election provoked an insomniac emotion in quite a number of my fellow citizens. I have taken this emotion into account. I must admit that I don't share it in the slightest and was struck by the magnitude and unanimity with which my fellow philosophers felt it – philosophers who themselves manifestly comprised (but they ought not have) a kind of echo chamber of all the 'intellectuals' and also a non-negligible part of the high-school students. In truth, this electoral result seems significant to me of the fact that, as I've said for many years now, this is a politically sick country. But, not seeing in the result any reason for losing my composure, I also saw that many people, including some that I love and value, thought such composure pathological. Emotion being for them an *antepredicative*, I thought it had better be analysed, and that it provided a good point of entry into the fiendish question of voting and 'democracy.'

Returning to the first point, here is what I propose by way of a procedure:

1. An examination and definition of the public affect in relation to its cause.
2. A critical examination of the names used to legitimate and confer political dignity upon this affect, to offer it a symbolic way out.
3. An identification of the general space in which the link between the public emotion, its cause, and its consequences was established, that is, the formulation of a problem that is ultimately the problem of voting.
4. A statement about this problem's general intelligibility and a radical displacement of its axiomatic position.

General Overview

The cause of the affect was that right *there*, where Jospin was expected, in came Le Pen. It remains to find out exactly what this *there* is – a subtle question pertaining to the numerical distribution of places.

The affect itself was registered as being somewhere between awareness of a threat (the affect, then, is in the register of fear: 'I fear . . .'; people were said to have been 'very scared') and the conscience of a stain, of an aberration ('I'm ashamed,' 'This is not possible'). But what relation does this have to the cause?

The legitimization of this affect was constructed around self-defence: defence of democracy and/or of the Republic. Was there any substance to this threat? And what did it profane exactly?

The symbolic 'solution,' which calmed the panic, was to vote for Chirac. But where did the supposed (moral) strength for that act come from?

The public space linking the affect (I fear, I'm ashamed) and its symbolic sedative (Chirac's triumph) was obviously the vote. It is imperative to understand the absolutely astounding subjective formula: 'Since Le Pen has occupied the place which Jospin should have occupied, now, where I would have otherwise abstained or voted for Jospin, I must vote for Chirac.'

Intelligibility requires that we relate the vote to something outside itself. So the questions are clear:

1. What is the reality of which some consider the vote to be a formalization and others a dissimulation? How is it that, a propos of the vote, we could pass from the solid maxim of May 1968 'Elections, arsehole trap', to the maxim that could be read at the demonstration of May 1 2002, 'I think, therefore I vote'?

2. Supposing that this reality includes Le Pen, isn't it possible that another way of dealing with Le Pen exists that cannot be reduced to the strange fanfare of voting for Chirac?

Cause and effect

To determine the cause of that public affect, it suffices to attempt the following eidetic variation: let's imagine Le Pen had received more votes than he in fact did on April 21, but that he came in behind Jospin. Then, we could bet there would not have been such emotion, nor such prolonged hysterics. No doubt the analysts would have voiced their concerns, as some indeed did after Le Pen maintained his level of support into the second round. But perhaps as a result, there would have been more of a relation to the real. And certainly less, if any, affective gesticulating.

Consequently, the cause of the affect was simply that Le Pen came in at a (certain second) place, and had nothing at all to do with the numerical impact of his candidature as such. In what, then, does this place consist? It is the place that is symbolically recognized as being 'in the race' for power: the stupefaction resulted from Le Pen's being 'in the race.'

It pays to think for a moment about the nature of places in the ballot. It clarifies how we should understand the idea of the symbolic equality between candidates. For, in reality, there is a fundamental distinction between merely 'being a candidate' and 'being a candidate in a position that indicates the possibility of having power'. Being in this kind of position is decided according to different criteria than is the case for simple candidature. We can see that a Le-Pen-candidate, and even a Le-Pen-with-a-very-good-score, made very little impression upon the masses, which is, moreover, regrettable. On the other hand, Le Pen's occupying the position he did unleashed a considerable affect, at least in certain strata of the population.

This means, of course, that this place is pre-coded. Certain people would argue that it is reserved only for 'democrats', for authentic 'republicans'. This is why, when it is obtained, as it was, by someone not regarded as being a democrat, by someone represented as heterogeneous to the coding of the place, then, just as whenever an infidel touches a sacred relic, it sparks off the public emotion of the guardians of the temple.

Hence it is simply false, at least in emotional terms, or in terms of the mass of opinion, to say that voting is an instance of the freedom of expression. For in reality what I shall call the homogeneity principle looms above it: anyone can be a candidate, but only those who are in line with certain norms may have a place pre-coded for potential power. In truth, this means those who one knows for certain will not do anything *essentially* different from those preceding them. The homogeneity principle is in fact what guarantees the *conservatism* of the vote, incarnated today by the alternation of the major parties. If your 'enemies' must also be able to be your successors in power, it is because you haven't taken any measures to render their coming impossible. Such is the so-called 'citizen's pact' that is constantly drummed into our ears: in the Chambers of

State the adversary's bed must always be made. This is to presuppose that the adversary isn't an adversary to the extent that one would block their road by taking even minimally serious measures. As Alain Peyrefitte said to the Socialists and Communists in power in 1981, when Mitterrand was making decisions about nationalizations: 'You've been elected to change the government, not to change society.' And the warning was well understood: from 1983 onwards, under Laurent Fabius, the orientation of the government became indiscernible from simple reactionary administration.

We ought to warn all those who became seriously troubled after April 21: in the end, they demonstrated in favour of the homogeneity principle, which was proved by the fact that they assuaged their turmoil by voting for Chirac. Since what was that vote's value, if not to say that, faced with the emergence of the apparently heterogeneous, what is essential is the common ground uniting Chirac and Jospin? And note that this principle of the homogeneous is global. If tomorrow another candidate that the *beaux quartiers* considered heterogeneous – let's say our honest Arlette Laguiller[11] – came in at a pre-coded place, we would certainly have another kind of public emotion, and how would you react to it? What would you do when the gigantic demonstrations to defend democracy against 'red' totalitarianism sprang up? As we know, bourgeois opinion is capable of causing an uproar. The demonstrations on June 30 1968 against the workers' and youth movement, and in 1982 in defence of l'Ecole Libre,[12] were much larger than that against Le Pen on May 1 2002.

The only reasonable conclusion is that, as regards decisive transformations in a country's politics, nothing will ever come to pass if left to a vote, because the homogeneity principle stands above it. And it is interesting to note that, in general, a partial but large mass of opinion, whether 'democratic' (in defence of free existential comforts) or directly bourgeois (in defence of property rights and earnings), will vouch for the principle in question in the streets. That is, it will vouch for continuing *just as before*.

Heterogeneous?

Le Pen was represented precisely as someone under whom we would not continue as before. But why, exactly? The question of the heterogeneous raises itself here and it is a difficult philosophical question. What is the threshold at which an entity may be determined as being heterogeneous to a given ensemble and its dominant predicates? Taking into account today's French parliamentary system, its personnel and its thematics, in what way is Le Pen heterogeneous to it? Let there be no misunderstanding: Le Pen is without doubt a scoundrel; he was trained at length in the inner circles of fascistic groupuscules in the 1950s, and, in his own words, was 'educated' by his activity as a torturer in the colonial army in Algeria. However, his personal identity does not suffice to define him really as heterogeneous to the parliamentary system. Does one dream of excluding Madelin, who steered the helm of a pro-Nazi small group appropriately called 'Occident'?[13] As to the general form of his action throughout the last decades, Le Pen has always argued that he has done nothing other than present himself for election. And that is essentially right. The National Front has a combat group, but so did the Communist Party. So no one on the left would be able to extract an argument from that fact in order to deny him the right to compete in elections. Hence we might say this (which is also my point of view): the fact that Le Pen was present at the second round of a French presidential election without having led a fascist militia into the streets means he is homogeneous to the French parliamentary system. Besides, in the second round 6 million people confirmed their vote for the leader of the National Front, thus proving without an inkling of doubt that for them he is a candidate just like any other.

But if Le Pen is homogeneous to our political system, then *it is the militants of emancipation who ought to be heterogeneous to it, so as to be really heterogeneous to Le Pen.* Elections should bear the responsibility for Le Pen's presence and not those who abstained. Hence the march should have been – as when the reaction utilized the vote of the *provinces profondes* to quell the uprising of May 1968 – to cries of 'Election, betrayal!' Or better still, 'Elections, what a pig-sty!'

But that is really far from what happened! Thus the question of the heterogeneous returns insistently. Indexing it to current political content proves difficult. What about the immigrants? But who among the mass of terrified democrats of April 21 has really worried about them? Has not even the harshest of successive bills worked to solder left and right together against the 'threat' of undocumented workers, universally marked as 'clandestine'?[14] Have we seen any of the 'anti-racists', so stirred up after the ballot, worry themselves about the plight of hundreds of thousands of workers deprived of their rights? And security?[15] Have we not seen the quasi-totality of the scribbling democrats rediscover with delight an awareness of security? Did we not read that a number of republican intellectuals cry out, in the school of the mayor of New York, for 'zero tolerance'? Have they not all joyfully consented to the disappearance of references to the worker in political discourse? Is not the idea that the word 'West' – formerly reserved for the extreme right wing – designates a superior civilization dominant everywhere? And is it not the case that all those democrats are now ready to fight in the name of that superiority against all the 'Muslims' on earth? On all of these points, Le Pen is homogeneous to the dominant governmental discourse. Besides, this is precisely why he can enter the ballot and parade on the television, whereas in the red years – between 1968 and 1980 – he and his like could not come out of their rat-holes without ten thousand militants forcing them back down.

So what? Suffice it to say that, when it comes to Le Pen, the general awareness of heterogeneity is purely ideological. For the mass of democrats, neither are the political methods he uses unrecognizable, nor is the political content he proposes inadmissible. He is only the promulgator of a discourse of self-preservation that, instead of being about democratic conviviality, is about a national archaism and its historical reality, Pétain. What is Pétain?

It is the cowardly conviction that shutting one's eyes in the face of a few atrocities makes it possible to maintain a more or less comfortable existence and, in any case, to avoid any risks, however mildly heroic. It is the conviction that things will remain essentially 'as before'. And what is parliamentarism – left and right wings alike! – in a secondary nation like France? Exactly the same thing: negative well-being without a project, without idea – or satisfied perpetuation. At bottom, Le Pen is the extreme end of the parliamentary system and this is precisely why he brings shame on the 'democratic' voters: he is like the hideous spectacle of what one is oneself, but taken to its extreme, or proclaimed rather than hidden. That is the true content of the bizarre slogan: 'Le Pen equals hate!' Do these people really like deprived immigrants, workers, sick Africans, war fraternities and enthusiastic political adventures, that is, everything that stigmatizes their electoral nightmare? There is nothing to warrant believing it. Instead, just as they have always done, moderate profiteers veil the chronic violence that shelters them from the real world and the vast anonymous masses with proclamations of love. But when someone declares, in all its rawness, the very thing their comfort presupposes, the thing they consent to in silence or through lies, they cry out that enough is enough and that they won't have any part in it.

The element of heterogeneity against which a small part of France raised their hands for two weeks was only the outdated, explicit, extreme, and in-your-face form of the thing this France tolerates in order to persevere in its being. It was in honour of this dreadful 'self' that a brief affect-storm – rather than being properly identified – was worked up in our minds.

Affect

The public emotion that accompanied Le Pen's occupation of a place that was pre-coded for someone else was presented as the identification of a danger. People were said to have been 'very scared'. Identifying this danger gave rise to a ridiculous and nearly inexplicable turgidity. Rumours circulated to the effect that Le Pen was assured of being elected. Bursts of feverish emails rang out around everywhere warning of fascism at the door. Petitions of 'resistance' unified all the intellectual corporations. Nevertheless we, the real militants, have had some reason to complain in that, for many years now, the attention paid to real Lepenist ideas and their governmental effects (iniquitous laws against workers without papers) has been only marginal. No 'resistance', or hardly any, has been forthcoming. Whence comes this barricading fever all of a sudden? Let's propose a rule: if the exercise of resistance is abstract, the suddenly unexpected is virtually infinite. Not normally worried by real Lepenism, but taken aback in their electoral sleep, the citizens, as they call themselves a little pompously, were prepared, like those who startle easily in the small hours, to imagine the most improbable tribulations.

On the other hand, there was an overall sense of feeling 'ashamed of France'. What was the content of that shame? As for me, I am ashamed of decades of successive French governments, and especially of hypocritical governments who persecute undocumented workers or lick the boots of belligerent Americans under labels such as 'leftists', 'socialists', or 'communists'. But here we are manifestly dealing with something else altogether. The shame, I think, came from the fact that the arrival of Le Pen – that extremist, odious image of a secret and subservient public conscience – into the second round was like a stain on the contemporary sacralization of the electoral institution. The shame was then supposed to have been 'effaced' by voting for Chirac. That is, the return of the usual routine – governmental alternation – restored the dignity of the fetish.

There are also many intellectuals, marked in this sense by a 'republicanism' *à la Chevènement*,[16] who have an inflated idea of France. For them it's the 'homeland of human rights', something that a number of foreigners also believe until that same 'homeland' expels them. For them it's the democracy *par excellence*. After April 21 some democrats went into convulsions remembering their arrogant lecturing to Jörg Haider's Austria and Berlusconi's Italy. Why is it that we have not ceased taking out overdrafts on our Revolution for over two centuries? It opened for us, nationally and internationally, a credit that one often believes is inexhaustible. The time has finally come – after Pétain, but also after Jospin (or Chirac: the same thing, as we saw with the vote) – to realize that this credit ran out long ago. Restoration France, the France of the *Versaillais*, Collaborationist France, the France of the colonial wars, contemporary French subservience: France is a disproportionately abject country. It is only saved by what constitutes an exception to it. Such was perhaps already the case with Robespierre, Saint-Just and Couthon,[17] although it was quickly overturned by that major figure of our national destiny, the Thermidorian; that is, the one who renounces his revolutionary enthusiasm and sells his rallying to the order of proprietors. The passage from 'Elections, arsehole trap', to the Western and democratic fetishism, and then to the vote for Chirac in order to 'save the republic', partakes of that eternal Thermidorian shift – alas, much more persistently French than our admirable insurrections.

Whether it be fear or shame, fear and shame: we oscillate between blind devotion to the vote, national hyperbole and panic-stricken gesticulating.

Names

In the political order, appropriate names are required to legitimize affects. And if that affect is a combination of panic and shame (dissimulating no doubt the most violent instinct there is: that of self-preservation), it is crucial that these names designate an entity that is both intangible and numerically consensual, the organization of whose defence they should forthwith provoke.

These names were: 'democracy' and 'the republic'.

Of the second – a national speciality (still milking 1792) – I will say that I've often wondered what it might possibly signify these days. I can see the rigour of the word when a section of the *sans-culottes* claim to take up the aristocracy *à la lanterne*, rise up in arms at the border to block the route to the monarchies, or invade the legal assembly to demand the purging of the indifferent. But today? The republic of whom, of what? That of the terrifying national massacre of 1914–18? That which voted to give full powers to Pétain? That of the atrocious colonial wars? Of Guy Mollet?[18] Of Mitterand? Of the pair of Jospin–Chirac? Or, then, of de Gaulle? To say that Le Pen 'threatens the Republic' is nonsensical. And evoking 'fascism' is evidently overblown, even if Le Pen's youth was nourished on the intellectual detritus of the thirties. Whoever saw the spirited Jack Lang,[19] given the task of commentating on the ballot on the television, saying 'fascism will not pass' has surely been vaccinated against all contemporary uses of the word 'republic'.

The word 'democracy' is obviously more complex, if only because, throughout the world, it names the system also called 'the West', that is, the civilization whose rampart is, as we know, the American Army and its Israeli mercenaries. This is the word that has worked to crystallize the consenting subjectivity and whose referent is intangible. Democracy: that is what Le Pen desecrated by being in a place reserved for those in the running for power. On the walls there were lyrical odes to this system of government, about which, however, one could not say that it has lifted us to the heights of the becoming generic of humanity. Around May 5, an immense graffito evoking Paul Eluard and the *Résistance* proclaimed: 'I write your name, Democracy!' The artist of the mural, however, did not dare write what was nevertheless to become the real object of his devotion: 'I write your name, Jacques Chirac!'

You'll remark that occurrences of the word 'democracy' became confused, since it was used to designate both that which Le Pen threatens and sullies, and that which Jospin lacked, preventing him from securing the place that, in the normal run of things, was reserved for him. It is indeed undeniable, as a number of idolizers of the said Jospin discovered while defending democracy, that during his reign this 'socialist' displayed constant scorn for the overwhelming majority of people who live and work in our country. So, one had not only to efface the shame that had been inflicted on democracy but at the same time to deplore Jospin's lack of it, for which the only solution on offer was Chirac – a veritable friend of the people, that one, a well-known democrat! We can say that the public emotion simply led its subjects down a labyrinthine path where 'democracy' and 'the democratic deficit', evil and remedy, cause and effect, constantly changed places. Nothing revealed this more clearly than the extraordinary declaration of Alain Krivine,[20] Trotskyist leader of the Ligue Communiste Révolutionnaire: 'Come Sunday I will vote for Chirac. Come Monday I will demonstrate for his resignation.' How about that for speaking forthrightly and drawing an intransigent democratic line! Naturally, the vote was held, but the demonstration will have to wait for better days.

It is because the sole function of the word 'democracy' was to sanction defending the vote against any occupation too hetero- geneous – that is, too revealing – of its symbolic space (in general, first and second places) that, without examining any political content, and speaking very vaguely of 'racism' and the 'facho',[21] which doesn't cost much effort, the dismayed democrats proudly claimed the right to say 'no!' Always commercially concerned to vaunt the merits of youth (which, as we've known for ages, refers only to those who have emerged in the period), various magazines accordingly baptized the demonstrations those of the 'no genera- tion'. Unfortunately, the essence of politics, especially when there is a real danger, resides not in the 'no' but in the 'yes'. It lies in examining various kinds of 'yes'. It resides in consenting to or affirming something. Saying 'no' to Le Pen completely avoids the question of what Lepenism is and how it is really spread. Opposing this diffusion can be achieved, not by saying 'no' to abstractions such as 'racism' or 'hate', but by saying 'yes' to entirely precise and rigorous political orientations, such as: regularizing undocumented workers; gaining complete independence from American imperialist adventures; affirming the factory as a political site; immediately organizing free healthcare for contagious illnesses, and especially for AIDS, throughout Africa. . . .

In fact, the famous 'no' authorizes us to pass in silence over the prior 'yeses', the 'yeses' of consent that have effectively authorized Lepenism to be everywhere. Consent to the persecution of those without papers, to detention centres, to American crusades, to the devastation of workers' lives by the petit-bourgeois Aubry 35-hour week,[22] and to millions of deaths in Africa. That is, consent to what was Le Pen's main slogan throughout the second round: 'feel at home *chez soi*', which was perhaps *the* consenting subjectivity of the overwhelming majority of the dismayed democrats of April 21 throughout the Mitterand/Jospin/Chirac years. And this consent remains the shameful subjective secret that the semi-affluent of our European societies dissimulate behind 'democratic' logomachy, a secret whose formula, as shared as it is unspoken, is: my comfort, my little bit of *jouissance* and leave me in peace!

What should be feared is that, concealed behind the (legitimate) disgust that Le Pen and his cronies inspire, an entirely different fear, intimate and abject, pursues its path: the fear that one day an unknown people, which is held at a distance, unnamed but massive, will come to ask for an explanation from those who have for so long consented to the fact that their visible fortune, their tranquil lives, their discussion as 'free' as it is vain, was paid for by the greatest indifference concerning the lot of generic humanity.

There can hardly be any other explanation for the speed with which commentators insisted on the alleged Lepenism of the workers and the poor. It is because, in the end, what would be really heterogeneous is the manifesting of an(other) idea of politics, for example, a politics of emancipation, a politics decided by ordinary people and not by the guardians of state, a politics not concerned with elections. Now such a politics would take root on the side of workers without papers, of free intellectuals, of ordinary wage earners, of people whose lives are constrained and difficult, rather than on the side of the 'editorialists' of *Le Monde* and *Libération*. What is better: it is starting to happen. So, notice how convenient it is to ward off these ordinary people by means of a 'no' which – justified by the dreadful Le Pen – ricochets nicely onto everything that aspires to inscribe workers and ordinary people in a politics veritably heterogeneous to the one dominating us.

This 'no' is only a symbolic, numerical, demonstrative consolidation of the essential 'yes' by which the middle classes of our country endorse the perpetuation of an ignominious political universe.

Granted it is more difficult to renounce these 'yeses', to change what one says 'yes' to, and to go from consent to militant affirmation or from comfort to truth, than it is to say 'no' for 10 days to the offence a fetish is declared to have suffered. This rebellious tone is only a pleasant and provisional form of getting one's thrills from the good old consent to what already exists, and from which sufficient pleasure is reaped not to wish for the coming of anything heterogeneous.

Paradoxes of the vote

Such an example of considering oneself heroic, whereas in reality one is simply conservative, provides us with a good introduction to examining the paradoxes of the vote. For example:

1. The vote is a formalism pertaining to freedom, indeed, some say, the formalization of political liberty itself, yet it is also

obligatory. We know it is officially obligatory in a number of countries. But, as we witnessed this time in the violent diatribes against abstention, for many it is also subjectively, or morally, obligatory. (That is, let it be said in passing, for many intellectuals and students, but not so much for ordinary people. For they abstained in still greater numbers in the June legislative elections. Little by little, 'democracy' is becoming a minority ritual.)

2. Equality of number is a law of suffrage, yet, as we have said, the decisive places are coded according to norms that transcend numbers.

3. There is a flagrant asymmetry between 'yes' and 'no'. The consequence of a 'no' is elimination and it is effective. On the other hand, what is played out with a 'yes' could not be more elusive. What commitments are elected members held to? Nothing of worth, in any case, which is even more so nowadays, seeing as the very notion of a 'programme' has been practically discredited. So, for the voter, there is a real of the negative sanction, but no measurable reality of success – excepting, as we've said, the reality of preserving the principal parameters of existence, that is, at least those that elected representatives exercise some authority over. Such is the secret of stale politicians: the only way to stay in power is to do nothing.

In these conditions, what is the meaning of the cult of the vote post-April 21? Precisely, that voting is the only political procedure known whose *immobilisme* (i.e. opposition to change) is a practically ineluctable consequence, excepting that which is demonstrably a law of nature. Phenomena as considerable and as dramatic as the destruction of rural France in a few decades, the dismantling of public services, schools included, the alibis found in obedience to European Union directives, and the follow-the-leader attitude in American wars, were never submitted to a vote, nor clearly chosen through one particular party. The vote does not bear on these capital questions, which are instead presented consensually by politicians as comprising simply what exists, and not as that which is decided (hence it is said: 'it's the modern world', 'the world as it is'). Similarly, certain decisions have to be taken in secrecy since they are not conservative enough to withstand the test of the vote (for example, France's commitment to Iraq during the long and extremely bloody war against Iran, a commitment that was really never made public). In other words, if important changes take place they do not do so in the field of the vote. Inversely, that which is in the vote's field is on the whole inalterable. What fascinates and brings about adhesion to the procedure of voting is this guarantee of a decision without object.

On the other hand, a politics encompassing real decisions, I mean emancipatory decisions, is entirely foreign to the vote, because by deciding something liberatory you are designated as being hostile to established interests, interests that, despite being in the minority, will make enough of a hullabaloo, and will have sufficient control over the instruments of propaganda, to ensure that you'll be replaced at the next election. And this will be all the more readily done, as people vote to persevere and not to become.

Linking politics to real decisions, those understood not as adhering to the nature of things but as consequences of a will, can only be done by submitting politics both to principles and to practices that depend directly on such principles, rather than to the very strange rule that submits everything to a count of votes.

The vote is in essence contradictory to principles, just as it is to every idea of emancipation and protest. Permit me an anecdote on this point: during those fatal 15 days, when the 'facho', Le Pen, contested the presidency, students from the Ecole des Arts Déc-oratifs produced numerous 'democratic' posters, just like their glorious ancestors of May 1968 produced revolutionary ones. The ancestors illustrated the adage 'Elections, arsehole trap', their descendants the adage 'Voting, it's great', or similar. Proof, then, that Heraclitus was right: one never steps in the same river twice. During this time, I caught sight of a green screen-print poster (for some time now green has been worn more willingly than red) hanging in the school's entrance proclaiming: 'A blank vote is no longer a protest vote.' I interrogated a group surrounding the masterpiece: 'All the same, you don't mean to say that to vote for Chirac would be a protest vote?' They granted that that would indeed be an exaggeration. 'Still less a vote for Le Pen?' I added. They exclaimed that I should not dream of it. 'So,' I said, 'if neither voting for Le Pen, nor voting for Chirac, nor voting blank is protesting you mean to say, and you should have written: voting is not protesting.' They did not agree except to balk at what they believed my conclusion to be. I gave chase, 'Are you democrats?' They smiled at the thought that I could possibly imagine the contrary. 'You find, then,' I continued, 'that voting is the major political act, that voting is what there is that is good?' This they confirmed with wide grins of self-satisfaction, and one of them explained to me, as if addressing himself to a slow intellect, that this is exactly what they wanted to say with their poster. 'But then,' I said, 'if voting is good, and voting is no longer protesting, then it is protesting which is bad. Is that what you want to say?' They would not be easily brought around. But, alas, that is exactly what they wanted to say. That was the real content of their emotion. As the libertarians of the nineteenth century said: 'To vote is to abdicate.' More exactly, today one should say: 'To want to abdicate is to vote.'

Passive and active number

The reason for the paradoxes of the vote is well known: it is its technical rationality, i.e. that which draws the result from a simple count, that which authorizes the infinite attentions of sociologists and political scientists – who are as concerned with numerical details and variations as the specialists of climactic history – and which works only to conceal massive irrationality. For why would number have any political virtue? Why would the majority, modifiable at will thanks to the ruse of infinite modes of balloting, be endowed with the attributes of a norm? Such approximations are simply not tolerated in other domains where human thought is at stake. Great scientific creators and innovative artists have been right, contrary to dominant opinion. Even violent amorous passions affirm themselves against mediocre social judgements. Is politics, and it alone, to be condemned to the conservatism of numerical means? Everything indicates that this cannot be the case. Since each time a capital political decision is to be taken, by everyone in their own name, the partisans of the just and the true are initially entirely in the minority, or even electorally insignificant. The *résistants* of the 1940s, those of the 1950s opposed to the sordid colonial wars, the 'leftists' of the 1960s and 1970s: all of them were absolutely in the minority just as are those who today see imperialistic ambitions and the spirit of servitude hidden beneath the mask of 'humanitarian interventions', or the 'war against terrorism'. And basically everyone knows that number, the majority, gained from blind lists at the end of the extremely unpolitical ballot box, has no real meaning.

The refuge, then, is the ambivalence of number, since we must distinguish the passive number, such as it functions at the ballot box, from an entirely other number, which is active, a number pertaining to demonstrations, mass strikes and, indeed, insurrections.

The active number, however large it is, is in reality always tiny with regard to the passive number. The demonstrators of May 1 2002 boasted of having numbered five hundred thousand. That was nothing compared either with the total number of voters, or with Le Pen's six million voters. In fact, the active number is not capable of being valorized except when the power of the collective will traverses it, as it takes the risk of an act, or of a tenacity of organization, above and beyond all considerations of averages or majorities.

Between April 21 and May 5, the democrats, having realized that a monster prospered in the fields of passive numbers – in fact, their own intimate monstrosity – but not thinking that perhaps this might have to do with the law of this kind of number – all passivity, I believe, is politically suspect – attempted to console themselves with a performance of active numbers. They 'took to the streets'. But their power was laughable, for by love of voting, they proclaimed the active number's servitude to the passive number.

The active number must be untied from all correlation to the passive number. A meeting, a demonstration, an insurrection: all of them proclaim their right to existence outside any consideration that is not immanent to that existence. Scoundrels have never found it difficult to prosper in obscure content, passivity, and the secrecy and anonymity of numbers. Hitler himself came to power through elections, and it was a regular assembly that elected Pétain.

This making the active number play the role of hollow auxiliary to the passive number, as on May 1 2002, is indicative of a state of consciousness lacking in hope. And all in all, the effect of that demonstration was, as we now know, simply nil. We got Chirac without the slightest democratic bonus. And the youth, like a small torrent in a dry region after a storm, disappeared into its bed.

Rousseau

Rousseau had already encountered the quandary of number in its relation to political will.

He is clearly opposed to voting in so far as it comes down to the designation of deputies, that is, to 'representative' democracy. His axiom – nothing less than that of the active number ('a demonstration is nothing beyond its act, as it is composed only of demonstrators who constitute its presentation') – states the following: 'The will cannot be represented.' That is why, for Rousseau, the British parliamentary system was nothing but camouflaged despotism: no sooner are the deputies elected than the people, he writes, 'is enslaved, is nothing'. The essence of politics, according to Rousseau, affirms presentation over and against representation.

Yet, on the other hand, he recognizes the strength of numbers, of the popular decision that is drawn from the majority of suffrages. The people gathers together, votes, and, says Rousseau, 'the greatest number obliges the rest'. The enigmatic link between passive totalization and decision is thus maintained: 'The declaration of the general will is drawn from the calculation of votes.'

However, it could not be said that Rousseau, so demonstrative in the details, manages to ground the authority of numbers. His argument, we know, is that the mutual destruction of individual wills working against one another gives rise to a vote that effectively concentrates the generality of a will. But what could the notion of majority voice possibly mean here, won as it is at the end of an obscure process of the reciprocal neutralization of individual wills (in sum, self-interest)? Who does not see that it would be magic were it suddenly to express the universal rectitude of political will?

Rousseau also saw the inadequacy of numbers when it comes to making really important decisions, since, he says, 'naming a supreme leader who suspends the law' is entirely legitimate when the 'freedom of the country' is at stake. The usage made of that insight by *les conventionnels* of the Committee for Public Safety is well known. And Marx himself repeated after them that, when on the verge of creation, dictatorship is the natural form of organization of political will. The reason is simple: what is the sole resource of those who have nothing, who control neither the apparatus of repression, nor that of propaganda? Without doubt, that unique resource is numbers, *but in the form of active disciplined numbers*. Yes, the only truly popular political arm consists in submitting the active number to a discipline of thought and action. And that is in general

foreign to the law of suffrage, for suffrage amounts to the disloca-
tion of discipline into the passivity of numbers. And does not
Rousseau himself indirectly recognize this in mentioning that,
when things get dramatic, recourse must be had to a single leader
as the symbolic materialization of citizenry discipline? And is that
not what Marx himself proposed under the guise of the 'dictatorship of the proletariat'?

Finally, for all these thinkers, electoral numbers are appropriate
when what is at stake is merely the tranquil perpetuation of the
passive calculus of interests and the maintenance of the homogeneous. But it is clearly inadequate when it is a question of acting,
founding, or when in the heat of an event.

The future

All this amounts to saying that the pompous formula employed the
day after Chirac's election, 'The Republic has been saved', has no
value whatsoever. For either there is no danger and exclaiming
we've been saved is absurd; or there really is one, and the number
of votes for Chirac will definitely not counter it. If there is a
problem with Lepenism in our country (and, more generally, a
problem of the extreme right wing in Europe), then both the
subservience of people's conscience and political incompetence
must be attacked by affirmative commitments that are untied to
electoral concerns and measured against principles alone. And the
principle of principles, for the modern philosopher, is the principle
of equality. Inventing the sites and procedures of a political work
internal to the popular masses; reviving the word 'worker' so that
the generality of the maxim of equality is applied throughout every
situation (workers' hostels, factories, streets, cities . . .): this is our
problem and our task. What is needed – and we should be in no
doubt – is a firm indifference to posts of state and a constantly
sustained cordial scorn for electoral prebends. What is needed is a

serene and declared supremacy of the active number over the passive number. What is needed is the wax Ulysses used to keep from yielding either to the songs, or to the sirens, or to the blackmail of 'democracy'. What are needed are new paths, since the key to invention is what, in the 1970s, was called *la liaison de masse*, which essentially means: doing politics directly with those it is made for in the first place, those for whom only the maxim of equality is capable of inscribing existence in its truth.

At bottom, it is about finding the new sites of the general will. Rousseau expressed it well: 'Individual wills tend by nature to preferences, and the general will to equality.' If we are to demonstrate the return of a general will, even on a single point, we must certainly sacrifice many preferences. This is where philosophy can help since, in its most general inspiration, it teaches us that the universality of truth is preferable to mere preferences. One is then happy, beyond the market.

5

The Law on the Islamic Headscarf [23]

1. A few pleasant republicans decided one day to argue that a law was necessary to ban girls wearing scarves over their hair. First, ban it at school, then elsewhere, and everywhere if possible. Did you hear me say a law? A law! The president of the Republic was as limited a politician as he was unsinkable. Totalitarianly elected by 82 per cent of voters, including all the socialists, people from whom a number of the pleasant republicans in question were recruited, he nodded in agreement: a law, yes, a law against a few thousand young girls who put the headscarf in question over their hair. The scabby, mangy brats! And they're Muslims too! That is how, once again, similar to the capitulation at Sedan, Pétain, the Algerian War, the double-dealing of Mitterrand, villainous laws against undocumented workers, France has stunned the world. After tragedies, a farce.

2. Yes, France has finally found a problem worthy of itself: banning scarves from a few girls' heads. One could say that the decline of this country is complete. The Muslim invasion, diagnosed long ago by Le Pen and confirmed today by some indubitable intellectuals, has met its match. The battle of Poitiers was a cakewalk, Charles Martel only a hired gun. Chirac, the socialists, the feminists and the Enlightenment intellectuals suffering from Islamophobia, will win the battle of the headscarf. From Poitiers to the headscarf: the reasoning is sound, and the progress considerable.

3. Grandiose causes require new types of arguments. Like this one, for example: the headscarf should be banned because it is a symbol of male power (the father, the older brother) over young girls and women. So we'll banish the girls who stubbornly persist in wearing it. In short: these girls and women are oppressed, so they must be punished. It's a little like saying: 'This woman has been raped, throw her in jail.' The headscarf issue is so important that it deserves a logical system with renewed axioms.

4. Or, on the other hand, this argument: it's the women themselves who freely choose to wear this damned headscarf, the rebels, the little brats! So they must be punished. Wait a moment: but isn't it a symbol of male oppression? Do the father and big brother play no part in the affair? So, where does the need to ban the headscarf come from? From the fact that it is ostentatiously religious. These brats flaunt their belief. Go stand in the corner with your back to the class!

5. So, either it is the father and big brother, and 'feministically' the headscarf must be torn off, or else it's the girl's sticking to her own belief, and 'secularly' it must be torn off. There is no such thing as a good headscarf. Bare heads! Everywhere! As it used to be said – even the non-Muslims said it – let everyone go out bareheaded!

6. Today's republic: down with hats!

7. Take special note of the fact that the father and the big brother of the headscarved girl are not simple parental accompaniments. It is frequently insinuated, and sometimes openly declared, that the father is a brutish worker, a poor devil come straight out of a village to be tied to Renault's assembly lines. An archaic bloke. And stupid. The big brother is a dope-dealer. He's modern, but corrupt. Sinister housing estates [*banlieues*]. Dangerous classes.

8. The Muslim religion adds to the defects of other religions this extremely serious fact: in France, it's the religion of the poor.

9. Viewed from this angle the headscarf is: the poor oppressing

the poor under the eyes of a poor God. 'Disgusting!' says the petit
bourgeois, whose affluence no longer believes in anything but its
self-perpetuation.

10. Someone who'll recognize himself here, and with whom I
debated the issue of the headscarf some years back, once said to
me: 'So you want hair to be a sexual symbol that for such ends
must be hidden?' I myself want nothing. But, lastly, remember
Baudelaire:

> O fleece! Curls rippling round the shoulders! Hair / Thick with
> the scent of langourous perfume! / What bliss! To shake it,
> kerchief – like – here, there; / Wake sleeping memories, waft
> them through the hair, / Filling, this night, our alcove's darkling
> gloom. / Devil! A fantasmatic Muslim! [*Diable! Une fantasmatique
> de musulman!*]

11. I remember the time when, by untying her hair (ah! softly,
impalpably falling onto her shoulders!) a woman made known her
amorous consent. Was that an affront to secularism? An imprisonment of femininity? Perhaps, perhaps . . .

12. Picture a high-school principal, followed by a squad of
inspectors armed with tape measures, scissors and books on
jurisprudence, on their way to the school entrance to inspect
whether or not the headscarves, skullcaps and other hats are
'ostentatious'. What about that large headscarf like a stamp
perched on a chignon? Or that skullcap the size of a two-euro
coin? All very suspect! The small one might well be the ostentatious
version of the big one. But what do I see now? Watch out! It's a top
hat! Alas! Questioned about top hats, Mallarmé once said: 'Whoever put on such a thing cannot take it off. The world would end,
but not the hat.' Ostentation for eternity.

13. Secularism. A rust-proof principle! Three or four decades
ago at school same-sex classes were forbidden, girls weren't
allowed to wear trousers, there was catechism, chaplaincy. Com-

munion was solemn, with the boys in white arm-bands and the pretty things under tulle veils. Real veils, they were, not just headscarves. And you want me to regard wearing that headscarf as criminal? That symbol of not keeping pace, of a reminder of the past, of a temporal entanglement? Ought we expel these young ladies who pleasantly mingle here today? Go ahead, let the capitalist machine grind on. Regardless of the comings and goings, the repentances, or the arrivals of workers from afar, capitalism will work out how to substitute the fat Moloch of merchandise for the dead gods of religions.

14. As it happens, isn't business the really big religion? Next to this, don't these staunch Muslims look like an ascetic minority? And are not the ostentatious symbols of this degrading religion to be read on trousers, T-shirts, sneakers etc., names like Nike, Chevignon, Lacoste? Is it not even pettier to be the sandwich-woman of a company at school than it is to be the faithful of a God? If we're to strike at the heart of the target, if we've got to think big, we know what's required: a law against brand names. Chirac, get to work. Prohibit the ostentatious signs of Capital, and don't flinch.

15. Ah what! Is it the duty of women to go nude? Is it imperative to have the thighs uncovered? Tits too? Pierced bellybuttons obligatorily bared? At a swimming pool in a provincial town, certain times were reserved to women only, whence the bathing and laughter of pious ladies who ordinarily shut themselves away. The mayor put an end to all this with a forceful argument: 'Women's bodies should not be hidden from view.' But of course! All women in the nude! And make it snappy!

16. Clarify something for me. What characterizes the feminist and republican rationality about what is and is not shown of the body across different times and places? To my knowledge, still to this day, and not only in schools, neither breasts, nor pubic hair, nor penises are shown. Should I get angry over the fact that these bits are 'hidden from view'? Should I be suspicious of husbands, lovers, big brothers? It wasn't so long ago in the countryside in

France – and it is still the case in Sicily and elsewhere – that widows wore black veils, black stockings, mantillas. One doesn't have to be the widow of an Islamic terrorist to do that.

17. But I understand that the obligation is tendentially toward nudity. The journalists of *Libération* have always hailed the coming of the miniskirt as an infallible sign of the imminent fall of totalitarianisms. The swallow of the miniskirt signals the spring of human rights. All excessive covering up of the body is suspicious. The battle for nude breasts at the beach was won by a knock-out. One cannot sell, it is impossible to sell, cars, caged canaries, concrete mixers or curlers except with a trading sign showing practically naked women.

Brassens, who twenty years ago considered himself to be 'the pornographer of the phonograph' today seems more prudish than a church mouse – if that. The so-called mice demand today, each one more loudly than the other, the right to homosexual marriage for their priests.

18. We have gone from the feminist slogan 'my body belongs to me' to the prostitutional slogan 'my body belongs to everyone'. Property, immanent to the first, led, unsound advice, to the second. From property to being put up for auction; the end result is great.

19. Curious, isn't it, the rage harboured by so many women feminists (in *Elle*, for example) towards a few girls in headscarves, to the extent that they went so far as to help give poor old President Chirac the Soviet-style score of 82 per cent, and then asked him to crack down on them in the name of the law? All the while, however, the prostituted feminine body is everywhere, the most humiliating pornography universally sold, and advice for the sexual exhibition of bodies crams the pages of magazines for teenagers.

20. A simple explanation: a girl *must* show what she has to sell. She must show what she's got to offer. She must indicate that hereafter the circulation of women shall obey the generalized model, and not a restricted economy. Pour scorn on the bearded

father and big brothers! Long live the global market! The generalized model, it's the top model.

21. It used to be taken for granted that a woman had the inviolable right to be able to undress in front of the person of her choosing. But no. Now, it is imperative to hint at undressing at all times, to be in a permanent state of undress. Whoever keeps covered up what she has on the market is not a loyal business-woman.

22. A propos of beards. We know that Luc Ferry,[24] that plumed minister, envisaged banning the beards of the elder brothers. From an egalitarian point of view this is fair: if one forces girls to show their hair, why not force boys to cut their beards? From the moment that hairiness becomes an affair of state . . . The union benefit would not have been negligible: a whole new hierarchy, the School Barbers, hidden in classes, shaving cream always at the ready. The unveiling of girls promises nothing as juicy. The Unveilers? The Undressers? The Strip-Teasers' Union? No. Quite impossible. Pity.

23. We maintain the following, quite curious thing: that the law on the headscarf is a pure capitalist law. It prescribes that femininity be *exhibited*. In other words, that the circulation of the feminine body necessarily comply with the market paradigm. It forbids on this matter – and with adolescents, the sensitive plate of the whole subjective universe – all *holding back*.

24. For some time, the declarations and films of a well-known director have manifested a real hatred of eroticism, a ferocious sexual indifference, an undertaker puritanism. All that camouflaged, as it must be these days, by steamy provocation. Officiating against the headscarf, this director basically says: 'So, we will make the ear lobe into a new erogenous zone!' And why not, dear director of sex? The creation or recreation of an erogenous zone; finally, some good news for the eroto-maniacs that we are!

25. Everywhere you hear it said that the 'veil' is the intolerable symbol of control of feminine sexuality. Is it that you imagine

feminine sexuality is not controlled in our day and age, in our societies? Such naivety would have really made Foucault laugh. Never has feminine sexuality been scrutinized with such meticulousness, had so much expert advice thrust on it, been subject to such fine discriminating between its good and bad uses. Enjoyment has become a sinister obligation. The universal exhibition of supposedly exciting bits is a duty more rigid than Kant's moral imperative. Besides, Lacan some time ago established the fact that, between the 'Enjoy yourselves, women!' of our gossip rags and the imperative 'Do not enjoy!' of our great-grandmothers, there is a strict isomorphism. Market control is more constant, surer, more massive than patriarchal control ever was. Generalized prostitutional circulation is more rapid and more reliable than difficult familial incarcerations, the mocking of which has, between Greek comedy and Molière, been cause for laughter for centuries.

26. In the nomadic vision of the world, where one rejoices at the incessant circulation and exchange of bodies, it is clear that a coin can think itself the freest thing in the world: it is what circulates the most.

27. The mother and the whore. Certain countries have made reactionary laws in favour of the mother and against the whore; in others, progressive laws have been made in favour of the whore and against the mother. However, it is the alternative between the two that must be rejected.

28. Not however by the 'neither . . . nor . . .,' which only ever perpetuates on neutral ground (i.e. in the centre, as with François Bayrou?) what it professes to contest. Saying 'neither mother, nor whore' is simply pathetic. As is 'neither whore, nor submissive',[25] which is quite absurd: is not a 'whore' generally submissive, and aren't they just? In France in the past, they used to be called *les respectueuses* (the respectful). The public submissives, all in all. As for the 'submissives' themselves, they are perhaps only private whores.

29. It always comes down to this: the enemy of thought today is

property. It is commerce, and such things as souls, but not faith. What should rather be said is that (political) faith is what is lacking the most. The 'rise of religious fundamentalism' is only the mirror in which sated Westerners consider with dread the effects of the devastation of minds that they've presided over. And, in particular, effects such as the ruining of political thought, which Westerners have attempted to organize everywhere, either under cover of insignificant democracies or with large reinforcements of humanitarian paratroopers. Under such conditions, secularism, professing to be at the service of different forms of knowledge, is but a scholarly rule by which to respect the competition, undertake training according to Western norms, and be hostile to every conviction. It is the school for consumer cool, soft business, free ownership and disillusioned voters.

30. Since the death of God, religions have become so incapacitated that, instead of trying to wipe each other out, as they had always done in obedience to their respective gods (who were all the more enraged when they were transcendentally the same), they have had to undertake to help each other out. The archbishop does not like it when the mosque is titillated. The imam, the pastor and the priest hold melancholic consultations. Even the rabbi and the pope get involved with one another. Much more than the war of religions and civilizations – that phantasmagoria for dissimulating plots of power and petrodollars – I believe in the International of moribund creeds.

31. Hence – obviously anti-Muslim – the law on headscarves bothers all the deputies of the right who owe a part of their prebends to the Catholic voters of the *provinces profondes*. To throw off the scent, the deputies made up the story that it was necessary to forbid ostentatious signs . . . of politics! Well, honestly! Are there any? Can you believe that there'll be, even in the depths of the darkest villages, even in the terrifying suburbs, a sweeping seizure of hammers and sickles? Of ostentatious Stalins, of headscarves bearing the likeness of the Great Helmsman? I do not believe that

such spectacles are generally to be seen during the lunch break. I heartily regret it, but that's the way it is. I myself sometimes went to give my large public seminars with badges, sometimes of the great Lenin, sometimes of my dear Mao. And, well, nobody remarked upon it!

32. One will never go into enough raptures over the trajectory of this singular feminism, which, from its quest to free women, has come to maintain today that this 'freedom' is so obligatory that it requires the expulsion of girls (and not a single boy!) solely due to their clothing accessories. Bewildering!

33. All the societal jargon about 'communities', and the combat, as metaphysical as it is furious, of the 'Republic' against 'communitarianisms' – all of that is utter nonsense. Let people live as they wish, or can, eat what they are used to eating, wear turbans, dresses, headscarves, miniskirts, or tap-dancing shoes; let them prostrate themselves whenever they like before worn-out gods, have themselves photographed bowing and scraping, or speak colourful jargons. Not having the least universal significance, these kinds of 'differences' neither hinder thought, nor support it. So there is no reason either to respect or vilify them. That the 'Other' lives somewhat differently – as amateurs of discreet theology and portable morality like saying after Levinas – is not an observation that costs much effort.

34. At the very most, the diversity of customs and beliefs is a surviving testimony of the diversity of the human animal, something that draws our attention in the same way that blue parrots or whales do, because the multiform force of life intrigues and charms us.

35. As for the fact that human animals group together according to their origins, this is a natural and inevitable consequence of the – most often miserable – conditions of their arrival (in France). Only a cousin or a village compatriot can, *nolens volens*, welcome you at the hostel at Saint-Ouen-l'Aumône. That Chinese go where other Chinese already are is a point that one would be obtuse to be

offended by, unless we are to return to the directives of the French Communist Party of 30 years ago: they demanded an equal distribution of the burden of immigrants among all the communes in the suburbs, that is, in communes of the left *and* of the right. 'Arabs', said these proletarian and internationalist comrades in sum. 'They are sending all the Arabs into *our* councils!'

36. Containing communitarianism and watching over the assimilation of Muslims today necessitates going further than the PCF previously dared. Let's demand that, in each large urban conglomeration, there are at most two Moroccan families, only one of them numerous, a sole moderate Malian family, a Turk bachelor, and a half-Tamil.

37. The only problem concerning these 'cultural differences' and these 'communities' is certainly not their social existence, habitat, work, family life, or school. It's that their names are vain as soon as what is in question is a truth, be it artistic, scientific, amorous, or, especially, political. That one's life as a human animal is forged from particularities, well, such is the law of things. When the categories of this particularity profess to be universal, thereby taking upon themselves the seriousness of the subject, then things regularly become disastrous. What matters is the *separation of predicates*. I can do mathematics in yellow underwear, and I can actively pursue a politics subtracted from electoral 'democracy' with rasta dreadlocks. This does not mean that the theorem is yellow (or not yellow) any more than it says that the directive under which we convene is dreadlocked. Nor, for that matter, does it lack dreadlocks.

38. Conversely: a truth, political or otherwise, recognizes itself in that fact that the principle of which it is a particular instance does not, as far as the principle is concerned, have anything particular about it. It is something that holds absolutely for whomever enters into the situation about which this instance is stated. This is how political militants, or those who demonstrate a theorem, or dream up a play, or live the enchantment of a love, all create singular

forms of thinking, forms of thinking that, from entirely disparate corporeal and mental supports, they can all share. Neither do sexual, linguistic, religious, psychological, or ethnic particularities enter as such into a truth process; nor do they present an obstacle to it. Before Saint-Just took it up, Saint Paul had already said it: when a truth is in question, particularity doesn't matter.

39. That school is said to be so threatened by a particularity that is as insignificant as a few girls' headscarves leads to the suspicion that what is in question here is not a truth but mere opinions, low and conservative ones at that. Have we not seen politicians and intellectuals declaring that, above all, school is there to 'educate citizens'? Gloomy programme. Nowadays, the 'citizen' is a bitter little hedonist, clinging to a political system from which every semblance of truth is foreclosed.

40. Might we not be preoccupied, in low and high places, by the fact that quite a number of girls of Algerian, Moroccan and Tunisian origin, their chignons tightly wound, austere demeanours, and doggedly at work, have become, with a few Chinese, who are no less bound to the familial universe, formidable heads of the class? Nowadays, it takes a lot of selflessness to be one. It could well be, then, that Chirac the Soviet's law winds up blatantly expelling some excellent students.

41. 'Enjoy unfettered.'[26] This 1968 stupidity never pushed knowledge forward at full steam. A certain dose of voluntary asceticism, the basic reasons for which we know thanks to Freud, is no stranger to the proximity between teaching and at least bare fragments of effective truths. So much so that a headscarf may end up being useful. When patriotism, that hard alcohol of apprenticeship, is altogether lacking, any idealism, even cheap, is welcome. At least, that is, for those who think that schooling has little to do with 'training' consumer–citizens.

42. Anti-headscarf maxims: 'School will perish before my secularity'; 'better a bare-headed illiterate than a headscarver of genius.'

43. In point of truth, the headscarf law expresses only one thing: fear. Westerners in general, and the French in particular, are no more than a bunch of shivering cowards. What are they afraid of? Barbarians, as usual. Barbarians both at home, the 'suburban youths', and abroad, the 'Islamic terrorists'. Why are they afraid? Because they are guilty, but claim to be innocent. Guilty from the 1980s onward of having renounced and tried to dismantle every politics of emancipation, every revolutionary form of reason, every true assertion of something other than what is. Guilty of clinging to their miserable privileges. Guilty of being no more than grown-up kids who play with their many purchases. Yes, indeed, 'after a long childhood, they have been made to grow up'. They are thus afraid of whatever is a little less old than they are, such as, for example, a stubborn young lady.

44. But most of all, Westerners in general, and the French in particular, are afraid of death. They can no longer even imagine that an idea is something worth taking some risks for. 'Zero deaths' is their most important desire. Well, they see millions of people throughout the world who have no reason to be afraid of death. And among them, many die for an idea nearly every day. For the 'civilized', that is a source of intimate terror.

45. I know that the ideas for which one is ready to die today are generally not worth much. Convinced that all gods withdrew long ago, it grieves me to see young men and women blowing their bodies to bits in horrendous massacres under the funereal invocation of something that has not existed for some while. I know, in addition, that those fearsome 'martyrs' are instrumentalized by conspirators barely distinguishable from the enemies they profess to be fighting. It cannot be repeated often enough how Bin Laden is a creature of the American secret services. I am not naive enough to believe in the purity, nor in the greatness, nor in any purported effectiveness of these suicide killings.

46. But I do say that the atrocious price being paid is above all that of the meticulous destruction of all forms of political ration-

ality by Western hegemons, an undertaking rendered practicable, notably in France, by an abundance of intellectual and working-class complicity. You wanted fiercely to liquidate even the memory of the idea of revolution? You wanted to uproot every usage, even allegorical ones, of the word 'worker'? Then don't complain about the result. Grit your teeth and kill the poor. Or have them killed by your American friends.

47. We have the wars we deserve. In this world numbed by fear, big bandits mercilessly bombard countries drained of blood. Medium bandits practise the targeted assassination of whoever displeases them. Small bandits make laws against headscarves.

48. They'll say it's less serious. Yes, of course. It's certainly not so bad. Before the Court of History, we will plead attenuating circumstances: 'As a hairstyling specialist, he only played a small role in the affair.'

49. Feeling better?

6

Daily Humiliation[27]

'Constant identity checks and questioning by police.' Of all the complaints made by the youth of this country in revolt, the omnipresence of police checks and being arrested in their everyday lives, this harassment without respite, is the most constant, the most widely shared. Do we really realize what this grievance means? The dose of humiliation and violence it implies?

I have a 16-year-old, adopted son who is black. Let's call him Gérard. No sociological or *misérabiliste* 'explanations' can be applied to him. He grew up in Paris, in all simplicity.

Between the March 31 (Gérard wasn't yet 15) and today, I have not been able to keep count of the police checks on him in the street. Innumerable – there is no other word. Arrests: six! In eighteen months . . . I call an 'arrest' being taken handcuffed to the police station, being insulted, being handcuffed to a bench, and left there hours upon end, sometimes for a day or two. All for nothing.

The worst aspects of persecution often lie in the details. So I'll tell you in a quite detailed way about the most recent arrest. Gérard, accompanied by his friend Kemal (born in France, therefore French, from a Turkish family), was outside a private high school (attended by young girls) at about 4:30 pm. While Gérard was displaying his gallantry, Kemal negotiated the purchase of a bike from a student from a neighbouring school. At twenty euros this bicycle was a bargain! Fishy, there's no doubt. Take note that, although he does not have many, Kemal has a few euros, because he works: he is a chef's assistant in a *crêperie*. Three 'young lads' come up to them. One of them, with a slightly distraught look, says, 'That's my bicycle, a guy borrowed it from me an hour and a half ago and didn't come back with it.' Oh no! So it seems the seller was a 'borrower'. Discussion ensues. Gérard sees only one solution: give the bike back. Ill-gotten gains bring nothing but trouble. Kemal resigns himself to the fact. The lads go off with the machine.

It is at this point that a police car, brakes screeching, pulls up to the kerb. Two of its occupants jump out and pounce on Gérard and Kemal, pinning them to the ground; they then cuff their hands behind their backs, and line them up against the wall. Insults and threats: 'Idiots! Arseholes!' Our two heroes ask what they've done: 'You know damn well! Turn around.' Still hand-cuffed, they are made to face the passers-by in the street: 'Everyone should see who you are and what you did!' A revival of the medieval pillory (they are exposed like this for half an hour), but with a novelty: it's done prior to any judgement, prior even to any accusation. Up pulls a police wagon. 'You're in for it when we've got you alone.' 'You like dogs?' 'There'll be no one to help you at the station.'

The 'young lads' say, 'They didn't do anything, they gave us the bike back.' Never mind, they're all thrown into the van, Gérard, Kemal, the three 'young lads', and the bike. Is the accursed bike the culprit? It should be stated that it wasn't. That's the last we'll hear of the bike. Moreover, at the station, Gérard and Kemal are separated off from the three 'young lads' and the bike, the three good little 'whites' are sent free back onto the streets. It's another matter for the black and the Turk. Now, they tell us, comes the 'worst' part. Handcuffed to a bench, kicked in the shins every time a policeman passed by them, insults, especially for Gérard: 'Fat pig', 'Filth' . . . This goes on for an hour and a half without their knowing what they're accused of and how they've become criminals. Eventually they're told that they are being kept in detention on suspicion of having committed a gang mugging fifteen days ago. They start feeling really sick, not knowing what will happen. Characteristics of police custody: the body search, the cell. It is 10 pm. At home, I await my son. Two and a half hours later the telephone rings: 'Your son is being held in detention on probability of gang assault.' I love that 'probability'. Meanwhile, a less complicit policeman says to Gérard: 'It doesn't seem to me you've been involved in any of these things. What are you doing here still?' A mystery, indeed.

As regards the black, my son, let's just say that no one recognized him. It's over now, said a cop, a little embarrassed. Accept our apologies. Where did all this trouble come from? A denunciation, again, as always. A supervisor from the girls' school had identified him as the guy who participated in this infamous mugging two weeks before. Wasn't he at all involved then? A black guy and another black guy, you know . . .

A propos of high schools, supervisors and informing, I'll mention in passing that at the time of the third of Gérard's arrests – as futile and brutal as the five others – his high school had been asked for the photos and school files of all the black students. Yes, you read that right – the black students. And as the file in question was on the police inspector's desk, I'd have to suppose that the secondary school, turned into a police agent, had carried out this curious 'selection.'

We were called well after 10 pm to come to pick up our son: he hasn't done anything; apologies are given. Apologies? Who would be content with that? And I suppose that those from the suburbs don't even have the right to apologies. Who cannot see that the mark of infamy they hope to inscribe in the everyday lives of these kids will have effects, devastating effects? And if the police intend to indicate that, after all, since they are stopped and checked for no reason, it might well happen that, one day, and 'as a group', they are picked up for something, and who would object?

We have the riots we deserve. A state in which what is called public order is only a coupling of the protection of private wealth and dogs unleashed on children of working people and people of foreign origin is purely and simply despicable.

Openings/Affirmations

The Power of the Open:
A Discourse on the Necessity of Fusing Germany and France

Let it not be thought that I am more opportunistic than I am. Trustworthy people can attest to my long-term commitment to a Franco-German fusion, long before, a propos of Iraq, the frightened restraint of Chirac and Schröder, badly seduced by the bombardier virility of Bush, only vaguely tabled the question.

Yet it is true that since this restraint, public occasions have multiplied in which one could make known this type of conviction. The most recent one, which gave rise to the speech you are about to read, was the necessity of celebrating the old Franco-German treaty in the many countries where German and French embassies are to be found. In Argentina, the embassies of both countries, as well as their cultural and linguistic institutions, the Goethe Institute and the Alliance Française, had recourse to my services, for which I thank them. On November 18 2003, before a strangely numerous public, and in the presence of the ambassadors and the directors of the above-mentioned institutions, I expressed myself as follows.

To start with, I would like to say that I am happy to be speaking here this evening of the conjoint spiritual destinies of Germany and France. Why? Because I believe that in the contemporary world the question of the relations between France and Germany is as decisive as it is complex. It is decisive, of course, for the Germans and the French. But perhaps it is also decisive, and in a shorter term than we think, for power, in both reality and in thought, in so far as its effects concern the entire world.

And so here we are in Argentina, in Buenos Aires, which is not just anywhere for the question that concerns us. Strange as it may seem, this 'here' matters greatly to Franco-German intellectual debate. I mean 'here' not only in the sense of the American continent but, more particularly, in the sense of Latin America, and, more particularly still, in the sense of Argentina. There exists here an intellectual, cultural and creative activity that is quite exceptional. There exists a concrete intensity of art and of thinking stretching from cinema to philosophy, including theatre, music and painting. And judging by the number of you here this evening, that keenness extends even to speeches about the intellectual destiny of France and Germany.

The Argentineans, whose country was on the verge of collapse, have shown to the entire world how, even in times of terrible crisis, even in times of terrible suffering, they did not abandon creation and thought. A striving spiritual resistance exists here for everyone to see. Today's Franco-German question, as well as being a question of political construction, is also basically a question of intellectual resistance, of a resistance in thought. In truth, if Germany and France go ahead with a union, with creation and action, Europe's spiritual destiny will be kept going.

As a concept and as a place, Argentina is, of course, unique. But, whilst being unique, it is also heir to the spiritual destiny of Europe. Argentina is thus concerned in its very core by what happens to Germany and France.

Let me express all that differently, as a variation. I will make use of a once celebrated but today unfortunately quite forgotten text, a text by Lenin. The title of the text is *The Three Sources and Three Component Parts of Marxism*. Lenin said: the three sources of Marxism are German philosophy, French revolutionary thought and English political economy.

Leaving the question of Marxism aside, let's pose the following question: how are we situated today with respect to these three sources?

Concerning the English or American economy, we have, as you know, had quite a fill. Indeed, from the newspapers and discourses, you'd think the economy was the only thing that existed. Of these three sources, then, the health of the latter is assured. In truth, the spirit of intellectual resistance today is to some extent a spirit of resistance to the global economy. I am not therefore going to say that this spirit is France and Germany's spirit of resistance to England and the United States. That would be a really petty and Eurocentric version of the situation. But the question of the spirit of resistance today surely has its focal point in the question of knowing what can resist being reduced to the planetary triumph of the Anglo-Saxon economy. So, when we interpret Lenin's text, the question becomes: how are we placed with regard to the great German tradition of philosophy and the great French tradition of critical and revolutionary thought? How are we placed in respect of the first two sources? And, more fundamentally, where are we with the relation between the two? It is here, without doubt, that the Franco-German question becomes highly significant.

I would say that there is, that there ought to be, a new Franco-German moment. Let me turn to the French and German ambassadors, who do us the great honour of being present here tonight, and toward the Embassies' counsellors and their directors, and toward the directors of the Goethe Institute and the Alliance Française, and let me thank them. Thank you for creating, here in Buenos Aires, a sort of fragment!

This fragment is part of a vast and difficult construction, a construction of a new Franco-German moment. For this new Franco-German moment, whose beginning, or at least the hint of its becoming, is visible from time to time, is a moment of global intellectual resistance. It is a moment of resistance to the barbarous reign of the pure economy that supports a politics of war and fuels the devastation of consciousnesses.

Let's take a minute to reflect upon what a Franco-German moment is.

I think that there have been three kinds of Franco-German moment throughout history. The first kind is the Franco-German wars. The years 1815, 1870, 1914, 1940, are all great moments. 'Great', that is, in the sense of terrible. The moment of 1914, for example, was a literally foundational event for the twentieth century. It was a moment during which the ferocious fighting between France and Germany practically destroyed European civilization. A little like Athens and Sparta destroyed Greek civilization during the Peloponnesian War. I won't give my opinion, before our ambassadors, on the question of knowing who was Sparta and who Athens in 1914! That said, you must be a fierce enthusiast for heroic massacres to long for that kind of Franco-German moment.

The second kind of Franco-German moment, of Franco-German link, comprises the great commercial, financial, industrial and agricultural exchanges. These exchanges include everything from coal and steel to electronics and rockets, not to mention corn and beer: everything that is stirred up and activated by powerful finance, and that has worked toward creating our magnificent single currency, the euro. You are no doubt aware, and it is important, even if we don't make the economy the alpha and omega of the destiny of peoples, that there exist no two large countries in the world as merged through material exchange as are France and Germany today. We, Germans and French, are, in any case, brothers through merchandise.

We might say, then, concerning what Lenin held to be the third of the constitutive sources of Marxist thinking, that is, British and American political economy, that France and Germany already constitute a sort of unity. So, the crucial thing here is to ask if the medium of that Franco-German economic unity can and should be something other than the English language. A material basis is necessary for every process, but that does not create a new spirituality; it does not create any possibilities for the cultural renewal of European space, nor, via this process, for renewal of the entire planet's space. When all is said and done, it does not create any kind of new language, taking language in the broad sense as that which acts as a vehicle for a novel capacity for thought. And the proof is that the language of this economic unity isn't new: it is a kind of English jargon, an anglicizing *patois*. That's why it's necessary to refer to the third kind of Franco-German moment, after wars and great material exchanges. These are the intellectual, cultural and subjective exchanges. This story is basically one about the German admiration for French clarity, French lightness. This admiration goes from Goethe to Brecht, via Nietzsche and many others. But it is also a story about the French fascination for German profundity, for German vision, a fascination that can be observed with Baudelaire and is still there in some of our most recent thinkers, such as Jacques Derrida, Maurice Blanchot and many others. This here is a veritable Franco-German space whose history has often been attempted or described, but which is almost enigmatic in its tension and in its grandeur.

We know, for example, how that *chef d'œuvre* of French literature, Diderot's *Rameau's Nephew*, became known in Europe thanks to Goethe's German translation of it. We know too that, while Diderot's book remained ignored in France, the character of the nephew was formed in Hegel's *Phenomenology of the Spirit* into what Deleuze calls a 'conceptual personage', that is, the proper name of a figure of universal consciousness. But in the opposite direction, we know how after the terrible abysses of the Second World War, Nietzsche, Wagner and Heidegger, having all been prostituted in various ways by Nazism, found shelter and disciples in France. They became, in brief, French artists and thinkers of German language, just as at one time Diderot had been a German writer of French language. This is where our most profound spiritual history lies. Am I going to say, then, in playing the game of nationalities, that my Ambassador, his Counsellors, the Alliance Française, and myself are clear and light as Frenchmen and women? Or that the German Ambassador, his Counsellors, the

Goethe Institute, and my friend Gernot Kamecke are, as Germans, profound visionaries? The psychology of peoples is a perilous art and you know well that it would always be possible to turn it around, because this Franco-German spirituality, which exists in its enigma, also allows for crossed destinies. More than that, however, I think that the situation is new. I think that French–German relations can and ought to enter into a new political and material era; and, therefore, that the dialectic of the link of creation and of thought between France and Germany can and must transform itself. And I would like to say in what way this might occur, if not according to the laws of the economy and of history, then at least according to my wishes.

You know that following the period of the great Franco-German wars, which I recalled a moment ago, there has been a half-century of peace in the European context.

A philosophical meditation on the context or framework in which things happen is always essential. What can we say about this framework today?

Certainly, we can say that Europe is a necessary framework, a great given of our history. However, for those of us who search for the new in thought and look at Europe as a possible frame of spiritual inventions, it remains a very narrow framework.

First, Europe leaves aside quite a number of partisans in our intellectual resistance in the world. For example, the Argentines, who have many rights – at least as many as our Turkish friends – to assert their candidature for the EU, at least if we conceive the European framework more broadly than in the sole terms of economic geography.

Further, Europe is subjugated in imperious fashion to a market dynamic and is inserted in a bureaucratic edifice of great complexity. But when all is said and done, we must admit that today's European framework is without true popular impetus, i.e. without subjective force. Europe unquestionably has an objective weight in the world, but the subjective weight of that Europe does not measure up to its reserve of power. And it is naturally that subjectivity that interests us, that solicits us. Now, that absence of subjectivity in this advancing, developing, growing construction – that absence of subjectivity is confronted with a new situation in the world.

Today, we are in a time after the collapse, without struggle, of the Soviet system, in a time of extraordinary consequences of this collapse, such as the fall of the Berlin Wall and the constitution of a new Germany. After all that, what is left? What is there that serves as a world?

On one side, we have the hegemony of the United States of America, a hegemony that, with the understatement character-istic of French classicism, I would characterize as being 'occa-sionally somewhat brutal'. And then, on the other side, we have some great human collectivities slowly attaining power through terrible efforts, terrible tests, which our old countries also once knew, and from which they drew part of their power: wars, civil wars, hard work, poverty, despotism, and devastation of nature. Yes, these great countries are at present enduring much hardship, they are rising up, standing up like still half-crouching giants: China, India, your neighbour Brazil, South Africa . . . And so, what are we? What are we Europeans? What are we subjectively in this new figure of the world? What is our role? What is our historical function?

I am convinced that, if our existence in thought, our spiritual existence, is to measure up to what is under way, to the post-Occidental world being born in power, effort and suffering, then a creative gesture is necessary, that is, a gesture that takes up again and raises our long history. A striking newness is necessary, one of those historical decisions that inflames our subjectivity and which above all creates new possibles.

Of this I am convinced: this decision must be the fusing of Germany and France into a new unity. I hesitate to say into a new state, because beyond this fusion, we aim for more, for far better, than the old form of the state. Let's just say the fusion is to create a new figure, a new space.

Yes, a sort of material and intellectual fusion of Germany and France is today's task. The moment is coming, or has already come, in which we should think this: Germany and France, or what are today called Germany and France, should not only take steps toward each other. Germany and France should and will have to pass into one another.

I'll tell you my philosophical wish: it is that France and Germany desire one day to be, before the world, no more than a single power. In a moment, I'll say a little about what I think that power ought to be. I'll say that it ought, in my view, not at all be a power of closure or of a withdrawal into itself; it should be the power of something that is open, the power of something that proposes itself to all.

What is France? Let's talk a little about France before deciding on its disappearance(!), its disappearance into a Germano-French opening. When I was quite young, one of my masters, Louis Althusser, said to me: 'France is a country crushed by its overly long history.' I thought he was right then, and that he is even more right today. France has such a long history that now, like someone become very old, it has a sort of overly tranquil certitude of its own existence. France often irritates other countries by the extent and calmness of its certitude. France exists and will always exist. But perhaps France does not ask itself enough if that survival is really an existence. France often believes that in the eyes of the world it incarnates a set of abstract principles, yet it often happens that it forgets concrete ones. France is like a weary grandeur, and that weary grandeur secretly aspires to a new birth.

I would readily compare France to a city named Orsenna, a city from a very beautiful book that without doubt some of you know, Julien Gracq's *Le Rivage des Syrtes* [*The Shore of the Syrtes*].[28] In *Le Rivage des Syrtes*, Julien Gracq magnificently presents to us a sleeping city that perseveres in its being, but which, in reality, silently aspires to invasion, destruction and termination. If only something new would finally happen! Even if that something new is terrible! Even if that something new is death! As old Danielo, the character who has plotted Orsenna's entry into war, says at the end, already knowing the war to be lost: 'A boat rotting on the shore; whoever casts it to the waves . . . could be said to be unconcerned about its loss, but not at all unconcerned about its destination.' Should I say, then, that to desire the fusion of Germany and France is like desiring to cast the rotting boat of my old Gallic country to the waves? Ah! The case of France is without doubt less romantic, its stability is more peasant-like. But the problem is of the same nature. Let's employ a slightly trivial expression. One might say about France what one says of certain fruit: still very good but a little overripe.

What to say now of Germany? Let me, Mister Ambassador, speak about it from the outside. Germany is a country that is forever haunted by the torment of its identity. This is perhaps one of the resemblances it shares with the Argentina welcoming us today. The issue is the torment of the question of identity. Germany is a country that asks itself perpetually, explicitly or secretly, what Germany is. It is no coincidence that Heidegger, that oh-so-German a thinker, said that the subject was a being for which what is in question is its being. Germany is a country where it is a question of Germany. And that is why Germany is the exact contrary of France. France is as sure of itself and of what it proposes, affirms and makes exist as Germany is uncertain.

Germany has always hesitated, oscillated between two contrary forms of historical existence. On the one hand, a kind of sub-existence, such as, for example, at the time it was still divided into principalities, whereas the other great European states were forging ahead with centralization. But also, no doubt, in that long Cold War period, during which the two Germanies had to behave like the two best students of two classes, the class of the United States and the class of the Soviet Union. And, on the other hand, we find a mythological super-existence of Germany, such as, for example, at the time when Germany thought it was the new Greece. Or worse still, when it proclaimed the creation of a Thousand-Year Reich, devastating the whole of Europe in the attempt.

If France is a weary grandeur, I would readily say that Germany is a hackneyed question. Hackneyed by too much alternating between sub- and super-existence.

So I believe the moment has arrived to exchange our predicates and, in so doing, to put an end to the weariness and the torment. Let France suppress itself and give Germany the gift of its historical certitude. Let Germany suppress itself and give France the gift of its genius for disciplined anxiety. As such, we shall, in the first place, obviously be engaging in the construction of a new political unity; but, in my view, this would above all be about forming the support for a new dialectic of thought. And I believe it would be one that measures up to our world.

Personally, I don't believe that a heterogeneous Europe lacking any real subjective influence is equal to our world and the terrible developments that threaten it. This construction, undoubtedly necessary, links together disparate pieces, but is not concerned with their interiority or intellectual solidity. Nor are the things that France and the French, and Germany and the Germans, have become, those ancient and limited things – those nationalisms of old weary figures and old hackneyed questions – equal to the task. We should, we contemporaries of the terrible world that is being created, put an end to the pendular movement between the construction of subjectively inert and impotent bureaucratic space and nostalgia for national grandeurs whose virtues are exhausted.

In this context, the decision I am talking about, and whose path I cannot know, but that I know must come – the decision for a new figure of Franco-German union – is a legitimate decision. It does not contradict any other construction; quite the contrary: it would bring into the world a new sense of the possible.

Understand: when I speak here of attaining real power by putting France and Germany together, I am not at all thinking of the creation of a new border, of a new enclosure; I am not thinking of a self-contained space. I am thinking of a new figure, of an invention that is at once transnational yet affirmative. That is, a figure of something that would be open in the coming world; something that, like life, is open to all. An open novelty, a unity, but a unity exposed to its own *ouverture*.

The great German poet Rilke, who is also a little French, spoke magnificently about the open in the eighth of the *Duino Elegies*. So, since we are here in Argentina contributing to the creation of a Franco-German moment, I thought it appropriate to have us listen to the beginning of Rilke's Eighth Elegy in the three languages that unite us here today: the poem's original language, German, and the French and Spanish translations. Permit me this poetic moment of French–German construction. And to begin with, the German.

(*Here one must picture the reading of the Eighth Elegy, and its simultaneous translation into Spanish.*)[29]

Mit allen Augen sieht die Kreatur
das Offene. Nur unsre Augen sind
wie umgekehrt und ganz um sie gestellt
als Fallen, rings um ihren freien Ausgang.
Was draussen ist, wir wissen aus des Tiers
Antlitz allein; denn schon das frühe Kind
wenden wir um und zwingens, dass es rückwärts
Gestaltung sehe, nicht das Offne, das
im Tiergesicht so tief ist. Frei von Tod.
Ihn sehen wir allein; das freie Tier
hat seinen Untergang stets hinter sich
und vor sich Gott, und wenn es geht, so geht's
in Ewigkeit, so wie die Brunnen gehen.
Wir haben nie, nicht einen einzigen Tag,

den reinen Raum vor uns, in den die Blumen
unendlich aufgehn. Immer ist das Welt
und niemals Nirgends ohne Nicht:
das Reine, Unüberwachte, das man atmet und
unendlich weids und nicht begehrt. Als Kind
verliert sich eins im stilln an dies und wird
gerüttelt.

My turn. I shall give Maximine's translation, which is somewhat removed from the original text, but inspired.

Tous les regards, de tout ce qui vit, regardent vers l'ouvert.
Seuls nos yeux, comme tournés à l'envers, tel un circle de
pièges, empêchent toute issue.
L'au-delà du cercle, nous ne le connaissons
qu'à travers le regard des bêtes.
Car dès la plus tendre enfance, nous orientons le petit
d'homme vers les ombres derrière lui, et non vers l'ouvert,
si profond dans l'expression des bêtes.
Libres, sans la mort.
Ah, elle! Nous ne voyons qu'elle!
La bête libre a toujours sa perte derrière elle:
devant elle, Dieu. Ainsi lorsqu'elle va, c'est en tout éternité,
comme vont les sources.
Nous jamais nous n'avons, pas un seul jour, devant nous
le pur et simple espace
dans lequel les fleurs ne cessent de s'épanouir.
C'est encore et toujours le monde:
jamais ce nulle part où le néant n'existe pas,
où la pureté, sans regard sur elle-même, se respire et se
connaît, à l'infini, sans l'ombre d'une convoitise.
Voici qu'un enfant s'y perd dans le silence:
Il s'en trouve bouleversé.

With all its eyes the creature-world beholds
the open. But our eyes, as though reversed,
encircle it on every side, like traps
set round its unobstructed path to freedom.
What is outside, we know from the brute's face
alone; for while a child's quite small we take it
and turn it round and force it to look backwards
at conformation, not that openness
so deep within the brute's face. Free from death.
We only see death; the free animal
has its decease perpetually behind it
and God in front, and when it moves, it moves
into eternity, like running springs.
We've never, no, not for a single day,
pure space before us, such as that which flowers
endlessly open into: always world,
and never nowhere without no: that pure
unsuperintended element one breathes,
endlessly know, and never craves. A child
sometimes gets quietly lost there, to be always
jogged back again.

At issue here is what Rilke calls the 'open', and in this elegy he poetically ascribes to it three figures. These three figures are three crucial examples of what, for him, is subtracted from the closure of the world. The open is the space freely left to that which is, and is not, like the past, always behind us. And it isn't always ahead of us either, like the thick construction of the world. These three examples are the animal, the child and the lover. The animal, the child and the lover are the great figures that organize the most secretive movement of Rilke's elegy, this great German, who also wrote poems in French.

Let Rilke's poem serve us as a guide for what I might one day wish to come from a fusing of Germany and France. This fusion ought to create, not so much a new state, or new industrial conglomerates, which are certainly necessary, but a new child, a new animal and a new love.

Let's start with a new animal, a new historical animal, something that would not exactly be a nation, but would not be anything other than a nation. It would be situated between the nation and the complete deposing of old national traditions. It would not exactly be a country, but not anything other than a country. It would not be globalized, but would not exactly be anti-globalized. It would be an original ensemble, and therefore a creation. On this point, we might refer to the French philosopher Gilles Deleuze. Gilles Deleuze explains very well how when two very different, very heterogeneous, things articulate themselves to each other, fit into one another, we get a radical innovation that is neither one nor the other but the monster of the two. Before you tonight, I wish for us to be up to the task of creating, finally, something destined to the whole world, open to the whole world, the monster of France and Germany.

A new child, too. A new child because we are dealing with something that, naturally, will have to educate itself, that will have to grow up by itself, that will have to bring itself up; something that would no longer be subject to the discipline of the past, of Germany's past hackneyed by too many questions, or of France's past, wearied by too many certitudes. Instead, it would have to invent its own education.

We come from old countries, unlike our host this evening, this Argentina that, quite naturally, is still a child-figure of history, bathing anxiously but without weariness, in the childhood of history. We come from old countries, but perhaps by putting ourselves together, by uniting our great ages, we shall become the child contained in this old man. Reversing the course of time, we shall transform the great historical crushing overwhelming us into something innocent and innovative. I really believe that this something original and new can be a new historical child, as it can be a new historical animal.

And lastly, it can be a new love between peoples. These days peoples persist in largely ignoring one another, in ignoring one another far too much, in being indifferent toward one another, some glorious exceptions notwithstanding. A decision of this kind cannot but create new possibilities as regards the bonds and the friendship between peoples. In questions of love and friendship, it matters greatly to know whether one is the same or not; to live in difference or to live in the decision of non-difference. With the decision of fusion, something would be moved deeply, disrupted. We would know that we are 'the same'; and we would have to deal with learning and living this element of the same. This loving apprenticeship would propose to two peoples a new manner of relating to each other.

Of course, it is not possible to imagine this new animal, this new child and this new love, all remaining imprisoned behind a great wall. Rather, at issue here is a simple trace [*trace*] on the surface of the earth, and above all on the surface of Europe. This Franco-German unity I dream of is like a line that is to be drawn and not like a fortress that is to be built. Everyone can cross the line; everyone can score the line. However, everyone must see it too; see it in its new existence. Everyone must see that it is an inscription, a trace, the trace of a site of thinking; a trace that sublates, in the sense of '*aufheben*', in the sense of '*surmonter*', our disagreements and our agreements; a trace that shows what in our agreements is hackneyed, and in our disagreements is out of date.

This idea of the trace, of a new line which would envelop two peoples and their contrary histories and predicates, naturally makes me think it would be something like a stroke of justice that we would be opening up around us. Moreover, in the Eighth Elegy that you've just partly heard, Rilke says about the animal, one of the figures of the open, that it is 'infinite, inapprehensible, unintrospective, pure', and that it speaks in this regard, regarding the open, of the '*au-delà du cercle*'.[30]

So, obviously, I am thinking about Brecht; I am thinking about

Brecht's great play called *The Caucasian Chalk Circle*, which is a play about justice. Brecht is also a little French. My dear German friends, please allow me these successive annexations, which are only preparatory to our fusion. Brecht is a little French in the precise sense that, if you look at the text of one of his very first plays, *In the Jungle of Cities*, you'll find entire passages of Rimbaud purely and simply incorporated into the freshness of the German language, as if they were born in it. The young Brecht was absolutely fascinated by the figure of Rimbaud. On many an occasion he used to say that his ideal of writing is that of the French eighteenth century. Moreover, it is an old German idea that the writing of the French seventeenth century produced a transparency and a vitality that no German could ever grasp. However, we French, we think that there is something of speculative German depth that remains forever inaccessible to us.

The proposition is thus to exchange all that, to merge all that. We shall introduce German depth into clear French rapidity and German discipline into the liveliness of French critique. Then, by some mysterious transfigurative chemistry, the two ambassadors present here today will merge into one another, and throughout the world there'll be *Alliances Franco-allemandes, Goethe–Diderot Instituts*.

In this sense, it would be a true European trace, or the trace of something that Europe could deploy around this trace and this opening. It would be the trace, open to the whole world, of a new Caucasian chalk circle. We shall produce it, I hope, without provocation but resolutely, in an ultimately spiritual act, without which there is nothing. A spiritual gesture, assured but friendly, one that we would be able to call the trace in Europe of the Franco-German chalk circle.

Thank you.

Third Sketch of a
Manifesto of Affirmationist Art

A much longer version of this text, one different in spirit, was given in 2001 in Venice as part of a conference called 'The question of art in the third millennium'. It was organized by Germs under the direction of Ciro Bruni. An even longer version, in a style no doubt driven by sarcasm, was published in the conference's proceedings, Utopia 3, *in 2002 by Germs Éditions. The present version, moderated, and unencumbered by the rhetoric of* Empire *(too indexed nowadays to Negri's bestseller) is essentially the outcome of a talk I was invited to give at the New York Drawing Center by the Center's director, Catherine de Zegher. The occasion of the talk was the publication of number 22 of* Lacanian Ink, *which is edited by Josefina Ayerza. This issue also features the English translation of my small book* Of An Obscure Disaster, *which was published in French in 1991 by Éditions de l'Aube. It is likely there will be further versions. Work in progress.*

Our force of resistance and invention demands that we renounce the delights of the margin, of obliqueness, of infinite deconstruction, of the fragment, of the exhibition trembling with mortality [*tremblante à la mortalité*], of finitude and of the body. We should, and therefore we can, proclaim the existence in art of something that, for the poor century now under way, no longer exists: monumental construction, projects, the creative force of the weak, the overthrow of established powers.

We should oppose all those who want only to terminate, the

entire cohort of last men, exhausted and parasitical, and their infernal 'modesty'. The end of art, of metaphysics, of representation, of imitation, of transcendence, of the work, of the spirit . . . Enough! Let's proclaim at a stroke an end to all ends, and the possible beginning of all that is, as of all that was, and will be.

The vocation of art, in all its forms, is, against the grain of its current tendency [*déclinaison*], toward inconsistent multiplicity, to take up once again the uninhibited, immoral, and – when successful – fundamentally inhuman, energy of affirmation.

Let's proclaim again, over and against humanity, the artistic rights of inhuman truth. Let's again accept to be transfixed by a truth (or a beauty: it's the same thing), rather than consent to governing as justly as possible the minor modes of our expression.

What is at issue is affirmation. And that is why this sketch is that of a manifesto of affirmationism.

The domination of romantic formalism

Let's propose to call postmodern – why not? – all representations of artistic production that come under the banner of a spectacular exhibition of desires, of fantasy and of terror; and under the banner of abolishing the universal, that is, the total exhibition of particularisms and the historical equality of formal means.

Yes, that's just how it is: we can refer to as 'postmodern' that which bears witness to the unlimited and capricious influence of particularity. Two types of particularity exist: there is communitarian, ethnic, linguistic, religious, sexual, and so on, particularity; and then there is biographical particularity, the self as that which imagines that it can and must 'express itself'. I submit that postmodern products represent the latest form of subservience of art to particularity. I shall, then, distinguish between communitarian and ethnic products, including their sexual subdivisions, on the one hand, and products of the ego, on the other.

The products that the gourmets of commerce seek most are precisely those that cleverly combine both kinds: within a recognisable ethnic and sexual framework, they are however of an egoism that is as playful as possible.

No one shall be denounced; each will recognize his own.

So, here is our diagnosis: revisited in a fairly long historical perspective, it can be said that postmodern products – pinned to the notion of the expressive value of the body, for which posture and gesture win out over consistency – are the material form of a pure and simple regression to romanticism.

For us this question is of the utmost importance. From among the vast mass of references that it calls forth, and that the affirmationists to come will gather together and edit, allow me narcissistically to single out one of my own texts. In the first chapter of my *Handbook of Inaesthetics*, I proposed a distinction between three basic schemata concerning the relations between philosophy and art. I called 'didactic' the one that claims in Platonic or Stalinist fashion to subject artistic activity to the external imperative of the Idea. The second – which I called 'classical' – subjects art to the natural rule of pleasing forms and, in the manner of Aristotle or Louis XIV, confers on it the practical virtue of tempering the passions, rather than a mission to truth. I called the third 'romanticism', where, on the contrary, art is presented the sole free form of descent from the infinite Idea to the sensible and, with Heidegger and certain fascisms, requires philosophy to prostrate itself before art.

I maintained that the twentieth century had not really innovated in relation to this decisive knot between material acts and ideality, that it had not really proposed any new figure of art considered as an independent form of thinking. Here is the text:

> The avant-gardes were nothing but the desperate and unstable search for a mediating schema, for a didactico-romantic schema. The avant-gardes were didactic in their desire to put an end

to art, in their condemnation of its alienated and inauthentic character. But they were also romantic in their conviction that art must be reborn as absolute – as the undivided awareness of its operations or as its own immediately legible truth. Considered as the harbingers of a didactico-romantic schema or as the partisans of creative destruction, the avant-gardes were above all anti-classical.[31]

A little further on, I concluded:

The global situation is basically marked by two developments: on the one hand, the saturation of the three inherited schemata [that is, didacticism, classicism and romanticism], on the other, the closure of every effect produced by the only schema that this century applied, which was in fact a synthetic schema: didactico-romanticism.[32]

I am convinced that the 'we' to come, the affirmationists of this century just under way, will be hardly tempted to revoke this judgement. It is by taking this judgement as a point of departure that this 'we' shall form the contours of its own and definite affirmation in the arts.

Of course, the affirmationists will defend the totality of really contemporary artistic production against all the current reactionary attacks. We pour scorn on all those who use temporary theoretical weaknesses to try to impose a restoration of the *pompier* heritage,[33] or of something even worse. But it is not a question of blinding ourselves to the problem we share: domination in all the arts by figures of egoistic and communitarian expressiveness, which is only a degraded didactico-romanticism, a kind of avant-garde without the avant-garde. In a certain way, this is of a pair with the renascent pompierism. Pompierism today proffers violent technologized affects and a grandiose decorative style, and it dominates Hollywood cinema as well as certain sectors of architecture and multimedia colouring [*coloriage*]. But the artists of the postmodern circuit oppose to this nothing but weak classicism, the sole resource of which is Spinoza's statement: 'We do not know what a body can do.' With this meagre communion to the dying, a number of them (a majority?) continue to seek in the paroxysms of particularity, be it ethnic or egoistic, the means to proclaim both the ruin of the classical conception of art, and the absolute affirmativeness of subjective expression, be it public or private. Whatever its modalities, then, the motif of expression has saturated artistic acts with romanticism, the only known variations of which are a lugubrious romanticism or a playful romanticism; respectively, one that speaks of the morose end of the human and one that claims to be throwing a party and breaking out.

We will never understand what constrains us and tries to make us despair, if we do not constantly return to the fact that ours is not a world of democracy but a world of imperial conservatism using democratic phraseology.

What is there to say about today's world? A solitary power, whose army single-handedly terrorizes the entire planet, dictates its law to the circulation of capital and images, and loudly announces everywhere, and with most extreme violence, the Duties and Rights that fall to everybody else. Valets and rivals – Europeans, Russians and Chinese – run after it. At times in disagreement on the means, they do not cease to show their agreement on the basics. For they have no other idea of the world to turn to good account.

Moreover, the thing that, under the imposed name of 'terrorism', appears most to oppose the hegemony of the brutal West, for which 'democracy' is a spiritual ornament, is in reality an organic part of it. Some nihilistic criminals indiscriminately killed thousands of New Yorkers. This mass crime is evidently an avatar of contemporary pathology. It is the cold *mise-en-scène* of a hackneyed motif: the outcry of inspired barbarians against the sated imperialists. The American Army and the 'terrorists' are simply playing out the same old and bloody historical scenario about a civilization encircled by brutes.

Now, we need only think of Rome to recall that a solitary power which believes itself to be the incarnation of civilization lays out two directions for art. On the one hand, there is a kind of rowdy celebration of its own power, a morbid and hackneyed representationalist intoxication, which is offered to the people as opium for its passivity. Such are the Circus games, the strict equivalent of which today is professional sport, and the musical and cinematic culture industry. This sort of amusement deals in wholesale. Corresponding to today's numerous torture victims and gladiators of the arena is the business of doped athletes and colossal media budgets. This art is *l'art pompier*, the art that turns the lugubrious power of the Empire into the subject of own increasingly allegorical and grandiloquent games and fictions. The natural hero of that art is the Killer, the *serial killer* torturer. In short: the perverse gladiator.

On the other hand, there is a meagre sophistication, itself worked over by a sort of formalist excess, which attempts to oppose to *pompier* massiveness the unctuous discernment and subtle perversity of people who, without overly suffering from it, pretend to withdraw from general circulation. Such art is romantically morose: it insists on the impotence of retreat as a kind of nihilistic delectation. It readily invokes great forests, eternal snows, bodies rendered supple by some natural or oriental wisdom. But this art is as much an art of the twilight as *art pompier*. Indeed, these two constitute a couple in the same way that the circus trumpet and Martial's deliciously obscene epigrams constituted one; in the same way as did the flamboyant rhetoric of generals and the ascetic preaching of the Christians in the catacombs.

The multiform desolation of vast sections of contemporary art, in total symmetry to the *pompier* art of massive image-commerce, lies in the fact that it is basically nothing but romantic formalism.

It is nothing but formalism in so far as it is presumed that a single formal idea, a single gesture/movement, a single dead (boring) craft, is sufficient to distinguish such art from commercial mass production.

It is nothing but romantic in so far as what is reactivated and worked over, although in growing anonymity, is the motif of individual expression, of the *mise-en-scène* of supposedly sublimely singular ethnic and egoistical particularities. That is in so far as the energy of bodies is considered to be that which redeems us from conceptual disembodiment. As a result, what returns, but this time devoid of miracle, in the boredom of exact gestures/movements, is either an art linked to a notion of redemption, or art as a suffering and radiant exhibition of the flesh, that is, art as the carnal installation of finitude.

In truth, romantic formalism has always been the artistic orientation appropriate to powers that are established and drawing to a close. And our age is just that: a unique and multiform doctrine (economic liberalism and political electoralism) that for the first time incorporates the quasi-totality of the human species in the distribution of its fortunes and constraints. Yes, our time is that of a unique doctrine, and of the consensus that has been formed around it under the strange label of 'democracy'. Well, every single doctrine of this type is desperate and nihilistic, since all it proposes to the human multiplicity is the absurd perpetuation of its obscene order. Further, the artistic subjectivity that it induces pertains solely to this nihilism and to this obscenity. It is a subjectivity that busies itself with formalizing the sublime despair of bodies delivered to enjoyment of the Unique. Lenin had already remarked that during times when critical and revolutionary political activity is very weak, what the sorry arrogance of imperialism produces is a mixture of mysticism and pornography. That's exactly what we are getting today in the form of formal romantic vitalism. We have universal sex, and we have oriental wisdom. A Tibetan pornography: that would fulfil the wish of this century, which is putting off inventing its birth.

Affirming the Great Twentieth Century

Artists have long thought that the resolute destruction of the romantic schema and all of its vitalist and naturalist paraphernalia was the imperative of the day. Affirmationists lay claim to the singularity of a critical genealogy. Throughout the twentieth century, great artists of all arts attempted to free art from the hold of romantic expressiveness and to endow it with its necessary *coldness*, in the very sense that Mallarmé had already called forth the poetic Idea, for its suddenly appearing, like a constellation, cold with forgetfulness and obsolescence. These often isolated artists slowly composed configurations that have become legible only today. They advanced the will of a thought-art that would tolerate neither finitude, nor the flesh, nor redemption. They advanced an art that is just as allergic to obscurantist hypnosis as it is to the pornographic stupidity of festive performances. An art that is neither that of Buddha, nor that of a desire caught between the fair and the morgue. An art that is effectively other than romanticism, an art capable of measuring up to what the poet Alvaro de Campos, the heteronym of Fernando Pessoa, called a 'mathematics of being'.

The tautest, most unremitting, and truest art of the twentieth century made an attempt to test out the notion, as Alvaro de Campos once again said, that 'Newton's binomial is as beautiful as the Venus de Milo.' Which is to say: this art tried to seize the real with the same impersonal rigour as that of mathematics. We can name some heroes of this attempt, all of whom were invariably opposed to successive neo-romanticisms, such as that of the surrealists, or, worse still, the situationists, to say nothing of the contemporary corporealists and vitalists. The list – we shall mention only those no longer with us – is arbitrary, and only indicates the apparent absence of contour of that which, in the dead sky of the century, sketches our constellation. The affirmative constellation.

There are the great affirmationists, the best, those who did not need to know they were; those who by themselves, by their acts, opened out entire configurations, in their principle as well as in their implementation: Pessoa for the poem, Picasso for painting, Schönberg for music, Brecht for theatre, Zadkine for sculpture, Chaplin for cinema, Faulkner for the novel, Cunningham for dance . . .

But we shall not forget Stevens, who affirmed the possibility of capturing the appearing of being in the poem; Mandelstam, who seized everything that formed a sacred symbol in the immensity of the corpse of Time; or Celan, who affirmed the transpoetic possibility of the poem 'After Auschwitz'.

We shall celebrate Berg, who asserted the complete possibility of opera beyond its apparent death, and Bartók, who perpetuated the experimental, contrapuntal and rhythmic force of the string quartet. Messiaen, too, who affirmed the embodiment of the innocent, contemplative life in a sort of sonorous slowness by means of subtle masses and temporal tangles; while, for his part, Webern constructed the mystical value of sophisticated silences.

We shall laud the proclamation, made by both Malevitch and Mondrian, of the ontological certainty of geometries, and the affirmation, made by Kupka and Rothko, of the power – oh drapery of the soul! – of great and pure contrasts of sufficient colour. We shall say: Kandinsky, legitimacy of the connection of signs! Pollock, enclosed effervescence of the infinite act!

We shall praise you, Pirandello, fecund decision of duplicity, illusion's aptitude for the truth. And likewise Claudel, stirring up conservative dissatisfaction as far as the summit of the heavens.

Richier's idolatrous insects; Moore's colossal pregnancies; Brancusi's pure signs!

Other affirmations: Woolf's enveloping vision of ephemeral totalizations; Mansfield and the benediction of the morning; Beckett and the ascetic relentlessness of the desire to exist; and you, fraternal Malraux, who ensnared history in the web of your rhetorical celebration.

Murnau: revelation of the power of dreams contained in the juncture of the frame and lights. Welles, tortuous, poetic arrangements of visibility . . .

Let's stop this exercise, which is absurd except in so far as it points out that nothing in the list falls under any nomination that could be identified with a school, other than that each work's singularity carries within it, although in disparate directions, the desire – against all romanticism, and with reference to this tenebrous century – for something that would ultimately take on the form of terrestrial affirmation.

Proclaiming the maxims of affirmationist art

We do not want, in naming what moves us, to hand out prizes. We want to make visible the genealogy of an axiomatic. An axiomatic that posits this: at the dawn of the century, we should recreate artistic desire in its incorporeal rigour, in its anti-romantic coldness, in the subtractive operations by which it holds most tightly to the imageless real, which is the only cause of art. In subtraction art destines the real it encounters to all people, negating the influence of particularity. Subtraction is the modern method for integrally affirming the universal.

This is, then, the axiomatic of an art that is neither ethnic nor egoistic. It is the axiomatic of an art that is as delocalized, as ambitious, as impersonal, and as naked for universal thought as the trait by which, thirty thousand years ago, the non-temporal signs of bisons and tigers were etched in the shadows of caves – a trait which, in its very nakedness, forever affirms the inhumanity of the Beautiful.

The affirmationist axiomatic only sets out the minimal but still entirely abstract conditions that were actively distributed in the still non-sketched constellation by the artists of the century, conditions under which art remains rebellious to imperial power, at the same time as it overcomes the romantic duplicity of the funereal and the playful. This is the duplicity that Victor Hugo, in claiming to be representative of it, very appropriately named that of the sublime and the grotesque. Because if it is not *pompier*, then today's art is exactly that: of a sublimeness forcibly obtained by means of the grotesque. It is the sterile grimace of an impossible-to-find sacralization; the insipid gesticulation of the self.

It is against these hasty colourings in by an insufficient devotion to the inhumanity of the time that we are trying to recreate the rights of an independent affirmation.

1. Art is not the sublime descent of the infinite into the finite abjection of the body and of sexuality. It is on the contrary the production, by the finite means of a material subtraction, of an infinite, subjective series.

We affirm that in art there are only works. And that a work is always finite, complete, as complete as possible. The myth of idleness is post-romantic; it is a kind of boredom with the finite in the name of a vague infinite. Instead, what is particular to art is to induce an infinite subjective possibility, which depends on the finitude of the work. This is indeed why our thinking, in accordance with a recreated subjectivity, still takes Aeschylus and Lucretius as a point of departure. The idea of the ephemeral is believed to be new, but it only amounts to aligning art on consumable commodities, on the wear and tear of products, which is the material basis of the Empire. To affirm the work is to resist Empire at the same time as avoiding any kind of pompier *praising of its power. It is to affirm the powerful powerlessness of the work, its fragile and implacable singularity.*

2. Art cannot be the expression of a particularity, whether ethnic or egoistic. It is the impersonal production of a truth that is addressed to all.

The schema of expression assumes that each person, as artist, is a kind of ineffable singularity. As one says today: 'I want to be myself' or – the tribal version – 'We want to create, to recreate our own culture.' The unfortunate thing is that this will is preformed, and that the 'myself' that comes to pass does not distinguish itself in any way from 'everyone'. It is the same with 'cultures', which are nothing but restored products, recycled obsolescences. All that is desperately average . . . But precisely, the only thing established powers like are statistics and opinion polls, because they know that nothing is more innocent and powerless than an average. They know that each individual, the anyone, is only an interchangeable animal. We affirm that, through artistic labour, it may come to pass that this animal becomes the chilled support of a universal address. The human animal is in no way the cause of this address; it is only its site, or one of its sites. The artist as individual is only a living being ascribed to a subject that, since it takes the form of an artwork, is a subject of the sensible and has need of such matter. But once the subject-work has been laid out we can completely forget about its transitory individual support. Only the work is affirmative. The artist is the neutral element of that affirmation.

3. The truth of which art is the process is always the truth of the sensible *qua* sensible, that is, the transformation of the sensible into the event of the Idea.

What distinguishes art from other truth-processes is that the subject of truth is extracted from the sensible; while in science the subject of truth is extracted from the power of the letter; in politics from the infinite resources of the collective; and in love from sex as differentiation. Art makes an event [fait événement] *of what lies at the edge of what is given to perceptual experience* [du donné], *that is, at the edge of the indistinctly sensory, and it is in this respect that it is an Idea, that is, in so far as it turns what is there into what must come to pass within the finitude of the work. In art, the Idea is imposed through the transformation of what can be perceived into an improbable imperative. To force to see something, as if it was practically impossible, something that is anyhow clearly visible, is precisely what painting does, for example. Art affirms that at the same point of an impossible-to-be-felt, the Idea holds on, as sensed in the sensible effects of the work.*

4. There is necessarily a plurality of arts and, whatever the imaginable intersections might be, there is no imaginable totalization of that plurality.

This merely stresses the fact that the changing of evidence into an imperative is issued within the sensible. Now, nothing unifies the sensible other than the individual animal subject and its organs. But art is indifferent to this empirical unification, since art deals with the sensible region by region, and produces its own non-empirical and non-organic universal subject. So there can be no art that is sensibly indistinct. We declare that the multimedia motif of a multisensory art is a motif without true destiny. All it does is project the obscene uniqueness of commerce – that is, the monetary equivalence of products – onto art.

5. All art comes from impure forms, and the purification of such impurity makes up the history of artistic truths and of their exhaustion.

Form is that which endows the sensible evidence with a new vibration, such that it dissipates this evidence and changes it into a fragile ought-to-be [devoir-être]. Form is initially always impure, because it is suspended between the initial sensible givens and its vibration, between recognition and misrecognition. For a long time, that's how it was with figuration: this is an ox but not exactly, and above all, one must really see it to believe it. Whereupon art persists in purifying the impure, in dedicating itself ever further to its duty of visibility as against the mere evidence of the visible.

6. The subjects of artistic truths consist in the works that compose them.

If this were not so, artistic truth would indeed consist in the authors and their evidence, or their expression. And so there would be no universality, no duty in art. There would only be reflections of ethnic and egoistic particularities. The only true subject is that which comes to pass: that is, the work on the basis of which evidence is suspended. The affirmative subject of non-evidence alone is the work.

7. Such compositions are infinite configurations that, in the artistic context of the time, comprise generic totalities.

Here we are referring to the subjects that are initiated by a historic event of art, i.e. to the complex that is composed of the works of an innovative series. Thus we are referring to serial work in music, to the classical style between Haydn and Beethoven, to the years in which Cubism was active, to the post-Romantic poem, and to thousands of other things. These are the subjective collections or constellations of works that we call configurations, and which comprise the real figures of artistic truths. A configuration is that which is neither nameable nor calculable in the anterior situation of the art in question. It is what happens outside of all prediction and outside of all predicates. That's why the totality thereby produced is generic; it affirms, at a given moment, art as a pure universal genre – art as subtracted from every previous classification.

8. The real of art comprises an ideal impurity as the immanent process of its purification. In other words, art has as its prime material the incidental contingency of a form. Art is a second formalization of the emergence of a form as formless [*informe*].

This statement simply restates the preceding ones from a different angle. At first, what is there is an impure formal idea that changes the evidence of some perception and of some interior intuition into a problem, into an imperative. Then, there is a refinement of impurity, as the form is detached from impurity and becomes ever emptier. That is why one can say that it is characteristic of an artistic configuration or truth-in-becoming to pass through a second formalization whereby the impurity is eliminated from the impure form, or the formless itself is made into a form. This is done until the moment where nothing more of the real holds, for lack of empirical evidence, for lack of impurity. When a configuration loses its affirmative power, it is accomplished.

9. The only maxim of contemporary art is not to be 'Western', which also means that it should not be democratic, if democratic signifies complying with the Western idea of political liberty.

Here we come to the present situation. Yes, the sole problem is to know if the artistic imperative can be freed from Western imperatives of circulation and communication. Western democracy indeed is circulation and communication. True art is therefore that which interrupts circulation, that which communicates nothing. An immobile and incommunicable art; that is the art we need, that is the only art that is addressed to all, that does not circulate within any pre-established circuit, and does not communicate with anyone in particular. Art must augment in each individual the non-democratic means of liberty.

10. A non-Western art is necessarily an abstract art in the following sense: it is abstracted from all particularity and it formalizes this act of abstraction.

For the struggle against expressiveness, against Romantic formalism, all that there is is the dynamic of abstraction. This rule is a very old one, but it is especially relevant to our situation. Everything comes down to this: to invent a new sensory abstraction. It is true that we barely know how. Scientific practice, at least, or especially mathematics, can instruct us. After all, this is the path that was taken by people during the Renaissance, and also by painters at the beginning of the twentieth century: they turned to geometry. And we should also turn to geometry, which has changed a great deal. For it is less a substitution of forms for their schema than it is a logic of the hidden invariants in every deformation. We should affirm, in art, the idea of intelligible deformations.

11. The abstraction of the art which is, and which is to come, does not take any particular public into consideration. This art is tied to a proletarian aristocratism: it does what it does, and it does it without factoring in persons.

We proclaim that all the institutional and sociological speculations about the art public must be left aside. Sociology, even when critical, is only ever an auxiliary of the democracy of the West. Art need not concern itself with its clientele. It is unbendingly for all, and its address bears no empirical signification within it. Art is made, and says what it does, according to its own discipline, and without considering anybody's interests. That is what I call its proletarian aristocratism: an aristocratism exposed to the judgement of all. The great French theatre director Antoine Vitez had a beautiful expression to designate the art of theatre. He would say that theatre is 'elitism for everyone'. 'Proletarian' designates that which, in everyone, and through the discipline of work, co-belongs to generic humanity. 'Aristocratic' names that which, in everyone, is subtracted from every evaluation carried out in terms of averages, majorities, resemblance, or imitation.

12. The art that is, and the art that is to come, should hang together as solidly as a demonstration, be as surprising as a night-time ambush, and be as elevated as a star.

Here is what provides the abstract basis for these three images. The work to come must be as solidly linked as a demonstration because it must oppose the perpetual mobility of the market in the imperial world with the inflexibility of a principle of consequence. *The work to come treats relativisms and suspect doubts with disdain. It explores its affirmation right to the end.*

The work to come must be as surprising as a night-time ambush because it makes an event of a previously unknown real. The work imposes this real, this piece of the real, violently upon whomever is seized by it. The work does not make it circulate, does not communicate it. It imposes it, necessarily with a little touch of terror.

The work to come must be as elevated as a star because it desires the atemporal coldness of an invented form. It is not fraternal, or corporeal, and does not place itself in the half-heartedness of sharing. The work of art to come considers itself above imperial commerce.

The difficulty of art today is that there are three imperatives and not simply one. There is the imperative of the consequence, that is, a logical imperative, one that pertains to the mathematics of being. There is the imperative of surprise, that is, of the real, or of the exception. And there is the imperative of elevation, that is, the imperative of the symbol, or of distance.

It is often the case that works can be admitted under one or two of the three imperatives. But today the great problem of form is really to combine the three. That is what will decide the work to come.

We shall leave the last three maxims in their conclusive starkness.

13. Art today constitutes itself by propping itself up on that which, for communication (both media and commerce), does not exist, or barely exists. Art abstractly constructs the visibility of this non-existence. That is what binds all the arts to the following formal principle: the capacity to render visible for all that which, for media [*médium*] and commerce, and so also for everyone but from another viewpoint, does not exist.

14. Contemporary power, in the assurance it has of being able to control the entire expanse of the visible and the audible through commercial laws of circulation and democratic laws of communication, no longer has need of censorship. It says: 'Everything is possible', which is also to say that nothing is. To abandon oneself to this authorization to enjoy is done to the detriment of art and of thought. We must be relentless in acting as our own censors.

15. It is better to do nothing than to work formally toward making visible what the West declares to exist.

Notes to Part One

1 The Femis is the École Nationale Supérieure des Métiers de l'Image et du Son in Paris. *Translator's note.*
2 The editorialist in question here is Jean-Marie Colombani, director of the daily *Le Monde*. In the aftermath of the attack on the Twin Towers, Colombani wrote an editorial for the September 12 2001 issue of *Le Monde* entitled 'Nous sommes tous Américains!' *Translator's note.*
3 Badiou is referring here to an article published in *Le Monde* on October 4 2001, by Monique Canto-Sperber, entitled 'Terreur Injustifiable'. She is more generally known in France for her peculiar brand of 'moral philosophy' and her work on Greek philosophy. Monique Canto-Sperber is Director of the École Normale Supérieure in Paris. *Translator's note.*
4 In English the French 'Occidentale' is translated by 'Western', but although the latter clearly designates the developed world, it does not resound as strongly with the second religious (Christian and Jewish) sense of the former. Thus in Anglophone countries it makes little sense to call a political group 'the Western Party', whilst in France during the 1960s and 1970s, as Badiou recalls, 'Occident' was the name of an extreme right-wing party. *Translator's note.*
5 'Bougnoule' is a racist name employed in France to designate North Africans or Arabs. *Translator's note.*
6 Jacques Julliard, for many years a historian at the EHESS and then later executive director at the *Nouvel Observateur*, is, among other things, famous for having successfully propagated the anti-Third-Worldist agenda of the so-called *nouveaux philosophes* at the level of the mass media. This 'debate', first launched in the pages of the *Nouvel Observateur* in 1978, basically posits the existence of an *a priori* propensity to radical evil to arrive at the conclusion that all socialism in the Third World will end in bloody dictatorship. Bernard Henry-Lévy, one of the most prominent of the *nouveaux philosophes*, has taken media manipulation to new heights. So

much so that he is no longer referred to by name, but marketed by his brand name BHL. Pin-up boy of the media, who have designated him 'France's greatest intellectual', he might be seen at any given moment on the cover of *Paris Match*, in the windows of many bookshops, and on several chat shows at once. *Translator's note.*

7 Badiou's 'Of an Obscure Disaster: On the End of the Truth of State', was first published in English in *Lacanian ink*, 22, Fall, translated by Barbara Fulks, 2003, pp. 58–89. *Translator's note.*

8 André Glucksmann, Romain Goupil and Pascal Bruckner together published an article in *Le Monde* on March 10 2003, calling for the French to support the American military intervention in Iraq. Bernard Kouchner joined them in their 'military moralism' and they came to be known as 'la bande des Quatre'. *Translator's note.*

9 This is a word play that does not work in English. *Translator's note..*

10 The original French slogan is 'Elections, piège à cons.' *Translator's note.*

11 Arlette Laguiller, member of the European Parliament from 1999 to 2004, was also a candidate at the French presidential elections of 2002, obtaining 5.72 per cent of the vote. She is the spokesperson of the Trotskyist organization Lutte Ouvrière. *Translator's note.*

12 The bourgeois École Libre movement of 1982 succeeded in stopping the planned nationalization of French's Catholic schools. *Translator's note.*

13 Alain Madelin co-founded an extreme right-wing group called Occident, which lasted from 1964 to 1968, being replaced by Groupe Union Défense and Ordre Nouveau. Later, he became a disciple of Friedrich Hayek and embraced free-market ideology, presiding over the Démocratie Libérale Party, which today forms part of the conservative umbrella group, the UMP, that currently dominates the French parliamentary scene. *Translator's note.*

14 Undocumented workers, or 'les sans-papiers', as they are referred to in France, have been the subject of a series of increasingly discriminatory laws endorsed by both the left and right wings of the parliament. The campaign against these most precarious of workers began in France in 1977 with an end to family reunification, but entered a new phase in 1993 with the introduction of the Pasqua laws which established a specific status for 'illegals' living in France. Indeed, as Badiou's *Organisation Politique* tirelessly point outs, the consensus of French parliamentarism today is precisely structured around creating a group of individuals who, though they constitute part of the situation, are effectively treated as politically non-existent. The OP has organized a series of campaigns against this criminalization of ordinary workers and the replacement in political discourse of the word 'worker' by that of 'immigrant'. Against these laws designed to protect the interests of French capital, the OP

upholds the universal maxim 'everyone who is here is from here'. *Translator's note.*

15 In French 'sécurité' is used politically to designate law-and-order policies, policies of defending and protecting what already exists and the stepping up of police intervention. *Translator's note.*

16 Jean-Pierre Chevènement is a French politician and the Honorary President of the Mouvement républicain et citoyen. He regularly invokes the 'republican model' and openly subscribes to the Jacobin tradition. Along with some other prominent figures on the French parliamentary left, such as Lionel Jospin, he has been key in promoting the notion that 'sécurité' is a value of neither the left nor the right; that is, it should be a value of the left *as well as* the right. *Translator's note.*

17 Georges Couthon formed with Robespierre and Saint-Just a sort of triumvirate of the Committee for Public Safety. He remained faithful to his political ideals until the end, preferring to triumph or to die with Robespierre rather than to flee. He was guillotined with Robespierre and Saint-Just the 10th Thermidor (July 28 1794). *Translator's note.*

18 Part of the so-called 'Front Républicain', Guy Mollet of the French Socialist Party (SFIO) initially espoused peace with Algeria but upon coming into office performed a quick about-face. Under his command the numbers of French troops in Algeria was doubled within 6 months of his taking office in 1956. He, moreover, refused any dialogue with the Algerian FLN. In October 1956, he also committed France to join forces with the English and the Israelis in the Suez expedition, after Gamal Abdel Nasser had nationalized it. *Translator's note.*

19 Jack Lang is a French politician and member of the French Socialist Party. As former Minister for Culture, the eternally tanned Lang – friend of the stars – is a particularly odious example of what the French call *la gauche caviar*, roughly translated as 'champagne socialists'. *Translator's note.*

20 Alain Krivine, a one-time member of the European Parliament, was one of the 'Old guard' from 1968. He retired from the political bureau of the LCR in March 2006. *Translator's note.*

21 During the two rounds of the French presidential elections, slogans such as 'Le Pen, facho, le peuple aura ta peau' (Le Pen, you fascist, the people will have your hide) and 'Le Pen, facho, Chirac, escroc' (Le Pen, fascist, Chirac, crook) were common. *Translator's note.*

22 One of the initiatives of the Jospin government, under the initiative of the Minister Martine Aubry, involved the reduction of the working work to 35 hours. The *Organisation Politique* has kept a close eye on the (often devastating) effects this has had on the most vulnerable workers due to the employers' strategy of conceding a reduction of the working week 'in

exchange' for greater flexibility in working hours. See their publication *Le Journal Politique*, available online at www.organisationpolitique.com. *Translator's note.*

23 A large extract of this text was published in the February 22/23 2004 edition of the daily *Le Monde*. The law of March 15 2004 bans the wearing of headscarves, turbans, skullcaps, or other 'ostentatious' signs of religious affiliation, at school, on the pretext that such acts are not in conformity with the secular principles of the French Republic. *Translator's note.*

24 Luc Ferry, a lightweight philosopher, is known in English-speaking countries as having co-authored with Alain Renault *French Philosophy of the Sixties: An Essay on Antihumanism*, trans. Mary. H.S. Cattani, Massachusets UP, 1990, a conservative–liberal attack on ''68 thought' in all its manifestations. He was the French Education Minister in the government of Jean-Pierre Raffarin from 2002 to 2004.

25 The slogan in French is 'ni putes, ni soumises'. It comes from the name of a movement that emerged in France after the France-wide 'Marche des femmes contre les ghettos et pour l'égalité' on March 8 2003. The mission statement of the movement is to 'diffuse the values of the secular republic . . . the only basis on which we can all live together'. Starting as a legitimate protest movement against forms of violence suffered by women in the *banlieue*, NPNS, rather like the movement SOS Racisme, rapidly became instrumentalized by the establishment parties and is one of the most virulent opponents of the *hijab* and any forces on the left who oppose the anti-headscarf legislation. *Translator's note.*

26 The French slogan is 'jouir sans entraves', and has been actively pushed in the media and by those who wish to cast May '68 as a movement of 'libertarian individualism,' i.e. who wish to deprive it of its political character by reducing it to an essentially hedonistic movement. On the various treatments of May '68 in France see Kristin Ross, *May '68 and Its Afterlives*, Chicago UP, 2002. *Translator's note*

27 This text was first published in *Le Monde* on November 15 2005, at the time of the riots in the housing estates around Paris and throughout France. *Translator's note.*

28 Julien Gracq, *Le Rivage de Syrtes*, Josi Corti, 1951.

29 For those who are interested, I've included both the original German and French translation in addition to the English one. As it was impossible to find an English translation that matched the spirit of Maximine's 'inspired' translation, I've opted for one of the most faithful renditions. For the English and German texts see: Leishman and Spender, *Duino Elegies: the German text / Rainer Maria Rilke; with an English translation, introduction and commentary by J.B. Leishman & Stephen Spender,*

Hogarth Press, 1963. For the French see: Maximine, *Élégies de Duino*, Actes Sud, 1991. *Translator's note.*

30 I've left the French here because it is more appropriate to the theme of the *trace*, and the reference to Brecht immediately following, than the English translation. *Translator's note.*

31 Badiou, *Handbook of Inaesthetics*, trans. Alberto Toscano, Stanford UP, 2004, p. 8.

32 Ibid.

33 Originating in the mid-nineteenth century, the term *pompier* ('fireman' in English) was applied pejoratively to French academic art (more particularly pretentious history painting) of the time. The term *pompier* is said to derive from the similarity between the helmets of firemen and those worn by the Greek gods and neoclassical heroes depicted by classical artists. *L'art pompier* is cast by its detractors as academic, imitative and vulgarly neo-classical. *Translator's note.*

Part Two
Uses of the Word 'Jew'

Introduction

For the last couple of decades, the intellectual situation in France has been marked by countless discussions about the status to be accorded to the word 'Jew' within the divisions of thought.

Undoubtedly, this has to do with the suspicion, based on some indubitable facts and some contrived ones, that anti-Semitism has made a 'return'. But had it ever disappeared? Or is it not rather crucial to see that a considerable change has taken place in the nature of anti-Semitism's forms, criteria and inscription in discourse over the last thirty years? Recall that in 1980, after the attack on the synagogue in rue Copernic,[1] the prime minister in person, and in all calmness, distinguished between those victims who had gone to worship and the 'innocent French' (*sic*) who were only passing by. Besides distinguishing between Jews and French with a kind of false concern, the good Raymond Barre appeared to mean that a Jew blindly targeted by an attack must be guilty in some way or other. People said it was a slip of the tongue. Instead, this amazing way of looking at the situation disclosed the subsistence of a racialist subconscious directly from the 1930s. Today, as regards the uses of the word 'Jew', such discriminatory confidence would be inconceivable at the level of the state, and one can only be unreservedly glad of it. Calculated anti-Semitic provocations and false discriminatory naivety, such as denials of the existence of gas chambers or the Nazi destruction of the European Jews, have today been taken in by, or confined to, the extreme right. So, although it is quite incorrect to say that anti-Semitism has disappeared, it is fair to maintain that its conditions of possibility have altered, to the extent that it is no longer inscribed in any sort of natural discourse, as was the case during Raymond Barre's time. In this sense, Le Pen, in France, is the somewhat jaded custodian of a historical anti-Semitism that public opinion of the 1930s accepted as entirely commonplace. All in all, it may well be that this new sensitivity to anti-Semitic acts and inscriptions is a basic component of the diagnosis that anti-Semitism has made a 'return'. Thus this return might for a large part be simply an effect of a significant and favourable lowering of the threshold at which public opinion no longer tolerates this sort of racialist provocation.

Below, I shall return to the issue of the birth of a new type of anti-Semitism, one articulated on conflicts in the Middle East and the presence, in France, of large minorities of workers of African extraction and of Muslim persuasion. For now, suffice it to say that the existence of this type of anti-Semitism is not in doubt, and that the zeal with which some deny its existence – generally in the name of supporting the Palestinians or the working-class minorities in France – is extremely harmful. That being the case, it doesn't seem to me that the data, which are freely available, are such that they justify raising a full alert, although it should be clear that, on such questions, the imperative of vigilance admits of no interruption.

What constitutes the point of departure for the present collection,[2] what has sparked its existence, is not the obviousness of anti-Semitisms, old and new. It is a debate with further-reaching consequences, or rather a debate that is to be settled beforehand, including by those who agree that the slightest anti-Semitic allusion is not to be tolerated. Indeed, what is at issue is to know whether or not, in the general field of public intellectual discussion, the word 'Jew' constitutes an exceptional signifier, such that it would be legitimate to make it play the role of a final, or even sacred, signifier. It is evident that tackling the eradication of forms of anti-

Semitic consciousness is done differently, and with a different subjectivity, depending on whether we consider these forms of consciousness to be essentially different to other forms of racial discrimination (e.g. to anti-Arab sentiments or to the segregating of blacks to their communitarian activities); or whether – given certainly distinct and irreducible historicities – we consider that all forms of racist consciousness alike call for the same egalitarian and universalist reaction. Further, this shared repugnance of anti-Semitism must be distinguished from a certain philo-Semitism which claims not only that attacking Jews as such amounts to criminal baseness but that the word 'Jew', and the community claiming to stand for it, must be placed in a paradigmatic position with respect to the field of values, cultural hierarchies, and in evaluating the politics of states.

Suffice it to say that, regarding the question of old and new anti-Semitisms and the process of eradicating them, there are two conflicting approaches, where what is at issue is to know what a contemporary universalism might consist in and whether it is compatible with any kind of nominal or communitarian transcendence.

Today it is evident that a strong intellectual current, featuring bestselling publications and considerable media impact, indeed maintains that the fate of the word 'Jew' lies in its communitarian transcendence, in such a way that this destiny cannot be rendered commensurable with those of other names that, within the registers of ideology, or of politics, or even of philosophy, have been subject to conflicting assessments.

The basic argumentation, of course, refers to the extermination of European Jews by the Nazis and their accomplices. In the victim ideology that constitutes the campaign artillery of contemporary moralism, this unprecedented extermination is held to be paradigmatic. In and of itself the extermination would underpin the political, legal and moral necessity to hold the word 'Jew' above all usual handling of identity predicates and to give it some kind of nominal sacralization. The progressive imposition of the word 'Shoah' to designate what its most eminent historian, Raul Hilberg, named, with sober precision, 'the destruction of the European Jews' can be taken as a verbal stage of this sacralizing of victims. By a remarkable irony, one thereby comes to the point of applying to the name 'Jew' a claim that the Christians originally directed against the Jews themselves, which was that 'Christ' was a worthier name than all others. Today it is not uncommon to read that 'Jew' is indeed a name beyond ordinary names. And it seems to be presumed that, like an inverted original sin, the grace of having been an incomparable victim can be passed down not only to descendants and to the descendants of descendants but to all who come under the predicate in question, be they heads of state or armies engaging in the severe oppression of those whose lands they have confiscated.

Another approach to this type of fictive transcendence is historical. It claims to show that the 'Jewish question' has defined Europe since the Enlightenment era, such that there would be a criminal continuity between the idea Europe has of itself and the Nazi extermination, which is presented as the 'final solution' to the problem. Further, there would be a basic continuity between the extermination and European hostility to the State of Israel, the prime evidence for which would be the constant support – in my view really inconsistent, but let's leave that aside – the European Community gives to the Palestinians. Europe would be enraged by the fact that the 'final solution' was defeated in the last act by the sudden appearance, on the balance-sheet of the war, of a Jewish state. As a result, there should be a legitimate distrust of everything Arab, for in starting out from support for the Palestinians we soon come to an undermining of the State of Israel, then from that undermining we come to anti-Semitism, and from this anti-Semitism to extermination – the logic, in short, has to be good.

In the texts that follow, I would like as far as possible to document a position utterly irreconcilable with the above assertions. I will submit a position that is avowedly my own. On such issues, and taking account of the passions that inevitably emerge with every dispute over the power of a collective nomination, it is better to state straight away that one is only speaking for oneself, or, more precisely, in one's own name.

Obviously, the key point is that I cannot accept in any way the victim ideology. I clearly explained my position on this point in my little book *Ethics* in 1993. That the Nazis and their accomplices exterminated millions of people they called 'Jews' does not to my mind lend any new legitimacy to the identity predicate in question. Of course, for those who, generally for religious reasons, have maintained that this predicate registers a communitarian alliance with the archetypical transcendence of the Other, it is natural to think that Nazi atrocities work in some way to validate – in a terrible and striking paradox – the election of the 'people' that this predicate, so they say, gathers together. Furthermore, it would be necessary to explain how and why the Nazi predicate 'Jew', such as it was used to organize separation, then deportation and death, coincides with the subjective predicate under which the alliance is sealed. But for anyone who does not enter into the religious fable in question, the extermination brings to bear on the Nazis a judgement that is absolute and without right of appeal, without in any way establishing any supplementary value for the victims, other than a profound compassion. In passing, I submit that veritable compassion does not concern itself in the slightest with the predicates in the name of which the atrocity was committed. As such, it is all the more wrong-headed to think that an atrocity confers a surplus value on a predicate. Neither can an atrocity work to provide any kind of special respect to anybody who today expects to take shelter under such a predicate and demand exceptional status. Instead, from those limitless massacres, we should draw the conclusion that every declamatory introduction of communitarian predicates in the ideological, political or state field, whether criminalizing or sanctifying, leads to the worst.

Less rational still is the claim that we can find means in the Nazi gas chambers with which to confer on the colonial State of Israel – set up in the Middle East (and not in Bavaria . . .) – some special status, a status other than the one that all colonial states have already had conferred on them for some decades, and that comes down to saying simply that they represent a form of the oppression of impoverished peoples that is particularly detestable and very rightly obsolete. The question of what was to become of these states was certainly complex, and has historically been worked out by a whole range of solutions. The French colonizers quit Algeria *en masse*, where their families had often resided for more than a century, whilst the European colonies of South Africa, despite the frightful racist practices of apartheid, are presently collaborating in the new South Africa founded by Nelson Mandela. I don't know what will become of the State of Israel, a situation of more recent date than the other two. My point is simply that the developments of this state can only be thought rationally by refraining from justifying its existence – which, whatever you might think, really is carried out on the Palestinians' backs – with continual reference to sinister episodes of Europe's history.

Let me add something of a more affective note. It is wholly intolerable to be accused of anti-Semitism by anyone for the sole reason that, from the fact of the extermination, one does not conclude as to the predicate 'Jew' and its religious and communitarian dimension that it receive some singular valorization – a transcendent annunciation! – nor that Israeli exactions, whose colonial nature is patent and banal, be specially tolerated. I propose that nobody any longer accept, publicly or privately, this type of political blackmail.

An abstract variation of my position consists in pointing out that, from the apostle Paul to Trotsky, including Spinoza, Marx and Freud, Jewish communitarianism has only underpinned creative universalism in so far as there have been new points of rupture with it. It is clear that today's equivalent of Paul's religious rupture with established Judaism, of Spinoza's rationalist rupture with the Synagogue, or of Marx's political rupture with the bourgeois integration of a part of his community of origin, is a subjective rupture with the State of Israel, not with its empirical existence, which is neither more nor less impure than that of all states, but with its exclusive identitarian claim to be a 'Jewish state', and with the way it draws incessant privileges from this claim, especially when it comes to trampling underfoot what serves us as international law. Truly contemporary states or countries are always cosmopolitan, perfectly indistinct in their identitarian configuration. They assume the total contingency of their historical constitution, and regard the latter as valid only on condition that it does not fall under any racialist, religious, or more generally 'cultural', predicate. Indeed, the last time an established state in France believed it should call itself the 'French state' was under Pétain and the German occupation. The Islamic states are certainly no more progressive as models than the various versions of the 'Arab nation' were. Everyone agrees, it seems, on the point that the Taliban do not embody the path of modernity for Afghanistan. A possible of modern democracy then, is that it count everyone, without factoring in predicates. As the Organisation Politique says in relation to France's reactionary laws against undocumented workers: 'Whoever is here *is* from here.' There is no acceptable reason to exempt the State of Israel from that rule. The claim is sometimes made that this state is the only 'democratic' state in the region. But the fact that this state presents itself as a 'Jewish state' is directly contradictory. We can say on this point that Israel is a country whose self-representation is still archaic.

Taking a different approach, I shall generalize the claim. I shall maintain that the intrusion of any identity predicate into a central role for the determination of a politics leads to disaster. This should be, as I've already said, the real lesson to be drawn from Nazism. Since it was above all the Nazis who, before anyone else, and with a rare zeal for following through, drew all the consequences from making the signifier 'Jewish' into a radical exception – it was, after all, the only way that they could give some sort of consistency, in their industrial massacre, to the symmetrical predication 'Aryan', the particular vacuity of which obsessed them.

A more immediately relevant consequence is that the signifier 'Palestinian' or 'Arab' should not be glorified any more than is permitted for the signifier 'Jew'. As a result, the legitimate solution to the Middle East conflict is not the dreadful institution of two barbed-wire states. The solution is the creation of a secular and democratic Palestine, one subtracted from all predicates, and which, in the school of Paul – who declared that, in view of the universal, there is no longer 'Jew nor Greek' and that 'circumcision is nothing, and uncircumcision is nothing' – would show that it is perfectly possible to create a place in these lands where, from a political point of view and regardless of the apolitical continuity of customs, there is 'neither Arab nor Jew'. This will undoubtedly demand a regional Mandela.

Lastly, there is no question of tolerating the anti-Jewish diatribes, uttered in the name of colonial guilt and the rights of Palestinians, that circulate in a number of organizations and institutions that are more or less dependent on identitarian words such as 'Arab', 'Muslim', 'Islam' . . . This anti-Semitism could not be passed off with give-and-take for a progressivism that settles for little. Besides, we already know the story. At the end of the nineteenth century in France, certain 'Marxist' worker organizations, notably of the school of Jules Guesde,[3] saw nothing wrong with the vulgar anti-Semitism that was very widespread at the time. They thought that anti-Semitic affairs, and notably the Dreyfus affair, did not concern the working class, and that to engage in them would distract from the principal contradiction between bourgeoisie and proletarians. But it soon became obvious what fuelled this concern to stick to the 'principal contradiction': in 1914, Jules Guesde, in the name of narrow-minded nationalism and a hatred of the 'Boches', entered into the sacred union that organized the military butchery. One dialectic for another, it will be recalled that a correct treatment of the principal contradiction most often consists in publicly assuming responsibility for managing a 'secondary' contradiction. Today, some among us are visibly tempted, in the name of the principal character of the contradiction between North and South, or between Arab peoples and American imperialism, to find all sorts of excuses for transforming (legitimate) opposition to the activities of the State of Israel into open and frank anti-Semitism, which is intolerable, and should not be tolerated. All the less so as the actions of progressive Israelis, who constantly show proof of a rare courage, have been crucial to advancing the situation in Palestine.

It's true enough that, to anyone wanting to eradicate such circumstantial anti-Semitism, it would be helpful if the State of Israel were no longer referred to as the 'Jewish state', and if everywhere it was agreed that a strict separation should be maintained between, on the one hand, religious, customary and private uses of an identity predicate – the words 'Arab' and 'Jew' as much as 'French' – and, on the other, its political usages, which are always harmful.

In the meantime, we can try, from our respective approaches, to agree upon a meaning for the word 'Jew' that would have universal import. The documents collected here are very different in date, form and origin. They should be read as constituting a trajectory unified by a single limit-point: a universalism that, as the becoming of a subject that, while not disregarding particularities, goes beyond particularisms; that within this going beyond accords none the least privilege; and that does not internalize any injunction to glorify communitarian, religious, or national labels.

As such, I've put the texts in an order that is quite simply chronological. In the appendix, there is a text that is not by me but by a friend, Cécile Winter. To my mind, the keen interest of this text is that it lies at a point which is not, and cannot be, one where I am situated. Cécile Winter engages in an intimate wrangle of a

1

Israel: the Country in the World where there are the Fewest Jews?

This text was published under this title in June 1982, the time of the Israeli assault on Beirut. It appeared in number 11 of Le Perroquet, *a journal founded by Natacha Michel[4] and myself in 1981 and which continued until 1988. Complete collections of it are still available. It is a collection that in my opinion contains invaluable documents about the combat led by those of us who saw right away the quagmire Mitterrand and the Socialist Party would get us into. The article was illustrated by a photo of the bombing of Beirut captioned: 'Can a warplane be Jewish?'*

I don't much like to speak about the 'Jewish question', as did Marx and Sartre, because the absolute atrocities the Nazis committed in the name of the 'final solution' have adversely rebounded on the very notion that there is a 'question' to which it would be appropriate to give a response. I might add that, on this issue, one ought to speak, absolutely, in one's own name, with one's own voice. As regards questions, I start from this: there are Jews. I do not ask why there are, nor where they come from, because such stories of origin and provenance are in themselves dubious. 'Jews' is the name of our real, a glorious name of our history – especially of our philosophical, scientific, artistic and our revolutionary history. And I say this: Hitler proposed to eliminate Jews in their physicality. His will was completely criminal, including what of such a crime must remain hidden, clandestine. The Nazi administration officiated over regulatory extermination under false pretences, wanting, purely and simply, to cut out an essential part of Europe, until such point as the only thing remaining would be to observe the *fait accompli*: the Jews have disappeared.

To do this, Hitler glorified, multiplied, the name 'Jews'. He everywhere ascribed things to the hand of the Jews. He made the incessantly named Jew into an emblem – the black emblem of his politics of universal conquest. Once the Nazis were defeated, the name 'Jew' became, like every name of the victim of a frightful sacrifice, a sacred name. And with good reason. Whether they had fought for and alongside the Jews for liberation from the Nazis, or whether they had to atone for the shame of tolerating the genocide, people developed an entirely new relationship with the Jews, not an inverted anti-Semitism, nor a simple tolerant friendship, but a conviction as to the very pronouncement of the word 'Jew', and as to what had been taken away with it of the essentials of history.

Hence, horrifically affected in its physicality, sometimes, like the Jewish communities of Poland, to the point of having its ancient reality exterminated, the Jewish identity has triumphed through a historical glorification of its name, and through a new strength of belonging and interiority. That this name has a major link to our thought and our history is something that has become clearer to all, since everyone can clearly see that it was no accident that the most barbarous imperialism, the most radical anti-thought, set out, in order to secure its reign, by corporeally exterminating Jews and by spreading their name around as a kind of evil signifier.

In my view, no greater threat weighs upon the name of Jews today than the politics of conquest, of physical liquidation of Palestinians, of massacring Arab schoolchildren, of dynamiting houses, and of torture, currently pursued by the State of Israel. Today, in accordance with what created its sacred renaissance after the Second World War, this name can have no meaning unless it is radically extricated from the State of Israel, and unless it is proclaimed that, in its current form, this state is incapable of tolerating, or meriting in any way, the label 'Jew'. Moreover, if more and more Jews let themselves take the direction of this state, we must conclude that Israel is a country where there are ever fewer Jews, a country in the process of de-Judaization, an anti-Semitic country – in the sense, that is, that we readily say that the Parti communiste français is an anti-communist party.

It is little wonder that the principal threat to the name of Jews comes from a state calling itself Jewish. The external enemy, like the anti-Semitic Nazis, can tie up and kill your physical being. That is the law of war and terror. But the loss of a name and of meaning always comes from the inside. For it has to do with giving up on [*céder sur*] one's own essence, and every de-essentialization [*désentification*] follows an immanent process. The sacralization of the name of Jews has taken on the external form, colonial in nature, of the State of Israel. Of course, in some conceptions the sacred remains incomplete when it has no crown, sceptre, or empire. But this means that the sacred is in need of slaves, and that the Arabs and Palestinians are those slaves. Not only is that way of thinking wrong; it is foreign to everything that has been brought forth in our history under the name of Jews; it is foreign to everything that, with their communities, which were so irreducibly strong in being minoritarian, has appeared in the richness of its singularity.

Yes, the name of Jews is threatened by the Jewish state, but dramatic crises of meaning do not come about in any other way. The idea of Marxism and Communism was also most gravely thrown into crisis by the 'Socialist' state in the USSR and Poland. Further, the debate here is not one about anti-Semitism or philo-Semitism; instead it is about engaging in the creation and the power of a new stage of Jewish identity, one where a radical critique will be brought to bear on all assertions of Jewish identity that only produce its opposite: militarism, invasion, massacre.

The most recent sequence of Israeli state politics takes this threat to its extreme. For what lurks here is the realization of this inversion of meaning, which would be the project of a genocide of the Palestinians. Already, the will to disperse them at all costs, to drive them further and further away, to wipe them out on every occasion, to shoot at their children, is declared and undertaken with systematicity. A Palestinian Diaspora – terrible recommence-ment! – is being formed in the world today. Ought the name of the Jews, in straying furthest from its historical meaning, become the place from where the creation, in the abandoned former place, of a new 'wandering' begins? Ought 'Palestinian' become the new name of the true Jews?

I know that many Jews, including those in Israel (they are judged and imprisoned), do not accept that one day they will have to desert their own historic name. That is what grounds my convic-tion that the basic link between the thought to which I am heir and Jews will not be severed – which would be disastrous for this very thought.

On such issues, geopolitics is of little use. The West's undue leniency, Mitterrand's included, for Israeli barbarism proves to my mind the little respect they have for Jews: for these politicians, Jews are only voters, or Middle Eastern oil police. Likewise, the paralysis of the Arab states shows the little respect they have for the Palestinians, who for them are already the Jews of the Arab world. The basic anti-Semitism of all states consists of hostility to wander-ing, to minorities, to the universal, to revolutions. As for the Russians, we know what the story is there: anti-Semites at home, arms' dealers abroad.

However, the major call to denounce the anti-Semitism of the State of Israel comes from a totally different position. A 'goy' [non-Jew] says it passionately: to him, saving the name of the Jews is essential, since it has to do with his own conceptual and active determination.

I've never thought that one must be an immigrant to speak about immigrants, a peasant to speak about peasants, a woman to speak about women, or a Jew to speak about Jews. My intention is not to defend a Jewish identity. Indeed, Begin is organizing a general catastrophe: we must attack it at the root. If Begin and his mercenaries are Jews, if Brezhnev is a communist, then there has been a total destruction of sense. The truth is simpler and stronger: just as Brezhnev is an empire brigand, Begin is a state gangster. Communists and Jews, often the same individuals, deny them absolutely all use of their names.

2

The Destruction of the European Jews and the Question of Evil

Here I've included fragments from my book Ethics: An Essay on the Understanding of Evil,[5] *first published by Hatier in 1993 at the initiative of Benoît Chantre, who spurred on its writing day in day out.*

Although the idea of radical Evil can be traced back at least as far as Kant, its contemporary version is grounded systematically on one 'example': the Nazi extermination of the European Jews. I do not use the word 'example' lightly. An ordinary example is indeed something to be repeated or imitated. Relating to the Nazi extermination, it exemplifies radical Evil by pointing to that whose imitation or repetition must be prevented at all costs – or, more precisely: that whose non-repetition provides the norm for the judgement of all situations. Hence the 'exemplarity' of the crime, its negative exemplarity. But the normative function of the example persists: the Nazi extermination is radical Evil in that it provides for our time the unique, unrivalled – and in this sense transcendent, or unsayable – measure of Evil pure and simple. What the God of Lévinas is to the evaluation of alterity (the Altogether Other as incommensurable measure of the Other), the extermination is to the evaluation of historical situations (the Altogether-Evil as incommensurable measure of Evil).

As a result, the extermination and the Nazis are both declared unthinkable, unsayable, without conceivable precedent or posterity – since they define the absolute form of Evil – yet they are constantly invoked, compared, used to schematize every circumstance in which one wants to produce, among opinions, an effect of the awareness [*conscience*] of Evil – since the only way to access Evil in general is under the historical condition of radical Evil. So it was as early as 1956, in order to justify the Anglo-French invasion of Egypt, some Western political leaders and the press did not hesitate for a second to use the formula 'Nasser is Hitler'. We have seen the same thing again more recently, as much with Saddam Hussein (in Iraq) as with Slobodan Milosevic (in Serbia). But at the same time, we are insistently reminded that the extermination and the Nazis were unique, and that to compare them to anything else at all is a defilement.

In fact, this paradox is simply that of radical Evil itself (and, in truth, of every 'mise en transcendence' of a reality or concept). The measure itself must be unmeasurable, yet it must be constantly measured. The extermination is indeed both that which measures all the Evil our time is capable of, being itself beyond measure, and that to which we must compare everything (thus measuring it unceasingly) that we say is to be judged in terms of the manifest certainty of Evil. As the supreme negative example, this crime is inimitable, but every crime is an imitation of it.

To get out of this circle, to which we are condemned by the fact that we want to subordinate the question of Evil to a consensual judgement of opinion (a judgement that then has to be pre-structured by the supposition of a radical Evil), we obviously have to abandon the theme of radical Evil, of the measure without measure. This theme, like that of the Altogether Other, belongs to religion.

It goes without saying, of course, that the extermination of the European Jews is a hideous state crime, whose horror is such that whichever way we look at it, we know – unless we are prepared to stoop to repulsive sophistry – that we are confronted by an Evil that cannot in any sense be quietly ('Hegelianly') classified among the transitory necessities of the historical process.

I further accept, without reservation, the singularity of the extermination. The bland category of 'totalitarianism' was forged in order to group under a single concept the politics of Nazism and of Stalinism, the extermination of the European Jews and the massacres in Siberia. This amalgamation does nothing to clarify our thinking, not even our thinking about Evil. We must accept the irreducibility of the extermination (just as we must accept the irreducibility of the Stalinist party-state).

But then the whole point is to situate [*localiser*] this singularity. Fundamentally, those who uphold the ideology of human rights try to situate it directly in Evil, in keeping with their objectives of pure opinion. We have seen that this attempt at the religious absolu-tization of Evil is incoherent. Moreover, it is very threatening, like anything that puts thought up against an impassable 'limit'. For the reality of the inimitable is constant imitation, and by dint of seeing Hitlers everywhere we forget that he is dead, and that what is happening before our eyes is the creation of new singularities of Evil.

In fact, to think the singularity of the extermination is to think, first of all, the singularity of Nazism as a political sequence. This is the whole problem. Hitler was able to conduct the extermination as a colossal militarized operation because he had taken power, and he took power in the name of a politics whose categories included the term 'Jew'.

The defenders of ethical ideology are so determined to locate the singularity of the extermination directly in Evil that they generally deny, categorically, that Nazism was a political sequence. But this position is both feeble and cowardly. Feeble, because the constitution of Nazism as a 'massive' subjectivity integrating the word Jew as part of a political configuration is what made the extermination possible, and then inevitable. Cowardly, because it is impossible to think politics through to the end if we refuse to envisage the possibility of political sequences whose organic cate-gories and subjective prescriptions are criminal. The partisans of the 'democracy of human rights' are fond – with Hannah Arendt – of defining politics as the stage of a 'being-together'. It is with regard to this definition, incidentally, that they fail to grasp the political essence of Nazism. But this definition is merely a fairy-tale – all the more so since the being-together must first determine the collective [*ensemble*] concerned, and this is the whole question. Nobody desired the being-together of the Germans more than Hitler. The Nazi category of the 'Jew' served to name the German interior, the space of a being-together, via the (arbitrary yet prescriptive) construction of an exterior that could be monitored from the interior – just as the certainty of being 'all French together' presupposes that we persecute, here and now, those who fall under the category of 'illegal immigrant'.

One of the singularities of Nazi politics was its precise proclamation of the historical community that was to be endowed with a conquering *subjectivity*. And it was this proclamation that enabled its subjective victory, and put extermination on the agenda.

Thus we are entitled to say, in this case, that the link between politics and Evil emerges precisely from the way both the collective [*ensemble*] (the thematics of communities) and the being-with (the thematics of consensus, of shared norms) are taken into consideration.

But what matters is that the singularity of the Evil derives, in the final analysis, from the singularity of a political sequence.

This takes us back to the subordination of Evil – if not directly to the Good, at least to the processes that lay claim to it. Nazi politics was not a truth-process, but it was only in so far as it could be represented as such that it 'seized' the German situation. So that even in the case of this Evil, which I would call extreme rather than radical, the intelligibility of its 'subjective' being, the question of the 'someones' who were able to participate in its horrifying execution as if accomplishing a duty, needs to be referred back to the intrinsic dimensions of the process of political truth.

I might also have pointed out that the most intense subjective sufferings – those that really highlight what is involved in 'hurting someone', and often lead to suicide or murder – have as their horizon the existence of a process of love.

I shall posit the following general principles:

- that Evil exists;
- that it must be distinguished from the violence that the human animal employs to persevere in its being, to pursue its interests – a violence that is *beneath* Good and Evil;
- that nevertheless there is no radical Evil, which might otherwise clarify this distinction;
- that Evil can be considered as distinct from banal predation only in so far as we grasp it from the perspective of the Good, thus from the seizing of 'someone' by a truth-process;
- that as a result, Evil is a category not of the human animal, but of the subject;
- that there is Evil only to the extent that man is capable of becoming the Immortal he is;
- that the ethic of truths – as the principle of consistency of a fidelity to a fidelity, or the maxim 'Keep going!' – is what tries to ward off the Evil that every singular truth makes possible. [. . .]

When the Nazis talked about the 'National Socialist revolution', they borrowed names – 'revolution', 'socialism' – justified by great modern political events (the Revolution of 1792, or the Bolshevik Revolution of 1917). A whole series of characteristics is related to and legitimated by this borrowing: the break with the old order, the support sought from mass gatherings, the dictatorial style of the state, the *pathos* of the decision, the eulogy of the worker, and so forth.

However, the 'event' thus named – although in certain formal respects it is similar to those from which it borrows its name and characteristics, and without which it would have no constituted political language in which to formulate proposals of its own – is distinguished by a vocabulary of plenitude, or of substance: the National Socialist revolution – say the Nazis – will carry a particular community, the German people, towards its true destiny, which is a destiny of universal domination. So that the 'event' is supposed to bring into being, and name, not the void of the earlier situation, but its plenitude – not the universality of that which is sustained, precisely, by no particular characteristic (no particular multiple), but the absolute particularity of a community, itself rooted in the characteristics of its soil, its blood, and its race.

What allows a genuine event to be at the origin of a truth – which is the only thing that can be for all, and can be eternally – is precisely the fact that it relates to the particularity of a situation from the bias of its void. The void, the multiple-of-nothing, neither excludes nor constrains anyone. It is the absolute neutrality of being – such that the fidelity that originates in an event, although it is an immanent break within a singular situation, is nonetheless universally addressed.

By contrast, the striking break provoked by the Nazi seizure of power in 1933, although formally indistinguishable from an event – it is precisely this that led Heidegger astray[6] – since it conceives itself as a 'German' revolution, and is faithful only to the alleged national substance of a people, is actually addressed only to those that it itself deems 'German'. It is thus – right from the moment the event is named, and despite the fact that this nomination ('revolution') functions only under the condition of true universal events (for example the Revolutions of 1792 or 1917) – radically incapable of any truth whatsoever.

When a radical break in a situation, under names borrowed from real truth-processes, convokes not the void but the 'full' particularity or presumed substance of that situation, we are dealing with a *simulacrum of truth*.

'Simulacrum' must be understood here in its strong sense: all the formal traits of a truth are at work in the simulacrum. Not only a universal nomination of the event, inducing the power of a radical break, but also the 'obligation' of a fidelity, and the promotion of a *simulacrum of the subject*, erected – without the advent of any Immortal – above the human animality of the others, of those who are arbitrarily declared not to belong to the communitarian substance whose promotion and domination the simulacrum-event is designed to assure.

Fidelity to a simulacrum, unlike fidelity to an event, regulates its break with the situation not by the universality of the void, but by the closed particularity of an abstract set [*ensemble*] (the 'Germans' or the 'Aryans'). Its invariable operation is the unending construction of this set, and it has no other means of doing this than that of 'voiding' what surrounds it. The void, 'avoided' [*chassé*] by the simulacrous promotion of an 'event-substance', here returns, with its universality, as what must be accomplished in order that this substance can be. This is to say that what is addressed 'to everyone' (and 'everyone', here, is necessarily that which does not belong to the German communitarian substance – for this substance is not an 'everyone' but, rather, some 'few' who dominate 'everyone') is death, or that deferred form of death which is slavery in the service of the German substance.

Hence fidelity to this simulacrum (and it demands of the 'few' belonging to the German substance prolonged sacrifices and commitments, since it really does have the form of a fidelity) has as its content war and massacre. These are not here means to an end: they make up the very real [*tout le réel*][7] of such a fidelity.

In the case of Nazism, the void made its return under one privileged name in particular, the name 'Jew'. There were certainly others as well: the Gypsies, the mentally ill, homosexuals, communists . . . But the name 'Jew' was the names of names, serving to designate those people whose disappearance created, around that presumed German substance promoted by the 'National Socialist revolution' simulacrum, a void that would suffice to identify the substance. The choice of this name relates, without any doubt, to its obvious link with universalism, in particular with revolutionary universalism – to what was in effect already *void* [*vide*] about this name – that is, what was *connected to the universality and eternity of truths*. Nevertheless, inasmuch as it served to organize the extermination, the name 'Jew' was a political creation of the Nazis, without any pre-existing referent. It is a name whose meaning no one can share with the Nazis, a meaning that presumes the simulacrum and fidelity to the simulacrum – and hence the absolute singularity of Nazism as a political sequence.

But even in this respect, we have to recognize that this process mimics an actual truth-process. Every fidelity to an authentic event names adversaries of its perseverance. Contrary to consensual ethics, which tries to avoid divisions, the ethic of truths is always more or less militant, combative. For the concrete manifestation of its heterogeneity to opinions and established knowledges is the struggle against all sorts of efforts at interruption, at corruption, at the return to the immediate interests of the human animal, at the humiliation and repression of the Immortal who arises as subject. The ethic of truths presumes recognitions of these efforts, and thus the singular operation of naming enemies. The 'National Socialist revolution' simulacrum encouraged nominations of this kind, in particular the nomination of 'Jew'. But the simulacrum's subversion of the true event continues with these namings. For the enemy of a true subjective fidelity is precisely the closed set [*ensemble*], the substance of the situation, the community. The values of truth, of its hazardous course and its universal address, are to be erected against these forms of inertia.

Every invocation of blood and soil, of race, of custom, of community, works directly against truths; and it is this very collection [*ensemble*] that is named as the enemy in the ethic of truths. Whereas fidelity to the simulacrum, which promotes the community, blood, race, and so on, names as its enemy – for example, under the name 'Jew' – precisely the abstract universality and eternity of truths, the address to all.

Moreover, the two processes treat what is thus named in diametrically opposite ways. For however hostile to a truth he might be, in the ethic of truths every 'someone' is always represented as capable of becoming the Immortal that he is. So we may fight against the judgements and opinions he exchanges with others for the purpose of corrupting every fidelity, but not against his *person* – which, under the circumstances is insignificant, and to which, in any case, every truth is ultimately addressed. By contrast, the void with which those who are faithful to a simulacrum strive to surround its alleged substance must be a real void, obtained by cutting into the flesh itself. And since it is not the subjective advent of an Immortal, so fidelity to the simulacrum – that appalling imitation of truths – presumes nothing more about those they designate as the enemy than their strictly particular existence as human animals. It is thus this existence that will have to bear the return of the void. This is why the exercise of fidelity to the simulacrum is necessarily the exercise of terror. Understand by terror, here, not the political concept of Terror, linked (in a universalizable couple) to the concept of Virtue by the Immortals of the Jacobin Committee of Public Safety, but the pure and simple reduction of all to their being-for-death. Terror thus conceived really postulates that in order to let [the] substance be, *nothing* must be [*pour que la substance soit, rien ne doit être*].

I have pursued the example of Nazism because it enters to a significant extent into that 'ethical' configuration (of 'radical Evil') opposed by the ethic of truths. What is at issue here is the simulacrum of an event that gives rise to a political fidelity. Such a simulacrum is possible only thanks to the success of political revolutions that were genuinely eventural (and thus universally addressed). But simulacra linked to all the other possible kinds of truth-processes also exist. The reader may find it useful to identify them. For example, we can see how certain sexual passions are simulacra of the amorous event. There can be no doubt that on this account they bring with them terror and violence. Likewise, brutal obscurantist preachings present themselves as the simulacra of science, with obviously damaging results. And so on. But in each case, these violent damages are unintelligible if we do not understand them in relation to the truth-processes whose simulacra they manipulate.

In sum, our first definition of Evil is this: Evil is the process of a simulacrum of truth. And in its essence, under a name of its invention, it is terror directed at everyone.

3

A Dialogue between a Jew from Darzia and an Arab from Epirus

This is excerpted from my novel Calme bloc ici-bas, *published by Éditions P.O.L. in 1997. Here is a brief account of the scenario. Simon Symoens is a construction worker on the run after having escaped from prison. He wanders about in a country called Prémontré accompanied by a young child, David, who was placed in Simon's care by David's mother, Élizabeth Cathely, a terrorist killed by disease, and for whom Simon felt an obscure and violent love. Simon takes on the identity of a provincial radio station manager, Ahmed Aazami, who had spectacularly disappeared from public at the end of a rock concert. Slowly, he begins to identify with this character. Tracked down in the south of Prémontré by a police officer called Lancini, the false–true Ahmed Aazami seeks refuge for David and himself in the house of a man called René Fulmer, a Jewish mathematician from a great country of the East, Darzia. While the child sleeps, the two men have a long conversation. I've picked out the fragment of this conversation that pertains to Jewish identity.*

It was two in the morning; time no longer had any meaning. Aazami and Fulmer – one settled in an armchair like a Roman emperor after a day's battle (since when had Aazami listened to anyone not seated in an armchair? Since Audruick, since the interview with Aazami and Kwado Asara?), the other on his work stool, frenzied, his beard flat like a moving wall on which his head, if not his aucupating eyes, had been placed and partly hidden – wander, both of them, in their speech, such that the leaden weariness of the one and the excitation of the other converged on an analogy of intoxication [*ivresse*].

Certainly, Fulmer exercised discretion, which he was conscious was friendly, but he yearned to hear those stories – in his view consonant with the life story of his father, who himself had gone to an abstract death under the injunction of equality – so he had in any case succeeded in extorting from out of his interlocutor's mistrust, or at least from out of his suffering interiority, some snippets of information about his origins, Élizabeth, David's birth, Lancini, the tracking, the wandering. Not a lot, though. Aazami had disclosed neither his former name (which anyhow he was slowly forgetting himself), nor his country of origin (to which nothing held him any longer), nor the murder of that dragon, Frédéric Rassinoux (which he had put down, not without some malaise, to sheer necessity). Above all, he had, like whoever wishes to keep to himself the rule that orders the disparate fragments of the self, strictly avoided all mention of the other Aazami.

FULMER: How do you make it up to our young friend in the beret? On the run in the countryside from the police at the age of five! The first time that happened to me, with Isaac, I was fourteen. By the way, you put a beret on him. You don't see them often in Prémontré nowadays, do you?

AAZAMI (*off guard for the first time*): Boys in my country wear them.

FULMER: Your country?

AAZAMI (blushing): In Epirus.

FULMER: Epirus! I'm Jewish, you know. A Darzian Jew. That's why I love Epirus. You'll discover that I don't know anything about it. But I love it. I picture myself walking in the desert, and I meet a wise man from Epirus. And so, we talk about being, mathematics, about the desert as the ground of all that is.

AAZAMI (*somnolently relating common opinion*): The people in Epirus are against Jews.

FULMER: Precisely! They're against them because nothing distinguishes them from each other.

AAZAMI: What is a Jew?

FULMER: Imagine that there is a law which says that you are you, and that, in God's eyes, you alone are who you are. 'You' is something that comes from the mother. She was your 'you' before you, the 'you' that is recounted in books. My mother Sarah died this year. My own 'you' before me is dead; I am Jewish in the orphanage of the provenance of the word.

AAZAMI: I never knew my mother. Where I was born, you leave the country with your father at a very young age. You go back when there's money. But there's never enough there to go back.

FULMER: I'm sorry!

AAZAMI (*nearly sniggering*): I've seen a lot worse human misfortune! You can speak openly. It's important to be conscious of things. Élizabeth would say to me: 'I'll tell you about Robert, the worker. It does no good to anyone to be ignorant.' But perhaps knowing is bad too. She knew, and she died like a dog.

FULMER (*trembling a little*): 'Jew' is also often caught up in the worst misfortunes of humanity. But not alone. What happens is that someone gets up who says: if I alone am who I am, that's because this 'myself' is nothing but all the others. Which is the only solution. Otherwise, you remain imprisoned in substance under the fated eyes of God. Let's call 'Jew' the one who says in the name of all others that there is no law separating them. He is the one who grasps his own being to break the divisive law, and thereby exposes humanity to the universal.

AAZAMI (*who has been listening very attentively*): That doesn't work. For if you constitute the Jew in law, then when he says 'there's no law', he has the Jew commit suicide.

FULMER: Ah! You've put your finger on the paradox. There's no being in this affair; there is the paradox of the universal under an inherited name. The universal can take on the name 'Jew', which is absolutely particular. But note that the name of the universal is inevitably particular. If we mention some Jews, who should we name? Whether you speak of Spinoza, of Marx, of Freud, you see clearly: they are people who enjoin the thought of all to the strictest universality, and, in memorable founding acts, enacted a rupture with any and every end of the law that was somehow exclusionary or identifying. They say 'no one is elected, otherwise everyone is'. And they can say it precisely because they were the supposed bearers of the most radical election in the eyes of God. They can announce the dissolution of all identity because above all they paid the price for their own identity, which is the strongest, since it has come from antiquity, God, and exile. That's why they've attracted the hatred of those whose identity is so precarious that they must seek it in substance, land, and blood. It is not the identity of Jew that produces that hatred; it is the power that it accords to thought to dissolve identity. The Jew is not hated because he is the Other. The Jew is hated because he is the Same.

AAZAMI: And who's the guy who started that story?

FULMER: It has been around forever. But we should attribute it to Saul, Saint Paul. He is the greatest Ancient Jew.

AAZAMI (*knitting his brow as if searching for a distant memory*): I think my father said that Saint Paul was a Christian king. He cannot have been Jewish.

FULMER: Saint Paul founded Christianity, your father was right. But that's not the most important thing. I'm not Christian in the religious sense, not by any means, nor Jewish, nor, excuse me, Muslim. In fact, I am opposed to religions, absolutely opposed. I tell you this in all sincerity. Saint Paul was Jewish, and he said, before Spinoza, before Marx, and before Freud: 'The Law, because it separates, must be abolished. If there is religion, it is for everyone. There are neither Jews, nor Greeks, nor Romans; there is the potential thought for all.' He was a great Jew, then. The Jew is not the universal, which precisely cannot be. He is the one who, singularly, proclaims the universal.

AAZAMI: I knew a Jew who was a butcher. He didn't proclaim much.

FULMER: Of course. Most of the time vast amounts of Jews only assert their identity, like you and me. I call them virtual Jews. They pass on virtuality. Because it must necessarily be there, that powerful and detestable identity, to enable a Jew who is more than the Jews to come, such as Saint Paul for example. This Jew is the one that I call an actual Jew because his act of declaration is an act that a Jew is capable of doing. The virtual Jews ought above all not to be despised or renounced. They are like everyone else, no more, no less. They're people, that's all. There are Jewish-people like there are people-from-Epirus. Sarah, my mother, was rather virtual. She prepared the stew of inheritance. She thought that when my father Isaac was seized by the actual Jew that she'd have to prepare for the worst, and she wasn't wrong. My father was assassinated in the revolution of popular Delegates. It is the complicated coexistence of the virtuals and the actuals that historically weaves the paradox.

AAZAMI (*blindly*): And your own way of proclaiming consists in these sheets of calculations here.

FULMER (*delighted, moved*): I think so. I hope so. Lots of mathematicians are Jewish, lots aren't. Being a mathematician means proclaiming the universal straight up, without even taking a detour through the negative. Saint Paul and Marx, Spinoza and Freud, like all revolutionaries, like my father, have to engage in savage polemics; they have to wring the neck of the Law. In mathematics, you make straight for transparent being, the being of thought such as it is transparent to being that is. You don't negate anything. You actualize the Jew in a single blow, and, admittedly, with fewer personal risks.

AAZAMI: What do all your calculations say, then? My Jewish butcher didn't proclaim a lot, but he liked to count. Only everyone said that he liked counting his pennies.

FULMER: Between you and me is he the only one?

AAZAMI: It's true that Jewish or not, there's nothing to do with pennies in the evening other than count them. (*With brusqueness*) Were it not for David, I wouldn't count them.

FULMER (*smiling*): That's your way of actualizing the Jew that you will have had to be.

4

Saint Paul and the Jews

Here I've excerpted the start of chapter 10 of my book Saint Paul: The Foundation of Universalism.[8] *After a few necessary generalities about Paul's conception of 'ethnic' and cultural differences, I go on, counter to the common accusation that Paul established a Christian anti-Semitism, to give a detailed presentation of what 'Jew' signifies for the 'apostle of nations'.*

That hope is the pure patience of the subject, the inclusion of self in the universality of the address, in no way implies that differences should be ignored or dismissed. For although it is true, so far as what the event constitutes is concerned, that there is 'neither Greek nor Jew', the fact is that there are Greeks and Jews. That every truth procedure collapses differences, infinitely deploying a purely generic multiplicity, does not permit us to lose sight of *the fact* that, in the situation (call it: the world), *there are differences*. One can even maintain that there is nothing else.

The ontology underlying Paul's preaching valorizes non-beings against beings, or rather, it establishes that, for the subject of a truth, what exists is generally held by established discourses to be nonexistent, while the beings validated by these discourses are, for the subject, nonexistent. Nevertheless, these fictitious beings, these opinions, customs, differences, are that to which universality is addressed; that toward which love is directed; finally, that which must be traversed in order for universality itself to be constructed, or for the genericity [*généricité*] of the true to be *immanently* deployed. Any other attitude would return truth, not to the work of love (which is unity of thought and power), but to the enclosure of that mystical fourth discourse of illumination, which Paul, who intends to ensure the transmission of the Good News throughout the entire extent of the empire, does not want to see monopolizing and sterilizing the event.

This is the reason why Paul, apostle of the nations, not only refuses to stigmatize differences and customs, but also undertakes to accommodate them so that the process of their subjective disqualification might pass through them, within them. It is in fact that search for new differences, new particularities to which the universal might be *exposed*, that leads Paul beyond the evental site properly speaking (the Jewish site) and encourages him to displace the experience historically, geographically, ontologically. Whence a highly characteristic militant tonality, combining the appropriation of particularities with the immutability of principles, the empirical existence of differences with their essential nonexistence, according to a succession of problems requiring resolution, rather than through an amorphous synthesis. The text is charged with a remarkable intensity:

> For though I am free from all men, I have made myself a slave to all, that I might win the more. To the Jews I became as a Jew, in order to win the Jews; to those under the law, I became as one under the law – though not being myself under the law – that I might win those under the law. To those outside the law I became as one outside the law – not being without law toward God but under the law of Christ – that I might win those outside the law. To the weak I became weak, that I might win the weak. I have become all things to all men. (Cor. I.9.19–22)

This is not an opportunist text, but an instance of what Chinese Communists will call 'the mass line', pushed to its ultimate expression in 'serving the people'. It consists in supposing that, whatever people's opinions and customs, once gripped by a truth's postevental work, their thought becomes capable of traversing and transcending those opinions and customs without having to give up the differences that allow them to recognize themselves in the world.

But in order for people to become gripped by a truth, it is imperative that universality not be presented under the aspect of a particularity. Difference can be transcended only if benevolence with regard to customs and opinions presents itself *as an indifference that tolerates differences*, one whose sole material test lies, as Paul says, in being able and knowing how to practise them oneself. Whence Paul's extreme wariness with regard to every rule, every rite, that would assume the form of universalist militantism by making of it a bearer of differences and particularities in turn.

Of course, the faithful belonging to small Christian cells incessantly ask Paul what they should think about women's dress, sexual relations, permissible or prohibited foods, the calendar, astrology, and so forth. For it is in the nature of the human animal, as defined by networks of differences, to love asking questions of this type and even to think that they alone are really important. Confronted with this barrage of problems far removed from what, for him, identifies the Christian subject, Paul displays an inflexible impatience: 'If anyone is disposed to be contentious, we do not recognize that practice' (Cor. I.II.16). It is in fact of utmost importance for the destiny of universalist labour that the latter be withdrawn from conflicts of opinion and confrontations between customary differences. The fundamental maxim is *mēeis diakriseis dialogismōn*, 'do not argue about opinions' (Rom. 14.1).

This injunction is all the more striking in that *diakrisis* means primarily 'discernment of differences'. Thus, it is to the imperative not to compromise the truth procedure by entangling it in the web of opinions and differences that Paul is committed. It is certainly possible for a philosophy to argue about opinions; for Socrates, this is even what defines it. But the Christian subject is not a philosopher, and faith is neither an opinion, nor a critique of opinion.

Christian militantism must traverse worldly differences indifferently and avoid all casuistry over customs.

Evidently impatient to return to the topic of resurrection, but also concerned lest he alienate his comrades, Paul takes great pains to explain that what one eats, the behaviour of a servant, astrological hypotheses, and finally the fact of being Jewish, Greek or anything else – all this can and must be envisaged as simultaneously intrinsic to the trajectory of a truth and compatible with it:

> One believes he may eat anything, while the weak man eats only vegetables. Let not him who eats despise him who abstains, and let not him who abstains pass judgement on him who eats . . . One man esteems one day as better than another, while one man esteems all days alike. Let every one be fully convinced in his own mind. (Rom. 14.2–5)

Paul goes very far in this direction, so it's very odd to see him accused of sectarian moralism. The opposite is the case, for we constantly observe him resisting demands in favour of prohibitions, rites, customs, observances. He does not hesitate to say 'in truth, all things are clean [*panta kathara*]'. And, above all, he argues against moral judgement, which in his eyes is an evasion before the event's 'for all': 'You, why do you pass judgement on your brother? Or you, why do you despise your brother? . . . Then let us no more pass judgement on one another.' (Rom. 14.10–13).

In the end, the astonishing principle proposed by this 'moralist' can be formulated as: everything is permitted (*panta exestin*, Cor. 1.10.23). Yes, within the order of particularity, everything is permitted. For if differences are the material of the world, it is only so that the singularity proper to the subject of truth – a singularity that is itself included in the becoming of the universal – can puncture that material. No need to presume to judge or reduce that material so far as this puncturing is concerned: indeed, quite the opposite.

That customary or particular differences are what we must *let be* from the moment we bring to bear on them the universal address and the militant consequences of faith (which is to say *only* inconsistency with respect to faith, or 'whatever does not proceed from faith' [Rom.14.23], counts as sin) can be better evaluated by considering two examples, with regard to which the accusation of sectarian moralism, or worse, has often been made against Paul: women and Jews.

It has often been claimed that Pauline teaching inaugurated the era of the Christian origins of anti-Semitism. But unless one considers that breaking with religious orthodoxy by maintaining a singular heresy from within is a form of racism – which, all things considered, is an insufferable retrospective excess – it has to be said that there is nothing remotely resembling any form of anti-Semitic statement in Paul's writings.

The accusation of 'deicide', which, it is true, burdens the Jews with a crushing mythological guilt, is entirely absent from Paul's discourse, for reasons at once anecdotal and essential. Anecdotal because, in any case – we have already explained why – the historical and statist process of Jesus' putting to death, and thus the allocation of responsibilities in the matter, are of absolutely no interest to Paul, for whom only the Resurrection matters. Essential because, amply predating as it does Trinitarian theology, Paul's thought does not base itself in any way on the theme of a substantial identity of Christ and God, and there is nothing in Paul corresponding to the sacrificial motif of the crucified God.

It is rather in the Gospels, and above all in the last one, John's, that Jewish particularity is set apart, and the separation between Christians and Jews is insisted upon. After the Jews' long war against the Roman occupation, this probably helped elicit the goodwill of the imperial authorities, but it already serves to draw the Christian proposition away from its universal destination, paving the way for the differentiating regime of exceptions and exclusions.

We find nothing of the sort in Paul. His relation to Jewish particularity is essentially positive. Conscious of the extent to which the evental site remains, genealogically and ontologically, within the heritage of biblical monotheism, he even goes so far, when designating the universality of the address, as to accord Jews a kind of priority. For instance, 'Glory and honour and peace for every one who does good, the Jew first and also the Greek' (Rom. 2.10).

'For the Jew first [*Ioudaiōu prōton*]': this is precisely what marks the Jewish difference's pride of place in the movement traversing *all* differences so that the universal can be constructed. This is why Paul not only considers the necessity of making oneself 'a Jew among Jews' obvious, but also vigorously invokes his Jewishness so as to establish that the Jews are included in the universality of the Announcement: 'I ask then, has God rejected his people? By no means! I myself am an Israelite, a descendant of Abraham, a member of the tribe of Benjamin. God has not rejected his people, whom he foreknew' (Rom. 11.1).

Of course, Paul fights against all those who would submit postevental universality to Jewish particularity. He fervently hopes to be 'delivered from the unbelievers in Judea' (Rom. 15.31). It is the least that could be expected from him who identifies his faith only in being affected by the collapse of customary and communitarian differences. But in no way is it a question of judging the Jews as such, all the less so because, ultimately, Paul's conviction, unlike John's, is that 'all Israel will be saved' (Rom. 11.26).

The truth is that Paul mobilizes the new discourse in a constant, subtle strategy of displacement relative to Jewish discourse. We have already remarked that references to the Old Testament are as abundant in Paul's texts as those to the sayings of Christ are absent. The task Paul sets for himself is obviously not that of abolishing Jewish particularity, which he constantly acknowledges as the event's principle of historicity, but that of animating it internally by everything of which it is capable relative to the new discourse, and hence the new subject. For Paul, being Jewish in general, and the Book in particular, *can and must be resubjectivated.*

This operation finds a basis in the opposition between the figure of Moses and that of Abraham. Paul does not much like Moses, man of the letter and the law. By contrast, he readily identifies with Abraham for two very powerful reasons, both contained in a passage from the epistle to the Galatians (3:6): 'Thus Abraham "believed God and it was reckoned to him as righteousness." So you see that it is men of faith who are the sons of Abraham. And the scripture, foreseeing that God would justify the Gentiles by faith, preached the Gospel beforehand to Abraham, saying, "In you shall all the nations be blessed." So then, those who are men of faith are blessed with Abraham, who had faith.'

One sees here that Abraham is decisive for Paul. First, because he was elected by God solely by virtue of his faith, before the law (which was engraved for Moses, Paul notes, 'four hundred and thirty years later'); second, because the promise that accompanies his election pertains to 'all the nations', rather than to Jewish descendants alone. Abraham thereby anticipates what could be called a universalism of the Jewish site; in other words, he anticipates Paul. A Jew among Jews, and proud of it, Paul only wishes to remind us that it is absurd to believe oneself a proprietor of God, and that an event wherein what is at issue is life's triumph over death, regardless of the communitarian forms assumed by one or the other, activates the 'for all' through which the One of genuine monotheism sustains itself. This is a reminder in which, once again, the Book plays a part in subjectivation: 'He has called us not from the Jews only but also from the Gentiles. As indeed he says in Hosea, "Those who were not my people I will call my people, and her who was not beloved I will call my beloved" ' (Rom. 9.24).

5

Against Negationism

On 14 October 1996, Natacha Michel organized a day against negationism at the Collège International de Philosophie. A collection of the numerous inter-ventions was published by Éditions Al Dante under the title Paroles à la bouche du présent *in 1997. I've reconstructed mine here. It should be noted that at the end of the day some negationists intervened, as usual, in their own unctuous and violent way. They were put back in their place by the speakers and the public with the most extreme severity.*

This day, this intermediary, this time populated with writings, has constructed a site. A fleeting site, a disassembled gathering. But it is nonetheless a site: that is, if we understand by 'site' the provisional territory of some protocols of thought.

This site has tied together a declaration and three questions. The declaration, as that which is prior to all question, as unquestionable and, as it were, atemporal, is this: there were gas chambers and cremation ovens. There was an extermination of the European Jews. And it contained three politically decided, state-organized stages using methods integral to industrial war that Hilberg has documented once and for all. There was a stage for identifying Jews governmentally and juridically, that is, for making special status laws, for markings and bans; another stage for sweeps and round-ups, and for separating and isolating in ghettos comprising barbed wire and famine; and, lastly, a stage for transportation and mass murder in atrocious conditions. This is not a question of arguments or history: there were gas chambers, there was an extermination – this took place. Our declaration is only to maintain, face to face, that having-taken-place in its inviolability, that is, as subtracted from the obliquity of questions.

The questions were of another order. They are questions of relevance today, questions for us, questions to us.

The first question has been to ask who is it that today declares there were no gas chambers, no extermination of the European Jews? On this point we've seen that, since the extermination took place independently of all questions and verifications, these people in effect attempt to propagate a lie that is at once enormous and devious. Who are the promulgators of this provocative and devious remark? What is the truth of their message? We have seen that this truth is Hitlerian. For them, simply, Hitler did what he could, and to this day no one has done better. But the business remains unfinished. Total war against the Jews must be pursued. To deny the gas chambers is to say: they are still required, and always will be. Their negation of what took place, of what is for evermore, is in reality an 'ought'. One ought to be absolutely anti-Semitic.

The second question has been to understand why and how these second and third generation Hitlerites exist. We have looked into the complete historical and political background of this question. And we have seen that the obvious fact of the gas chambers and the extermination was not *declared*, politically, that it was displaced, or concealed, by arrangements that emerged at the war's end. And we've seen that, for this declaration to exist, it is imperative to construct another site from which to declare it, as we have done here today at this level. Second- and third-generation disciples of Hitler, total anti-Semites, have also, with tenacity and ruse, constructed the site of their counter-declaration in the propitious shadow of an insufficient or concealed declaration. And if they managed to become Nazi academics, it is because for a long while after the war the powers in place had no interest in identifying Nazism as a politics. To such an extent, indeed, that this politics, whose major plank is the extermination of the Jews, persisted under the academic mask of history.

The third question was: why, today, does negationism find an audience, accomplices and a suspect media orchestration? Why is the dominant attitude to it so defensive? Why is it accepted that it all has to do with history and memory, with argument and documents, when it has to do with declaring what took place, and constructing a visible and intelligible site for that declaration? We've talked about the things that oppose the construction of such an intelligible and visible site, not just all the old persistent oppositions, but also some new ones that have come along. In doing so, we've had to describe people for whom Israel and Zionism are considered to be so emblematic of Empire, of America, and of Evil that their position is indistinguishable from absolute anti-Semitism, that they must pursue, must take up again, an all-out war against the Jews; and, thus, that they proclaim that Hitler did not finish it off, did not win, that the extermination didn't take place, that there were no camps or gas chambers, so they are needed now. Further, we have had to speak about what it is that put our time in contact with the restricted *forms* of Nazi politics and its submissive national variant, Pétainism. That is to say, the re-emergence of a taste and a demand for special status laws, for raids, for marking and persecution; the presence, for a good while now, in governmental politics of this taste and this demand; the creation of names that brand and mark out for denunciation, arrest and imprisonment, like the name 'immigrant', or the name 'clandestine'. Finally, we've had to speak about what has rendered possible, with Le Pen, its extreme and independent form, that is, intellectual Hitlerism.

I would like in turn to talk, and in my own name, about the points that have been raised concerning the responsibilities of philosophy, responsibilities I share. That the extermination of the European Jews is a singularity – a properly unique and incomparable atrocity

– is indubitable; and many philosophers have fully recognized it as such. But the discussion was about, and is still about, the issue of knowing the nature of the relation to be articulated between thought and this singular atrocity, this crime. It seems to me that today we can distinguish three types of arguments that, in their attempt to confront the Nazi singularity, prove incapable of uprooting revisionism, that is, incapable of constructing the site of a declaration concerning what took place in its inviolability. We might perhaps refer to them as follows: the argument of the unthinkable; the argument of the interruption; and the argument of absolute Evil.

1. The argument of the unthinkable

This argument consists in maintaining that the gas chambers and the extermination can be preserved in their singularity and in memory only if they are upheld as unthinkable and unsayable, that is, only if they are taken as a limit-point beyond which the resources of thought dissipate. The idea here is that every attempt to think the extermination assumes that it can in fact be explained, clarified, related to something else, compared, and its genesis given, its causes revealed. It is argued that with such operations the extermination becomes desingularized, reduced to the common lot of the facts of history (and so indirectly legitimated), or else they create a space for its legitimation.

The mistake here concerns the identification of thinking. For not all thinking involves explanation, the revealing of causes, objective development. Thinking the Nazi singularity does not necessarily imply an objective type of thinking. Instead, it involves thinking the very possibility of what took place, thinking the possibility of a criminal politics; such thinking does not, then, grant what took place any causal necessity, and creates no space of legitimation. Rather, it maintains, in thought, a confrontation with what has taken place; in this respect, it might be said that, far from being unthinkable or unsayable, to think and to say the extermination is a duty.

2. The argument of the interruption

This argument comes down to saying that after the gas chambers, the extermination, Auschwitz, etc., it is no longer possible to maintain a line of thought that is in continuity with the Enlightenment, or with classical rationalism, because these atrocious singularities are partly the visible effects of the domination of scientific and technological rationalism, and partly the monstrous effectuation of its collapse.

The mistake this time undoubtedly concerns the apprehension of the singular. Since, if the Nazi singularity is the effect and measure of some historical apparatus – of technological rationalism, of mythical romanticism, of Western metaphysics or of the Enlightenment – it's because this singularity is not a singularity. In a sense, this is exactly the revisionist thesis, which itself is resolved to return all singularity – and in this case, the subjectivated history of total anti-Semitism – to history. We ought not to concede to Nazism what it aspired to be: a caesura and a millenary foundation; we ought not to concede this even by inverting the claim. Thinking Nazism and the extermination presupposes that we think its singularity as such, which in turn presupposes that we have the resources necessary for thinking singularity as that which is untied to every philosophy of history.

3. The argument of absolute evil

This argument assumes that coming to grips with the extermination presumes an intrinsic moral order, wherein the extermination is the prime example of a limit, or an absolutely pure point, of Evil. The treating of humans as simple matter and not as ends in themselves; separating them and burning them *en masse*; pursuing a denial of life to the point of naturalizing annihilation pure and simple: all that would constitute something like a historical paradigm in which every ethical figure had been destroyed, and the price to be paid when such figures pass into history. Such would constitute a historical Idea of Evil that is symmetrical to the transcendent Idea of Good. However, it can also be said that if Evil is the appropriate category for thinking Nazism and the extermination, then it is an abstract and circulating category that dissolves its singularity. For what happened was that Nazism slowly became a term of feeble opinion to be applied when and as needed: to Nasser or Milosevic, or Saddam Hussein, that is, to anyone held to be intolerable or inhuman. In ethical mediations on Evil, the incomparable and the singular become that which is constantly compared, referred to, and illustrated.

It seems to me, then, that neither the unthinkable, nor historical destiny and its interruption, nor ethics in its common meaning, can block revisionism and repetition. The encounter between thought and the extermination of the European Jews remains an imperative; and this imperative has neither to do with some memory without concept, nor meditation on the end of time, nor can it be articulated as the morality of collective life. Hard as this task is, the issue before us is to identify Nazism as a politics once and for all, and to maintain that criminal types of politics exist, types of politics that must be included in what thought thinks politics is, or can be.

But the issue here today is this inviolable point of departure, this declaration that seeks to have no common ground or discussion with negationists, not even to refute them. This took place. There were gas chambers; there was an extermination of the European Jews. We cannot allow the world to slide into a state where it becomes increasingly possible at any time to split hairs over this point.

For a world that debates, argues over, or puts into doubt, the gas chambers and the extermination is a world in which criminal types of politics prosper in the very denial of their having taken place.

To proclaim oneself against revisionism is also to proclaim oneself against all seemingly innocent or blind consent to sweeps, special status laws, round-ups, internments and persecutions. Not that there is the least common measure here. Simply this: these proclamations go hand in hand. They construct the same site of thought, like the precarious and disassembled one we've constructed here today.

Local Angel

In August 2003 at the European Graduate School held in Saas-Fee – in an unforgiving and splendid site in a glacial cirque of the Swiss Alps – and run by Wolfgang Schirmacher, I met Udi Aloni, a real Sabra, a poetic inhabitant of his native Hebrew, provisionally a New Yorker, author of films, essays and fiction. He showed us his film Local Angel, a very powerful vision of the situation in Palestine, one turned toward more than peace (it calls for a peace, of course), and toward more than a simple accord between parties (an accord it wishes for): a view that is turned toward the possibility of a new blessing that would be given to all in the same land, by the same god.

It is the deepest and most effective film I know of about this apparently intractable situation. Udi Aloni shows us that it suffices to look at what exists in an intelligent and accepting way in order for a certain evidence to become visible: that is, that the people living in this situation share intensely the generic position of humanity, and that that is precisely what torments them. Whether it is the interview between Udi Aloni and Arafat, the clarifications presented by Jewish theologians, or the violent grief of young rappers; whether the interminable military controls, the bomb attacks, the singing and dancing, the crowds in streets saturated with colours, or the man who sings songs of mourning and of love in Arab as well as in Hebrew: everything converges on the power to come of a recreated country. Udi Aloni, who quickly became a real friend, asked me what I thought of it and, just like that, quite unexpectedly, he filmed my reaction, which I've reproduced below. The English version of this improvisation figures in the booklet which accompanies the DVD of the film. Isabelle Vodoz transcribed it into French. I've reviewed it and added to it.

Local Angel is a very beautiful, very singular and very interesting film. However, I would like above all to speak about why it is an important film. We can unhesitatingly say that there is something beautiful and interesting in the subtle, composite and magnificent images it presents of New York, of the Palestinian territories, of men and women from different countries seized by the same and obscure truth. But the importance of Udi Aloni's work relates to the way it organizes an intersection between a subjective determination and an objective situation. The story certainly does not only deal with the Palestinian situation. It speaks in an inseparable fashion about his mother and exile. It deals with the distance between New York and Israel, which is the visible symbol in the universe of Udi's split consciousness – a split that can find its appeasement only in a thoroughgoing re-conception of the situation, in something which would be neither Israel, nor New York, and that we shall call 'Palestine'.

The film of course in no way avoids the terrible distress of the Palestinians, nor, more generally, questions about the war, about the violence and about history. However, what it makes visible is a sort of constructive interaction between two things: on the one hand, a subjective trajectory – what is a Jew who is nothing other than a Jew, whose intellectual site is the Great Tradition, but who finds himself torn between New York and his country of birth, because, such as it is, this country is still unacceptable to him? – and, on the other hand, an objective investigation of the political situation in its radicality – what to do when the violences and opacities seem to take away every foothold for affirmative action?

This interaction is most often absent in films dealing with political situations, or else it is undermined in advance by a prior taking of sides. That's why it is so frequently the case that such films are at once laudable and unconvincing. They fail to make a point of the universal, and therefore dialectical, signification of what they stand for. Immersed in the battle, they act, as Mao Zedong would have said, 'unilaterally'. Why do films that are honourably pro-

Palestinian, and anti-Israel, or anti-Sharon, often end up giving the
painful impression of being anti-Jewish? Certainly, to the extent
that Israel proclaims to be a Jewish State, it is all too easy to make a
leap from hostility towards the State of Israel to hostility towards
Jews. It is nonetheless unacceptable, and so these films end up
backfiring. If we are to avoid this kind of reversal, the universality
in the situation must be attested to – and this can only be done by a
subject that speaks in its own name and not in accordance with
preformed statist predicates. This is exemplarily the case in Udi's
film. Nothing dissimulates the fact that it is Udi himself who
unfolds the situation's sensible givens; and for that very reason
what this situation possesses of universal, of peaceful greatness, is
made dramatically manifest. For the way we arrive at this pacifying
universality – symbolized by the statue of an angel at the edge of
the sea (that's the local angel) – is not via the preliminary
distribution of combatants, but via Udi's complex wishes.

Of course, I know perfectly well that Udi operates from a radical
and real point of view that has nothing neutral or academic about
it. He is a militant. He is pro-Palestinian. He is a revolutionary. Yet
the importance of the film comes from the fact that he seeks a path
that would be acceptable to all actors in the situation, and not
simply to one of the parties. The film believes in the possibility of
finding something in the situation that could be an existential
symbol of peace for all. We cannot reduce this search to the point
of view of Palestinian militants, a point of view the film also names
and includes; nor can it be reduced to the point of view of Jewish
pacifists, once more also represented in the film, particularly in the
form of Udi's mother, who herself is a historic activist for the rights
of all people in Israel. Udi goes beyond this, especially beyond his
mother, because he knows both that the symbol of the universal
can be found in the situation only by inventing what has yet to be
said or seen, and that this invention cannot be summed up either
by the necessity of Palestinian struggle, nor by the necessity of
Jewish good will.

The conviction the film defends, and that opens onto what must be invented, is that a consideration of the situation from the standpoint of a real subjectivity, a subjectivity whose gaze is fair and simple, will enable us to know that those who proclaim a desire to live, at long last, in Palestine are the same as those who live and desire to live in Israel. In one sense, two different and even opposed names designate 'this same'. We know this 'same' to be traversed by significant empirical differences: differences in history, religion, customs, origin . . . But the honest and simple gaze sees this 'same' emerge from these differences. As soon, then, as we see that these people are the same, and in which sense they are the same, we can see something in the situation which is neither the victory of one side over the other, nor a sort of discussion or negotiation resulting in a precarious compromise lacking in any real thought.

What interests the film, the film's gaze, is neither victory nor defeat, nor interminable compromise, nor the continuation of war: it is *the construction of a new place*. Inasmuch as Palestine represents not only a local situation but stands in as a symbol of all humanity, the real intention of the film is to propose something like a new place for all the people living on earth. Looked at in a simple and honest way, the film establishes that the grand histories of States, of wars, of religion, and the small histories of individual men, women, Palestinians and Jews, etc., can find a sort of common point in the future, which is precisely a new place, a place at once concrete and spiritual, both entirely local and committed to the universal.

Let there be no misunderstanding: *Local Angel* is a very concrete film; it is infinitely sensitive, borne along by the singular colour of things like the sea, women, bodies and the tangible qualities of discourse. It is also a film that is attentive to voice and languages: Arab, English and Hebrew can all be heard in the rawness of life. It is not at all an abstract film, although it grants declarations and principles their fair part. It is, indeed, by this extreme sensitivity to the concrete that it becomes possible to find a way toward the construction of a new place.

The film tells us that, although the situation is 'objectively' terrible, full of death and violence, although it seems impossible that anything good might come of it, it can *always* be tackled from another angle, or be thought – including artistically – from a stance that includes all humanity. A different gaze sees in the heart of the Terrible that all the people living there are the same. Then, a new place can exist. *Local Angel* is the angel of a new place.

The film contains a very important subjective declaration about the possibility of reconciling, on the one hand, a god – not one of glory and power but a weak and suffering god – and the figure of a mother who protests and refuses. Let's say that Udi Aloni's problem is the gap between these two determinations. Is it possible to have, simultaneously, strong protest and revolt, and a god of weakness, of pity and compassion, that is, something like a Christian god? The simple and honest vision of the film is rendered possible precisely by that gap. Questions concerning the constructing of a new place always put into operation what we might call power and weakness. As such, a new Palestine cannot be the result of a victory or of a defeat. If you wish to create a new site, you must renounce the established distribution of powers. You must be, in the eyes of that distribution, at the weak point. So, Udi tells us, on the one hand, you have a god which is not the god of a single people but the god of all; and, on the other hand, it is imperative to do and to say something, because if a new place is to be created, one cannot be content with being simply passive and compassionate. This creation must certainly express its weakness, but it must further find the original path of a power of the weak.

At one point in the film, we see Udi Aloni in an encounter with Yasser Arafat. In politics, to speak to someone is to act. But, Udi wonders, and the film with him: what action would live up to the vision I have of constructing a new place? The classic forms of action – resistance, combat, aggression – that the situation seems to require do not live up to it. As Udi is not a simple pacifist, he knows as well as I do that when it comes to conflict-ridden situations a new political conception will not emerge from old ideas of continuing to struggle until victory or death. What's at issue is to find another path. In the film we can see that art, singers and love are all immanent determinations of a real conception of a political transformation of place. The gap separating revolt and the weak god is a gap where new means enable us to reach a new place.

So, we might rightly ask what the 'means' of Udi Aloni's vision are. These means are placed between four messianic figures: Walter Benjamin, Gershom Scholem, Shabtai Tzvi and Saint Paul. But all the same, I am under the impression that Udi is situated between a messianic figure and something that is not anti-messianic but perhaps non-messianic. With Paul, for example, we have a notion that is not contained in the idea of messianism, since at issue is the process of the coming of God himself, such as *it has taken place*. I don't think that Udi occupies a clearly defined place in relation to the Jewish spiritual tradition; rather he is between two clearly defined places and has to find a new solution.

In fact, it seems to me that in the film there is a fundamentally subjective idea, which is that, if we have to create a new place, it is also because we have to create a new Jew. It seems to me that beyond the rule of establishing a universal, something that would necessarily include the destiny of the Palestinians, Udi Aloni's real and secret project concerns the question: 'What is it to be a Jew today?' And the response does not involve the caretaking or the resurrection of an established identity; nor does it involve the renunciation of such an identity. The response is: the Jew of our time is to come.

7

Interview at the Daily *Haaretz*

This interview appeared in Hebrew in the culture and literature section of Haaretz, *an Israeli newspaper, on May 27 2005. It accompanied the publication of Adi Efal's Hebrew translation of my book* Ethics. *The conception, presentation and realization of the interview was undertaken by Schlomzion Kenan. I had the occasion to get to know her along with Udi Aloni during a summer's teaching at EGS. That's what she alludes to when in one of the questions she says 'in a course . . .' She is a philosopher and writer of fiction, and I thank her sincerely for giving me the opportunity to address the public. I likewise thank Adi Efal for her translating work. My responses to questions were given sometimes in English and sometimes in French. Schlomzion translated the interview into Hebrew. Isabelle Vodoz revised my English and translated it into French.*

Was the founding of a Zionist state a real event? What about the Palestinian uprising?

The founding of a Zionist state is a mixed reality, quite complex. On the one hand, it is an event that is part of a larger event, namely, the emergence of the great revolutionary, communist and socialist projects, of the idea of founding a completely new society. On the other hand, it is a counter-event that is part of a larger counter-event, namely, colonialism, the brutal conquest by people from Europe of new lands where other peoples existed. This creation was an extraordinary mixture of revolution and reaction, of emancipation and oppression. The destiny of Israel must be to separate out what constitutes it. The Zionist state must become what there was that was of just and new. It must become the least racial, the least religious and the least nationalist of states. It must become the most universal of all. And it must do so through an unprecedented act: create in itself its own Palestinian part as an integral part of what it is. Of course, to create this part, or to allow it to be, *beyond itself*, would entail confirming the dark part, the colonial and racial part, of its origins.

What has become of the fidelity to this event?

As I was just saying: maintaining fidelity to the initial event can only be done by separating out the components. For the colonial and racial part do not proceed from the event, but from the counter-event. This part does not propose the universal void of a creation, but the dreadful 'whole' of chauvinism and unending war. Israel must return to its universal vocation: create before the world a state grounded in principles, and not in a supposedly national, religious or racial substance.

So where does religion come in here?

Of course, what I am saying here concerning the Israelis goes equally for the Palestinians. Narrow-minded terrorism carried out under the word 'Arab', or 'Muslim', is the symmetrical term to the racial militarism carried out under the word 'Jew'. Besides, we know about the historical complicities between Hamas and elements of the Israeli secret service. These symmetrical forces work toward a sort of sharing of powers, to a division of areas of influence and existence. Against that, it is necessary to come to terms with the historical destiny between Israelis and Palestinians, and do it fundamentally in the same site.

So what is your solution to the Middle East problem?

It is the existence of a single, democratic, secular Palestine (or any other jointly chosen name), where names like 'Jew' and 'Arab' could be names of the multiple in the same place, names of peace. This would have such power for thought, such a political power, that the whole Middle East would be completely turned upside down.

What renders the imperative 'keep going' less mystical than the consideration of the face of the Other for Levinas?

For me, an imperative can exist only in a concrete situation. It can therefore never be brought back to the level of a general category, as is the case with Kant's morality ('act in accordance with the universal form of the moral law'), or the case with Levinas' ethics ('take the revelation of the face of the Other for the ethical sign of transcendence'). The imperative 'keep going' takes on a meaning only in the process of a singular truth, which is itself a becoming in a singular situation, in what I call a 'world'. For me, there is in reality no Subject *before* this singular process. Everything, then, is rational: either you do not keep going (your action, creation, love . . .) and you destroy the Subject in you; or you support the Subject, which is to say you keep going. Now, without a Subject the question of ethics does not arise. If you abandon, if you betray, you render ethics impossible right where it existed. As for love, there is nothing mystical or irrational about it. It is the existential construction of a thought of the Two; it is an intimate and creative experience of difference.

What precisely is the unnameable?

The inaccessible, or the non-manifest, are points of impasse for rational thought. It is the moment when so-called 'metaphysical' thought must yield. For me, the void is at the heart of every situation. But this void is perfectly thinkable by means of the purest rationality, that is, mathematics. I'd add that a great event (a revolution, a shattering scientific discovery, a sudden amorous encounter . . .) is precisely what renders the void manifest in the situation. A truth envelops this void; it presents it in the situation in which the void was formerly unrepresented. Thus, with workers' revolutions, there is a brutal presentation of the central void of bourgeois societies, which is precisely the political existence of workers. And with an amorous passion, there is the central void that separates the sexes, or simply the void separating any two individuals. Love reveals the void, works it over, peoples it with acts, with feelings, with new dreams. A new politics in the Middle East will give form and reason to the terrorizing void that disjoins those who proclaim themselves Jewish and those who proclaim themselves Palestinian.

In the preface to Infinite Thought, *a collection of your texts translated and presented by Oliver Feltham and Justin Clemens (Continuum 2003), the example is given of a historical situation in Australia about which your translator writes: 'Any representation of the content of the multiple "aboriginals" with reference to what it is to be Australian, would thus cause the unity of the situation to dissolve' (p. 26). Could one make an analogy with the representation of the multiple 'Palestinian bearers of an Israeli passport' with reference to what it is to be Israeli?*

The analogy is legitimate. I believe that many Israelis do not see that, henceforth, their existence is determined by that of the Palestinians. The same goes for the Palestinians. By this I mean that the existence of an Israeli people can no longer prop itself up solely with the word 'Jew', although this word remains fundamental. Nor do I believe that the existence of the Palestinians can prop itself up solely with the word 'Arab'. The future lies in a reciprocal identification through a sort of determination that is at

once internal and external. What would exist would be Israeli–
Palestinian. It would be a creation, a totally new, paradoxical
reality. The opposition between 'Jews' and 'Arabs' is an old and
murderous thing. An extraordinary innovation must be created
that would have universal power, that would astonish the whole
world: a site at once completely Israeli and completely Palestinian, and in the same place, in the same locales. I do not believe
in the 'solution' of a territorial division. It's as stupid as if a man
and a woman shared a house but had walls dividing each room.
Israelis and Palestinians are historically fiancés, fiancés by war, by
wars. I believe, likewise, that France and Germany, historically,
are fiancés by war. This is moreover why I put forward the
proposal in *Circonstances 2* that the two countries be fused, pure
and simple. The same goes for you, the Israelis and the Palestinians. Your bloody engagement is even more intimate than
France's and Germany's.

Why can one not speak of pure Evil?

If the Good is always relative to a truth procedure, and so always
linked to a singular concrete situation, there can be no pure Evil,
no timeless Evil. For Evil is dependent on the Good, and not the
other way round. Nazism is the evil of the epoch of twentieth-
century revolutions. It cannot be made to play the role of absolute
Evil, of ineffable Evil, etc. In order to understand this Evil, it is
essential that the complex history of the diverse politics throughout
the century to which it belonged be understood: the fascisms, the
communisms, the liberalisms, etc. To put it in a stronger way: in
order to understand Nazi politics as a politics of extermination of
European Jews, one must at the same time understand Zionism as a
revolutionary politics of creating a Jewish state somewhere *outside of
Europe*. Do not forget that Hitler's initial idea was precisely to
deport the Jews outside Europe. He thought about Madagascar
. . . Evil must be thought from truths, Nazism from revolutions, the

extermination from foundation. Otherwise, we lapse into the obscure fetishism of Evil.

In a course, you showed the sense in which Nazism is unfounded: the multiple 'Nazi' includes no foundational element other than itself. Nazism is a tautology. How then can something without any foundation exist?

When a reality is non-founded it can exist only by destroying something else. A racial tautology can exist only in war. Nazism aimed for the millenary reign of Aryans. But the Aryan doesn't exist. It is only a tautology of Nazi discourse that says: Aryans are Aryans. That's why the sole reality of the Nazi project was the extermination of that which, for the Nazis, was not Aryan. First up, the Jews, obviously, but the gypsies too, not to mention the Slavs. Nazi politics, as racial politics, is in reality a politics of unlimited war.

You wrote this about love: 'Enjoyment as such is inaccessible to the power of a truth, which is the truth of the Two.' And in a course you said the following: 'The fusion of two lovers is unfounded. This is why it involves destruction. The history of a love is a singular history. It is an invention that departs from the question of the Two. The reduction of Two to One institutes an unfounded Two which is the destruction of the veritable Two.' What is this 'One' that must not be named?

With love, one cannot desire the fusion of two lovers without going towards the destruction of love itself. Why? Because, as a truth, as a creation, love operates from the interior of sexual difference, even when this love is homosexual. Well, enjoyment is a sort of corporeal symbol, of symbol *en-corps*, of the fusion, the death fusion, of the two lovers. That's why I say that enjoyment must not be named or wanted in the case of love. It happens, and that's all. What must be desired, created, wanted, is a new practice of the world, a practice dominated by the Two, by the difference.

How could a Jewish minority survive in a Judeo-Arab state? Has that worked in the case of Yugoslavia?

It is perfectly possible for a 'minority' to survive in a multi-racial, multi-national and also multi-confessional state. And not only to survive, but to stand as a point of reference for all. In fact, to speak in terms of 'majority' and 'minority' is not at all necessary. A modern state is composed of all sorts of people. The fact that Israel has called itself a 'Jewish state' with an 'Arab minority' certainly presents a difficulty and a kind of archaism. The same goes for France. It was only in the sorry period of the Nazi occupation, with the Pétain government, that France was defined as the 'French state'. What happened next was that this 'French state' organized the deportation of Jews, the internment of Spaniards, etc. In Yugoslavia, the current situation is the result of an absurd and criminal war. The Europeans bear a grave responsibility for having accepted the destruction of the Federal State of Yugoslavia. As a result, we have 'national' states (Croat, Serb, Slovene, etc.) that are totally archaic, no less than would be the division of a small territory into a Palestinian (or Arab) state and an Israeli (or Jewish) state. The modern conception of a state is an open conception: a country is made up of all the people who live and work there. We have to accept, as a rule of peace, that a national entity be a kind of creative patchwork. There is no reason on this point to make a 'Jewish exception'. The argument traditionally advanced for such an exception evokes the singularity of the destruction of the European Jews by the Nazis. But there is strictly no relation between the Nazis and the Palestinians. The question of the destruction of the European Jews is a German and European question. If we are to come to a resolution of the Middle East problem, we must manage – and I know it's a difficult thing – to forget the Holocaust.

We can perhaps look at it differently, but forget it?

I'll be more precise, since the formula is ostensibly unacceptable. It is obviously necessary, not only for the Jews but for all of humanity, not to forget the destruction of the European Jews. What's at issue here is not exclusively a question of memory; it is a question of thought, of a great philosophical and political meditation. The key to the problem is to understand Nazism completely, not in a theological way (as an absolute Evil), but as a monstrous ideological project: the creation of a completely imaginary 'new man', by means of the very real eradication of all those who are alleged to represent the 'old man', which is once again completely imaginary. For very particular mythological reasons, the Jews (and some others) symbolized this old man for the Nazis. All this must be thought through, paying special attention to how a very real politics was able to be organized in the service of this ideology. But in this mediation there is no coherent place for the Palestinians, for the Middle East, or for the Arabs. All that is completely foreign to Nazi politics. The only thing we can retain here is a principle of universal scope: there is always something monstrous about determining a state from a racial, mythical, or religious point of view, or more generally, by appealing to particularity. That went as much for the German fascists as for the French fascists. It goes for the Serbs as much as for the terrorist conception of a 'Muslim state' (with Sharia, etc.). It goes for the Jews too. That is why, although the destruction of the European Jews ought never to be forgotten, it is nonetheless dangerous to tackle the concrete problems of the Israeli state based on this destruction. The memory of the Holocaust concerns all human beings. But paradoxically, in the concrete circumstances of the Middle East, we have to – strict asceticism – forget the Holocaust, since we are exclusively faced with the practical necessity of having to found a new kind of peace by means of a new kind of political subjectivity.

What do you think about the hypothesis that the current anti-Israeli tendencies in France come from an old type of anti-Semitism?

Mao Zedong said that everywhere, except in the deserts, there is a left, a centre and a right. It is the same thing in France on the Palestinian question. A small anti-Semitic right wing uses the often very brutal activities of the State of Israel as a pretext to speak out against Jews. A much more numerous, genuine left wing condemns the politics of Sharon, without ever forgetting everything that our political, scientific and artistic history owes to the genius of the European Jews. A cautious centre would like to be able to have a positive solidarity with all the peoples of the region. The best way to crush anti-Semitism is the active fraternity with the many Israelis who know that one day it will be necessary to become the brothers of the Palestinians.

8

The Master-Signifier of the New Aryans: What Made the Word 'Jew' into an Arm Brandished Against the Multitude of 'Unpronounceable Names'

Cécile Winter

This essay was written by Cécile Winter in 2004. It is the synthesis of a long meditation whose first formulations were pronounced at a conference in Lyon in 1992 as part of a seminar series organized by our mutual friend Lucien Pitti, who, alas, has since died. This conference was published in a journal called Le Croquant. *Centred on the destiny of the word 'Jew' after the war, and on the assessment of this history proposed by Claude Lanzmann's great film* Shoah, *Cécile Winter's text sketched some developments that are orchestrated and unfolded here to their most radical consequences.*

I emphasize that the present text, despite many efforts in which I've participated, was unable to find a place of publication until its inclusion in the present collection. For strict reasons of the general economy of this book, I've made cuts to it for which I bear total responsibility. The complete text can be requested from Cécile Winter via the publisher.

Cécile Winter is a doctor and AIDS specialist.

'I made this film', wrote Claude Lanzmann, referring to *Shoah*, 'to show that the European jews were exterminated as jews', 'because they *were* jews'.[9] The jews were exterminated as jews! Could the Nazi point of view have been put any better? The Jew, such was the Nazis' very idea, which they then worked to substantiate, starting with decrees and laws: what's a jew, who's jewish, is he/she a full jew, a half-jew, can one become a jew by marriage, etc.? First, the Nazis had to legislate with the care and meticulousness to be expected from the law in Europe (on this point see the opening chapters of Raul Hilberg's great work *The Destruction of the European Jews*); then, once the jews were well defined, they had to locate them, mark them, round them up, and finally destroy them; in sum, they sought in full awareness to accomplish the hard but necessary work whose worth – Hitler was sure of it – would be appreciated by posterity: to have rid the world of Jews 'as jews', 'because they were jews'.

If you say – like Hitler – 'The jews were exterminated as jews', 'because they were jews', what counts in this case, more than the fate of individual people, is the word 'jew'; what counts is the assumption and elevation – explicitly founded in and by the Hitlerian undertaking of thought and, then, of action – of a signifying entity called 'the jews', one that transcends the existence and the narratives of those to whom the predicate is applied. Before Hitler there were *jews*, very real individuals and peoples, whether religious or atheist, poor or prosperous, to each their own jew and to each their own jews – no predicate would have been able to mark out or gather together a group of jews in its entirety. It is Hitler who made the name 'Jew' into an Idea, his great Idea, and so into a signifying totality. He's the one who did the work for this idea by making a mythico-communitaro-racial soup. And now, seemingly, everyone has a duty to accept it, even venerate it, find it grand, untouchable and indisputable. 'The Jews' is now something, a word one is bound to recognize and respect, and before which one must bow – a master word, in effect. Were one to ask *why*, well, there would be no reason other than the work of Hitler! We are, then, to understand that there was a reason, and even a good reason, to kill these people. This good reason is 'the jews'. Indeed, since Lanzmann, the work of the Nazis has been elevated and even sacralized under the name of 'Shoah'. 'Shoah' has today become the compulsory common name for designating the Nazi oeuvre.

If you say, with Hilberg, 'the destruction of the European Jews', then at issue is a criminal politics deployed on a large scale. But if you say, 'the Shoah', you speak about a divine work, about the accomplishment of destinies, in which the dead, 'the jews', are victims offered up in sacrifice to a signifier transcending them. This comes down to validating, in politics, the right to mark and to decide the fate of people in the name of a signifier transcending them as individuals or as peoples, which *a priori* overqualifies them, as it were. That a transcendental overqualifier might mark out a group either 'as more' or 'as less' in no way alters the main point. And the proof is that in this conception the more and the less are reversible and complementary. For Hitler, the jews ought to be considered and treated as though they were subhuman, for if not they will inevitably become superhuman. Conversely, today, being jewish is supposed to grant one superior rights for fear of being treated as inferior, and in retribution for the suffering caused from being treated as inferiors in the past under this name.

That is because today, in perfect continuity with Hitler's invention, the word 'Jew' has become a transcendental signifier, an inversion by which the powerful of the day turn in a profit, a word brandished to reduce one to silence on pain of sacrilege. For whoever is hostile to the Nazi viewpoint, it has become an unsayable name. Hitler had perhaps not imagined any such triumph of his vision.

Today, we are able to retrace the stages of this triumph, which we hope is only temporary. It begins, after Germany's military defeat, at the famous Nuremberg trials. The German army is wiped out, Hitler is dead and Germany almost destroyed. But what is the story with the destiny of Nazism? Here, the famous trial is hastened so judgement can be passed and the file closed in order to proclaim a new era for nations and for humanity.

But, first, who passes judgement? It's the American Army. What gave the right to this Army to order the trial of Nazi criminals and make themselves its judge?[10] Apparently, their military victory gave them this right. We must keep that in mind. Right belongs to the strongest army. It was not to those who fought against Nazism, not even to the rare survivors of Nazi crimes, that it fell to pass judgement or to pronounce. The former were quite simply asked to go back whence they came, the latter had to be put up with being forever called 'victims' by the new discourse. The right to judge fell to the new power because this power decided it would be so. Here, then, it was the military victory of one power over another that was decisive, and not the defeat of Nazism. The question of Nazism was immediately confiscated, clamped down on.

What indeed did the American Army proclaim at Nuremberg? They said that the acts of the Nazis were so barbarous that they fell outside the legal framework, that they exceeded traditional methods of investigation, comprehension and judgement. It seems that the destructive Nazi undertaking warranted being enthroned in capitals. It was a Crime (and not a multiplicity of crimes) against Humanity (and not against a multiplicity of people). The capitals, majestic and intimidating, had the advantage of short-circuiting all inquiry, of immediately dispensing with the perspectives of detailed historical and political investigations like some bothersome cloud of flies. By undertaking an inquiry, by looking into the circumstances, you're inevitably led to encountering the protagonists, the tacit and cooperative accomplices, the indifferent and the *résistants*. But the capitals isolate Nazi activity, lift it above the world. The 'Crime' against 'Humanity', unique and separated, detached from circumstances, and therefore without any connections or relations, rises up, in truth, from the non-place.

For this reason, the role that the Anglo-American allies played in the work of Nazi destruction, with their tacit acceptance and resolute choice of 'non-intervention', has been completely obscured.[11] Szmul Zygielbojm, representative of the Bund in London and member of the Polish National Council in exile, wrote on May 11 1943, shortly before gassing himself in his London apartment:

> The responsibility for the crime of the murder of the whole Jewish nationality in Poland rests first of all on those who are carrying it out, but indirectly it also falls upon the whole of humanity, on the peoples of the Allied nations and on their governments, who up to this day have not taken any real steps to halt this crime . . . By my death I wish to make my final protest against the passivity with which the world is looking on and permitting the annihilation of the Jewish people . . . I know how little human life means in our times but since I could do nothing when alive, perhaps by my death I can help destroy the indifference of those who could save, perhaps at the last moment, those Polish Jews who are still alive.

This text was published in a book called *The Warsaw Ghetto Uprising*[12] and S. Zygielbojm's suicide is recounted in Jan Karski's *Story of a Secret State*, published in 1948.[13] It is the same Jan Karski who, interviewed in Lanzmann's film, tells us the content of the messages the ghetto's representatives gave him to pass on to the 'free world'. The Allies were asked to drop leaflets on some German towns stating that, if the extermination of the Polish Jews did not stop, a German town would be bombed. The Polish government in exile was asked to make this demand known to the leaders of the Allied forces, the Allied forces were asked to act on it, and the Jewish and Zionist organizations throughout the world, and especially in the United States, were asked to support it using every possible means. The message added that, though it was clear the Allies would defeat Germany militarily, there was something here that did not come directly under the logic of war: preventing the extermination of a people. Of course, Lanzmann neglected to ask Jan Karski to tell us about the welcome he received in London, but we know that the Polish Jews perished without any attempt to save them, and that afterwards the Allies savagely bombed not only one, but all the towns of Germany. It is clear, then, that the Anglo-American allies aimed only at attaining the goals of war and only went after German power, whereas the politics the Nazis carried out, and notably the systematic killing of millions of people, did not matter to them in the slightest, leaving them perfectly indifferent. Thanks to the discourse they pronounced at Nuremberg, with its emphatic capitals, their responsibility was never raised and all mention of these facts brushed aside, to the point that some fifty years later they appear as a revelation.[14]

Drawing a veil thus over the real history of the connections the respective parties had to the extermination of the European Jews was especially welcomed by the Zionists who had set foot in Palestine. Their supreme goal was to create their own State and from the war's inception their conscious and determined strategy was clear: take full advantage of this tragic affair. The first chapters of Tom Segev's book *The Seventh Million*, published in Israel in 1991, make all this plainly clear. The Zionist leaders were, from the outset, clearly conscious of the great moral advantage the destruction of the European Jews could bequeath to their future State.[15] Indeed, Tom Segev reports, the project of a future memorial of Yad Vashem had already been conceived in 1942:[16]

A former delegate to several Zionist congresses, Mordechaï Shenhabi, proposed in September 1942 that the Jewish Nat-ional Fund establish a memorial to the victims of the Holocaust, 'the war dead and heroes of Israel'. Not long thereafter, the projected memorial received the name it would bear when it was built some years later: Yad Vashem. Shenhabi's proposals led to discussions and letters, and a committee was set up to examine them. There was no clearer, more grotesque, even macabre expression of the tendency to think the Holocaust in the past tense: while the yishuv discussed the most appropriate way to memorialize them, most of the victims were still alive.

So that the moral benefit could be cashed in on, it was of utmost importance that the policy of capitalizing on the drama adopted by the Zionist leaders not give way to an inquiry. For this capital reason, the policy of elevating the Nazi Crime – and of subtracting concrete Nazi crimes and their interrelations as multiple-in-situation – adopted by the Americans at Nuremberg rendered a noble service to the Zionists. Diffuse sentiments of Western guilt, most legitimate in view of what had occurred, would go to accelerating the creation of the State of Israel in a unanimous display of opinion. Paying out 'compensation' is at most what our States know how to do when there is human death, and for that to happen there must, of course, be inheritors willing to collect payment and who are unconcerned about the price to be paid for it. The leaders of this brand new State were not concerned, as they had already shown; they were men of State. They had prepared the insignia of family mourning – including that famous memorial – and hoped to be able to boast of this heritage for a long time to come. So, their brand new State was named, with generally reverential assent, the 'Jewish State'.

But collecting the inheritance is one thing; forever continuing to draw interest on it is another.[17] In this respect, precisely, the ideological frame mounted at Nuremberg laid the foundations for a durable edifice. The 'Crime' against 'Humanity', the first, the incomparable and absolute, the inaccessible, definitive yardstick of all others, elevated its victims to exemplary status. The 'Victims', once jews, became 'Jews'. 'Jew', that is, turned into a metonymical signifier for Humanity, and – this time, in an unreachable sky – into the very point of intersection, the obligatory point at which 'Humanity' and 'Crime' meet. 'Victim' names this connection, and 'Jew' is the Victim par excellence. So, the 'jewish State' could become the 'Jewish State'.

With the passing of time, the more distant the European origins of the State of Israel became, the more it became a Middle Eastern State, a colonizing power, and then an occupying power, in a political and geographical situation no longer bearing any relation to the history leading up to its founding,[18] the more important it became to increase the upper case – continuing to draw on moral benefits from the destruction of the European jews depended on it – i.e. to establish the signifier 'Jew' 'in itself', as an unquestionable, atemporal, absolute signifier. Such were the efforts of those who, in France, found their vocation at the end of the 1970s as ideologues of the Western world. So, while the Six-Day War was being waged and the occupied territories established, while the PLO, which in everyone's eyes at the time represented the national Palestinian movement, called for a 'free, secular and democratic Palestine', the French current of the so-called new philosophers sought to restore and strengthen the American text from Nuremberg. They claimed that this text founded, over and against the obsolete pretensions to progress and to the good of the century preceding it, a new era of morality guaranteed by law and force in the combat against Evil – which always comes first. See, then, just how precious Hitler becomes when revised by Nuremberg, adorned with all its capitals. Quite indispensable. Would we have ever known Evil without him? Would we now dispense with the notions of 'Crime', of 'Humanity' and of 'Victims'? Moreover, whoever is accorded the title of Victim par excellence is not only exempted once and for all from every count, but is also granted the right to speak for all of 'Humanity' and to occupy the role of the universal arbitrator.[19]

The effect of making victims into Victims eventually leads to the curious argument according to which the Israelis would possess full rights to be bastards 'just like everyone else'. With the implication that, should you not recognize the right of Jews to be as racist, as paratrooper-like, as, say, the French, then you are anti-Semitic! But, to be precise, at issue is not their being 'just like everyone else', since it is claimed that the Israeli owners of the transcendental signifier should be able to exercise their rights to be paratroopers, racists and torturers in the absence of a right to criticism. It is mandatory not to criticize them, and even to approve of them on pain of lèse-master-signifièr.

At the time of the demonstrations in Paris against the American war in Iraq, some demonstrators bearing an Israeli flag with a swastika slapped on it were taken to court on charges of anti-Semitism![20] The scandal provoked by this association is understandable, although the word 'jew' was entirely absent here, except, of course, if it is identified with the State of which the flag is the emblem. But what is interesting is that it is precisely in Israel itself where there are frequent rapprochements between the swastika and the practices of the Israeli State. Over there, the poisonous character of the heritage of the signifying chain in question is pointed out and discussed. Thus, for example, in a recent book, *Towards an Open Tomb*,[21] Michel Warschawski discusses in great detail the uses made, in Israel, of the word 'Nazi' and its derivatives.[22] And again, a few days after the media publicized that fact that certain *done-for* Palestinians have numbers tattooed on their arms, B. Michael, himself the son of survivors, published a painful and severe article called 'From the Marked to the Markers'. He wrote:

> There is no doubt that the historical path of the jewish people through the sixty years that separate 1942 from 2002 could serve as material for impassioning historical and sociological studies. In sixty short years, from the ones who are confined in ghettos to the ones who do the confining. In sixty short years, from the ones who are branded and numbered to the ones who brand and number. In sixty years, from the ones who file along with their hands in the air to those who make others file along with their hands in the air . . . At last! We are no longer a different and bizarre people with a pale complexion and a wise air, but brutal soldiers like everyone else. At last, the equals of all other nations.[23]

Sometimes, this perverse reversal is completely conscious, as it was with that Israeli army superior who, the day before the invasion of the Palestinian refugee camps, explained to his soldiers that 'we must learn from the experience of others, including from the way the German troops took control of the Warsaw ghetto'.[24]

So, what was a real moral income for Israeli leaders has perhaps well and truly changed – with visible effects in the country itself – into a veritable public poison. Without the superimposition of the master signifier, indeed, the situation would be simply what it is. A colonial situation, a terrible situation, with racist laws, apartheid, colonizers with free rein, yes, true, but a situation not unlike others we've seen, and involving the resourcefulness of all those in it, surely no less talented than others. After all, apartheid in South Africa was much older and had an unenviable record of injustices and crimes. So, then, what would prevent an Israeli leader from naming Arafat as co-Prime Minister and for them to convene all their fellow Palestino-Israeli citizens for the creation, at long last, and covering the whole vast area, of a country that would undoubtedly be as rich as it would be powerful? Commissions, whose tasks would be nothing short of arduous, would be necessary to sort out yours from mine when the refugees finally returned to their unrecognizable and reconstructed homes. It would be nec-essary to bring to heel a number of rancorous beings who'd be armed and brazen for a while. This would make for a lot of problems, of course, but, to stick to the situation itself, there is nothing that cannot be envisaged, and much that is sensible. People would breathe: they would have a country. We could even bet that they would be relieved and jubilant. But the master-signifier induces an overdetermination that creates an obstacle. It aggravates the racism of the bearers of the word 'jew' with the merciless burden of a fiction that no real situation can relieve them of. This fiction hangs over the situation, blocking all respite, heralding destruction and death to the Palestinian people, and bearing disaster upon disaster for the Israelis themselves.

Yes, at this point in time, the signifier sent by Hitler, wanted by the Zionists, obligingly transmitted by the Americans, and then by their Western allies, to the 'Jewish State', is surely no longer a gift but a burden, its mark a sign of non-independence. For who owns the signifier today? Who is the master of the master-signifier?[25] Certainly not the Israeli leaders. It is a master-signifier of Western discourse, which, thanks to the detour via Israel, is back and doing the job in the service of its owners. That is, those who, although perfectly well identified and excellent in the art of discerning and crushing the smallest ant not convinced of their supremacy, are not easily named: the rich, the democrats or Westerners, the developed, the well-armed wing of Humanity, servicers of goods who know Good and Evil, pro-Americans, the Masters of Discourse, the in-any-case-we-deserve-better-than-others-and-things-must-remain-like-that-even-if-others-die-from-it. It was simpler to say 'Whites'. But we are no longer in an era of robust colonial empires. Hannah Arendt showed how Hitlerian discourse was rooted in colonial discourse and filled in for the lack of German colonies. It is amazing to see Hitlerian discourse now returning to the rescue, as modern purveyor of signifiers of supremacy, to distinguish the 'masters'.

Here, in order to illustrate this and to come full circle, is the portrait of one of today's masters, one of the pillars of the Bush government, who, I might add, was promoted after the writing of the article cited below to one of the most important posts in foreign politics, relating notably to American politics in the Middle East: Elliott Abrams. This Elliott Abrams was described in detail by Serge Halimi in an article called 'Victory of the Right', published in *Le Monde diplomatique*, August 2001.[26] At the time, President George Bush had just appointed Elliott Abrams to the position of Senior Director of the Office for Democracy, Human Rights, and International Operations. It is not completely clear how this appointment, which went unreported in the big media channels, coincides with the new era of universal law, morality, and tenderness sung by the strolling players of the International Criminal Court.

After having enumerated the base acts that this human rights specialist has either organized or tried to conceal, and in particular frightful massacres carried out under his direction by various death squads in South America under the banner of anti-communism, Serge Halimi concludes as follows:

> When we met him in February 1995 in a conservative think tank, the Hudson Institute, this declared partisan of the Israeli right-wing considered that the Palestinians had 'no right to a State.' He dreaded, moreover, 'an intervention by President Clinton in Iraq, because I do not think he has the firmness to finish it off.' Mr. Abrams would also have been favourable to the dismantling of programs in the US aiding underprivileged minorities: 'It is partly because I'm Jewish. The Jewish community has 30% of places at Harvard: even if we represent only 2% of the population.' These programs of positive discrimination have, according to him, 'exacerbated relations between races.'

At my conference, in 1992, the turn of a spiral that is still incomplete, I concluded by citing Celan from his 'Conversation in the Mountains':

> One evening, when the sun had set and not only the sun, the Jew – Jew and son of a Jew – went off, left his house and went off, and with him his name, his unpronounceable name . . . because the Jew, you know, what does he have that is really his own, that is not borrowed, taken and not returned – so he went off and walked along this road, this beautiful, incomparable road, walked like Lenz through the mountains, he who had been allowed to live down in the plain where he belongs, he, the Jew, walked and walked. Walked, yes, along this road, this beautiful road.[27]

Today, having come full circle, it's either one or the other: either the master-signifier, or the multitude of unsayable names. It falls to each to choose the master he wants to serve. In other words, having become an arm brandished against the multitude, the signifier 'Jew', master-signifier of the new Aryans, must be deliberately put aside. Whoever uses it does it clearly in the service of the new masters. Whoever does not want to make himself into their servant must decide to reject it, in order to take the side of the unsayable names. Szmul Zygeilbojm, Rudolf Vrba, Robert Wachspress, and Rabbi Benyamin, or Mordechai Anielewicz and Zyvia Lubetkin . . . There's no shortage of unsayable names; and it would be easy to extend the list, the list of those who have remained by choice with those that are allowed to live in the open, and who, by devoting themselves to those who are consigned to the depths, make the light of their name shine for all.

9

The Word 'Jew' and the Sycophant[28]

1

One could resist responding. One ought not to, perhaps. Or else, one could respond by looking at things from a bird's-eye view, as a very small symptom of the situation into which France has lapsed in recent times. *Circonstances 3* is a book for which Cécile Winter and I alone take responsibility. Yet the violence of the reaction provoked by this book must be placed in its political context. The fact is that the situation in France today is dominated by an unprecedented reactionary offensive against workers of foreign origin, the adolescents of housing estates, children's schooling, the health of the poorest and weakest, women with different customs, workers' hostels, the mentally ill . . . Every day we have to put up with reading that absolutely criminal legislative measures are being concocted. 'Sarkozy' is the name of a rampant process by which, step by step, and with violence, entire sections of the population are relegated to a status deprived of rights, and are offered up to the police as internal enemies. In this context, it is important to ask the following question: what is the desire of the petty faction that is the self-proclaimed proprietor of the word 'Jew' and its usages? What does it hope to achieve when, bolstered by the tripod of the Shoah, the State of Israel and the Talmudic Tradition – the SIT – it stigmatizes and exposes to public contempt anyone who contends that it is, in all rigour, possible to subscribe to a universalist and egalitarian sense of this word? I will submit, then, that this is an extremist faction that harbours the same political intent as that dominating French parliamentarism today, one that is oriented towards identifying, separating off and persecuting people that the state itself has constituted as the enemies internal to the consensus. The petty group of which we speak forms the intellectual extreme right wing of this deadly orientation, that is, in so far as it takes a subjective form that, as a rule, is more negative (the anti-Palestinian, anti-Arab element is essential) than positive; in so far as its intellectual mechanism is inevitably obscurantist (primacy of particularities, restricted nationalism, racism, religiosity without God); and in so far as its polemical practices belong to the various established genres of senseless repression. Natacha Michel has already brought to my attention the fact that the procedures of this petty faction accumulate all the known historical genres of public denunciation. Engaging in juridical and statist denunciation, they demand that an end be put to our 'impunity'. Engaging in MacCarthyist-type denunciation, they say we are totalitarian Bolsheviks. Engaging in a *latter-day* Soviet-style denunciation, they diagnose the manifestation of various psychoses in our writings. Natacha Michel remarks, with a sad humour, 'On all sides, I have passed into the other camp.' This accumulation is significant; it leads one to wonder what it is this faction is protecting, what it so fears losing whenever its monopoly over the usage, normativity and correlative associations of the word 'Jew' is undermined.

I will make the hypothesis that the aggressive promotion of the triplet Shoah–Israel–Tradition, or SIT, as the only acceptable content of the word 'Jew', and the ignorant, stubborn, personalized violence directed against anybody who proposes a different mode of signification and circulation the word, has to do with protecting a power: the power – very useful to the powers-that-be – of managing to subjugate this word to totally anti-working-class political and statist determinations, i.e., to a system of judicial and police control to which, little by little, everything that shows

intellectuals whose feebleness exasperates and misleads – with the support that a large part of public opinion lends to odious policies. I know better, a thousand times better than the extremist faction, of the connection between the word 'Jew' and the immense history of universal truths. In nullifying all the substantialist and racialist interpretations of it, in liberating it from any necessary connection to religious customs, in giving it a contemporary vivacity independent of fictitious narratives, in de-linking it from a state which sticks it in the mud of imperial particularities; in sum, in liberating the word 'Jew' from the triplet SIT, to which this faction tries to reduce it, I associate myself amicably with the work – undertaken by many others, whether or not they lay claim to the predicate 'Jew' – by which a new force of the word can and will emerge. For the moment, I see it hardened, stunted, its flag moth-eaten by the defences of reaction. My profound hope is, as firmly stated in *Circonstances 3*, notably with respect to Udi Aloni's film *Local Angel*, that this word shall be reanimated, reinvented, revived in a cycle of truth-procedures. And first of all, without doubt, in Israel, where the implementation of a state or a country that is shared by all the people living there, whatever their customary predicates might be, would constitute the major landmark of such a revival.

But with regard to this vision of things, the work this faction and its mercenaries engage in, work of sabotage, of propagating ignorance, of hatred of vitally important actions, and of spreading filth everywhere, cannot be left entirely to its own worthlessness. As tiresome and as partly vain as the labour might be, it is imperative to respond to certain attacks, clean up, stitch up, restore, call to read and to think. It is imperative to go beyond. It is imperative to put on our boots and clean out our Augean stables, so that one day we really may come to 'the splendid cities'.[29] It is a pity, a pity indeed, that *Les Temps Modernes* believes it should provide a base for such stables. But we must get stuck into it. We must dissect Marty. We musn't leave anything unfinished. Let's get on with it.

3

The practice of singling out great philosophers for public condemnation by specialists of lies, ignorance and insane mediocrity has a long history. The pair of Socrates and the petty characters who accused him of corrupting the youth, Anytos and Meletos, is inaugural. The technical name for these professional accusers is 'sycophant'. Eric Marty, never have been able to amount to anything significant by relying on his own powers, has made himself a sycophant of everything that had some allure in the works of thinkers of the 1960s and 1970s, a task to which – so true is it that this man is incapable of initiating anything at all – he was beaten by Renaut and Ferry.[30] The only pertinent passage of the acts of accusation that he levels against me in the latest issue of *Les Temps Modernes* is the one where – in incorrectly attributing its paternity to me – he paints his own portrait: 'the "glorifier" [of the word "Jew"] reveals his true face, and [is] equally a sycophant and an informer; [there is], at bottom, a synonymy between sacralization and stigmatization'. Well said, Marty!

Deceived by his craftiness, journals and publishers have permitted this yapper to bite the hams of Althusser, Genet, Agamben and Lacan. However, the very constancy of the yapping, spitting and attempts at biting with which I have been honoured is peculiar. No doubt this is the price to pay for the fact that after, alas, the passing away of many of those of the calibre the little yapper has bitten, I've become the most widely read and translated French philosopher in the world. A sycophant will always say to himself that in biting what has some value he might thereby make a little profit. Besides, we must recognize the fact that Anytos and Meletos had no chance of getting on in the world as it was without Socrates. Eric Marty has even less of a chance without me. So, this lover of pillow talk, malicious gossip, funfair diagnoses and carnival psychology, says, as he can: '[Badiou's] *jouissance* is never satisfied.' Indeed, I will never rejoice completely in so far as my thought

manages to withstand the test of time but must always drag along
its sycophant.

4

This Marty, who constantly dishes out lessons about 'reality' and
'history', is not only a sinister sycophant, but an incompetent and
lazy academic. Here are five examples; difficult to believe they are
so outrageous.

4a

In so far as Marty puts forward anything in his appalling diatribe, it
is that 'Jew' must be thought of as a name, and that I am perverse,
odious, melancholic, hateful, criminal, and, to cap it all, manic-
depressive, to maintain that it is a predicate. So, he says, lampoon-
ing my ruses and tricks: 'The title Badiou has chosen for his book is
deceiving; it is "*Uses of the name Jew*".' How inconsequential indeed!
Only, the title *is not* 'Uses of the *name* "Jew"'. Rather, in line with
my contention, the title is 'Uses of the *word* "Jew".' The severe
Marty has written twenty pages on a book whose title he has not
got around to reading!

4b

From among the list of base acts and 'maniacal escalations' (*sic*) to
which I am prone, the sycophant Marty likes to cite the rapprochement I make in my book, *The Century*, between the mysterious
slogan of the strikes of December 1995, 'All Together [Tous
ensemble]', and the last line of a poem by Paul Celan, 'Anabasis',
where at issue is the 'tent word: together'. This rapprochement is

obvious to anybody that nourishes themselves, as I have always done, on the poetry intrinsic to popular insurrections. Of course, linked as he is to the clique from the journal *Esprit*, which considered it the most pressing intellectual duty to launch a petition against the millions of people who marched through the streets of our cities,[31] Eric Marty loathes, abhors, finds absolutely intolerable, any mention of the strikes of December 1995, or any strike at all (he is repeatedly enraged by my references to the workers' strike at Talbot in 1982. No doubt he took the side of the pack of bosses and executives who leapt at the workers screaming '*les bougnoules au four!*' ['Send the Arabs into the ovens!']). And just look at him here remarking, after having spewed his bile over any communication between poetry and workers' uprisings, that, I quote, 'To all appearances, the poem by Celan to which Badiou alludes is to be found in *The No-One's-Rose.*' Bravo, professor Marty! You have traversed the appearances and made the allusions explicit! True, it wasn't too difficult: the poem to which Badiou 'alludes' is reproduced in its entirety on page 128/129 of the book mentioned by the sycophant, the German and French references to the collection are given with dates and the name of the translator, and then the poem is discussed in detail over nearly ten pages! To all appearances, Marty has not read *The Century* either. Spit first, read later. Or not at all.

4c

Badiou, Marty tells us, cites Saint Paul's universalistic statement 'there is neither Jew, nor Greek', but 'what Badiou omits to say . . . is that this universal is made possible only in and through the sacrifice of Christ, the event of the sacrifice'. One pinches oneself to make sure one's not asleep, that one's read correctly. Pardon? What? The author wrote a book – i.e. my *Saint Paul: the Foundation of Universalism* – wholly devoted to analysing the sense, for Paul, of the Christ-event, but 'omits' to speak about this event? There is more stupefying stuff yet to come. Roused by the profundity of his sentences, the sycophant teaches Badiou, as proof of his philosophical baseness, that Paul is proud of his Judaism. But of course! Badiou devotes to this point a whole chapter of the very book, i.e., *Circonstances 3*, that Marty wants to pulverize! More, the sycophant uses exactly the same quotes of Paul against Badiou that Badiou uses to establish that Paul still operates under the predicate 'Jew'. Badiou indeed presents Paul, and I quote him, as 'A Jew among Jews, and proud of it'! Marty then uses the Abrahamic affiliation of Paul's thought against Badiou. But in *Circonstances 3*, Badiou writes this: 'Abraham thereby anticipates what could be called a universalism of the Jewish site; in other words, he anticipates Paul'! Not only has Marty not read *Saint Paul*, but he has taken no notice of the fragment of it included in *Circonstances 3*. Since he likes reality, let's propose an empirical theorem that is a little more empirical, a little more verifiable than the fireside conversations between God and Jacob, or stories about Noah boarding all the animals in Creation into his Ark. The theorem can be formulated as follows: intellectual denouncers of the extreme right are often recruited from among incompetent and lazy academics.

4d

Similar to his denunciation declaring that Badiou's 'delirium', his 'madness', the core of his manic-depressive psychosis, consists in a relentless negation and diabolical elimination of all mention of the name 'Jew', the sycophant must convince the dazzled reader that, all of a sudden, under the pressure of these times in which the Jewish question 'insists, remains, knocks at the door', the prudent Badiou, who had remained silent on this point until recently ('Badiou had put the "Jewish question" aside, something for which one could, in some sense, thank him', says the crafty Marty, the insinuator, the demagogue), has finally revealed his dreadful symptom. This Badiou has suddenly come out with it! He has finally written the book of his shameful secret, which is that, day and night, he only dreams of negating the Jew. Unfortunately, *Circonstances 3* very concretely states a propos of the 'signifier' that Marty adores – contrary to the 'ordinary philosopher', i.e. Badiou, who is 'insensitive to the signifier' – that Badiou has not ceased offering his thoughts about the uses and effects of the word 'Jew'. Indeed, *Circonstances 3* is basically a collection of philosophical, political and literary texts, written and published over the last twenty years. Introductory passages to each text clearly indicate their dates and contexts. A propos of the text that the denouncers – whether Frédéric Nef in *Le Monde*[32] or Eric Marty in, alas, *Les Temps Modernes* – have most frequently cited, I clearly state that it dates from June 1982. Some twenty-three years before the publication of *Circonstances 3* . . . And as for the most discussed fragment – the text that has given rise to the most dirty-trade, out-of-context quoting, and misleading imputations – I clearly state that it is excerpted from my book *Ethics*, which had been published twelve years before in 1993, has since been constantly re-edited, and translated into fourteen languages, including Hebrew. And so forth. The sycophant does not once mention these dates and facts. The signifier? Only if it can be of use in the trial. Reality? Only if it has some chance to harm Badiou.

4e

Spitting on everything he possibly can, the sycophant naturally attacks the Organisation Politique. I've already said that *Circonstances 3* is not in any way a document of this organization. But, ultimately, I am one of its founding militants, and I believe I am capable of defending before anyone the claim that it is the only organization that today proposes an idea and a practice of politics that breaks with the asphyxiating consensus in which our country vegetates. Marty, who is never far away when the opportunity is presented to let fly with vulgar commonplaces, makes ironic remarks about the OP's size and audience, and I gladly leave to him his cult of everything that is big, fat, well established, and rigorously polled. But he deems it necessary to finish off this section of his police report with an allusion to Natacha Michel's most recent novel, *Circulaire à toute ma vie humaine* (Le Seuil, 2005), writing that this book 'traces the portrait of the least sinister of the petty gang [read: of the OP]'.

The trickery is outrageous, and we, Natacha Michel and myself, would laugh ourselves to scorn were the question not, at bottom, so serious. For Natacha Michel is actually one of the founders of the Organisation Politique, at the same time as being one of the greatest novelists of the last thirty years. To utilize the force of her prose against the force of her political commitment is rather a violent ploy. Anyone who has only skimmed through her very beautiful and very humorous novel, whether or not he or she knows anything about the history of French intellectuals, straight-away sees that her subject concerns the 'petty gang' of renegades; in other words, those who do business in complete abandon of emancipatory and revolutionary politics. When it comes to them-selves, these people thump their chests about having been into Maoism before they started receiving a retainer for their repen-tance. But when it comes to some unfortunate others, who might also be mad, and who recall a few principles, they hunt them down. Natacha Michel paints of these renegades – who constitute the matrix of the faction that we've been discussing, and who are all the more intensely real in being fictional – a rich portrait. Never again read Eric Marty, but always read Natacha Michel; that's the advice of the day.

With respect to the faction of real renegades – whether they consider themselves Jews or not is totally unimportant, what they are intensely concerned with is that nothing might come to recall their distressing militant past – 'Jew' has very often become a central protective signifier, and Israel the state of reference, for the base reasons that I mentioned in my book. One of this 'petty gang's' notorious regents was Benny Lévy.[33] And it is the petty gang, need I say more, of which Marty the sycophant in person is a spiritual member! In trying to have it believed, and in banking on ignorance to do so – for critics have more or less submitted *Circulaire à toute ma vie humaine* to that 'democratic' form of censorship that is silence – that the literary portrait of him and his kind is instead the portrait of those he wants to proscribe, Marty pushes his scorn of reading and readers, his hatred of precise signification, to quite revolting extremes.

5

In philosophy, Marty is simply worthless. Everything he says about my conceptions of what is a situation, an event, an encyclopaedic predicate, a name, a process of truth, a consequence, a decision, a subjective immortality, comprises a woolly and incoherent mass. In making his blanket denunciation, he fishes here and there for some fragments of sentences, some discordant words, and performs some operetta interpretations. I have given some evidence to show that Marty is neither attentive to 'reality', nor to the 'signifier', i.e., the one he so prides himself on tenderly protecting from the 'ordinary melancholic philosopher'. But with respect to the concept our Marty is neither ordinary nor extraordinary. He is equal to zero. He doesn't know anything; he doesn't read. He blindly pecks. He holds up police files, and everyone knows that these files are idiotic. Hence, often, very often, as I've already demonstrated, he thinks he must, by banging his fists on the table to dissimulate his ignorance, arrogantly contradict me with what he has discovered, but completely misunderstood, in my own works. In one of the

funniest passages, he administers to me a lesson on the distinction
between 'individual' and 'subject', a distinction which, he has
discovered (the night before?), 'is well known', lies 'at the heart of
the Jewish and Christian traditions', and 'runs throughout philosophy'. My word! With Professor Marty, I shall pass my baccalauréat.[34] In my text, which the sycophant incriminates, and which
in his opinion recalls the lessons learnt in that severe final-year
exam, the distinction between the individual ('the human animal',
as I call it) and the subject-of-truth is re-elaborated in such new and
such radical terms that the sycophant misses everything. It is even
as regards this re-elaboration that, among other examples (the
serial revolution in music, the amorous declaration, the founding
of modern algebra . . .), the status of the word 'Jew' is convoked.
Here Marty really loses what remains of any grip he may have had.
But in the end it is not so easy to understand a new philosophy.
One must read and continue to read, which has never been to the
taste of sycophants. After all *'ces choses là sont rudes / Il faut pour les
comprendre avoir fait des études'* [things like that are really tough / To
understand them one must have learned one's stuff]. Study, Marty.
Study my books. Start with *Circonstances 3*. It is a very clear and
persuasive book. Philosophy is addressed to everyone, really it is, it
is. Even to denouncers. They are the least capable of all, that's for
sure, so the hope of making oneself understood is very slim. But
philosophy, at least in my school, knows nothing of despair.

6

On the basics, may we, Cécile Winter and I, be read, slowly,
carefully. If we are read, then, whether or not one is in agreement
with us, one will be unable to go down the same path as the
Frédéric Nefs and the Eric Martys in their feigned fury, in their
aggressive stupidity. The question is too serious to leave to public
denouncers. Who and what are they protecting? I sketched my

response to this question at the beginning of the book. But in any case, since the heart of the indictment lies in making me say that I identify the word 'Jew' with the predicate used by the Nazis, or with the 'youpin' ('Yid') used by the Pétainist anti-Semites, I shall cut straight to the most obvious point regarding my position here. Leaving the sycophant aside for a moment, of whom I tire quickly, I have included below the response I sent to a letter from the psychoanalyst Jean-Jacques Moscovitz, who, trying to plumb my childhood (it's his job . . .), wonders why I have identified the word 'Jew' with its Nazi designation. Here is how I responded to him:

> Come on! You make yourself out to be more stupid than you are. It is not I who identify the word 'Jew' today with the word 'Jew' as it was used by the Nazis during the Occupation. That is indeed exactly what I am taking a stand against! As is Cécile Winter. Such an imputation is an almost perfect example of what I wrote in the letter I sent to the newspaper *Le Monde* after Nef's article: it is the turning of an antithesis into a thesis. For in public polemics today the word 'Jew' is immediately correlated – that is, not for me by any means, but for all those who want to raise it up *as an exception* – to what is called the Shoah. It is by way of the extermination, and by way of it alone, that these ill-advised defenders hope to put the word, and with it everything that lays claim to it, including especially the State that absurdly proclaims itself to be 'Jewish', beyond all evaluation. And, tell me, once one dispenses, as Nef does, with the possibility that there can be a universal dimension to this word, something I absolutely maintain (for 'Jew' as for all other predicates; yes, predicate, what else?), then on what basis could it be granted any sort of privilege? On the myth of the Alliance? On the policies – which are neither more nor less cynical and particu-larist than those of any other States – practised in Israel? On the infinitely divisible history of disparate communities? I laughed hard seeing that poor Nef, playing the baffled logician, taking

offence to the fact that, with respect to those who've called themselves 'Jews', I valorize their contribution to universal history, and hence to all peoples. It is this same aspect that I valorize in any community: since this is how a community's particular destiny, the creations it has made possible, communicates with the universal interest. And if not that, then what must we praise? Particularity as such? One particularity rather than another? Who doesn't see that this was precisely the path that all forms nationalism and racialism had to take? That this path's only substance is endless war is attested to by the facts, today as yesterday. I've said it before and I'll say it again: the word 'Arab', the word 'Palestinian', do not have, in this respect, any differential value.

In short: what is at stake – and this is the only voice calling us, the only way forward for peace – is to reduce all communitarian predicates to equality, whatever their historical, social, cultural, religious, etc., content may be. I am led to think that it is this equality that offends you as it does Nef. On this point examine, since such is your method, the depths of your own childhood . . . Personally, I have always been especially severe on all the inegalitarian characteristics that mark the uses of the signifier 'French' in contemporary polemics, especially when it comes to the so-called 'republican' camp. For one must start by putting one's own house in order.

Every national and/or racial claim makes a great case out of origins, of founding texts, of immemorial laws, etc. You need no instructing: 'My dear Badiou, go and look at the Hebraic texts!' No. Absolutely not. We are talking about here and now, about public opinion, about the political circulation of words. I will not refer the anti-immigrant uses of the word 'French' to Vercingetorix, nor the 'victimary' predication surrounding the extermination of the Jews of Europe to the destruction of the Temple by Titus, nor German nationalism to the Nibelungen. We have means to judge without having recourse to such genealogical

resources. That is what Cécile Winter and I have done, and
what, until now, the 'critics' have in no way found fault with. At
most they have made distortions and uttered insults.

7

More generally, the question is to know if we ought to let the
stylistics of the sycophant become an established norm of public
discussion in philosophy. This stylistics consists in diagnosing, in
whomever is being set up for public condemnation, a symptom
that is as repugnant as possible. The sycophant prepares the terrain
by reducing the supposedly great individual to the nudity of his or
her psychological misery. Intimate portraits and psychiatric diagnoses are all we get. For, in any case, the basic matter of his targets
of accusation, the sycophant does not read, or, if he reads, he
doesn't understand.

7a

Let's look at Marty at work in relation to me. He works progres-
sively, upping the dose of venom a bit at a time. Here is the first
sequence of the construction:

I am 'a philosopher in the most banal sense of the term, that is to
say, insensitive to the irony of his own propositions' (p. 26). This
'insensitivity' will take its course. Insensitive to the signifier –
Insensitive to the pain of others – Insensitive to everything.

I have a 'propensity to be satisfied with the most banal register of
discourse there is, that of generalities and of opinion' (p. 29). This
remark makes it possible to treat me as much as a paradoxical
madman as a banal lowlife. A good sycophant has all the irons in
the fire.

That the historical referent is for me 'a pure myth, is reiterated in an incantatory manner from text to text; it is an obscure bloc to which [Badiou] swears eternal fidelity, like a believer' (ibid). A mythologist and a theologian. Not one of the good theology, i.e., that of God's conversations with his elected people or with Jonah in the whale's belly. But one of a 'natural' theology: one deprived of all gods, one that says that a human being, by incorporating him- or herself into a truth-procedure, is capable of something he or she believed him- or herself to be incapable of, and that such is, at the same time, his or her experience of immortality. Madness that natural 'theology'! Marty is only capable of those things he is capable of. That is why he can do so little.

I produce 'a hallucinatory leitmotiv effect in philosophical discourse' (ibid). This is a very important 'hallucination'. To be scrutinized.

I 'put in my adversaries' mouths the realization of [my] own and obscure designs' (p. 32). What does that Badiou bloke want? He's fishy.

7b

The sycophant has put in place, underhandedly, the essential terms: banality, baseness, obscurity of intention, hallucination. In the second sequence he can get on with more explicit insults and more degrading associations.

My thesis (which is that of the adversaries that I designated, as mentioned above, but nothing stops the zeal of the sycophant) is 'literally mad' (p. 33). Psychiatry rears its head.

I am (for Cécile Winter, treated by the sycophant in a properly abject fashion. She will certainly tell it to him straight) the 'Doctor Mabuse who serves her as a master' (p. 35). That makes me the head of worldwide swindling operations.

I am also 'her Tartuffe' (p. 36). Why not? The love that binds us to eternal beauties/Does not stifle in us love of temporal ones.

I speak 'with the pomp of a Gallican priest' (p. 42). That's no easy matter for a Mabuse–Tartuffe.

I speak also 'with the stupid good faith of the son of a freemason institutor' (p. 43). Many thanks to my father and grandfather.

I am a *goujat* [a boor], but 'don't forget that, according to the *Littré*, the etymology of the word "*goujat*" is "goy"'' (p. 47). Well found! And what refinement!

7c

Everything is in place for the finale, the one that will turn me into the inevitable client of private clinics:

My *jouissance* is unbalanced, Marty knows it, and Marty declares it (!):

> [Badiou's] *jouissance* without doubt operates in the tiny interval where the fault falls back onto the partner, where the shame is the other's shame, where the crime becomes the responsibility of the accomplice or of the victim. His enjoyment can never be satisfied; it necessitates an acolyte just as much as it necessitates that the subaltern wear the stain. (p. 49)

What? We've seen this before, haven't we? One can picture Marty, his eye peeping through the keyhole with his behind up in the air! And if he can't see anything, he makes it up. All the same he didn't sneak by the door for nothing.

My *jouissance* is 'a *jouissance* that is insatiable; it is maniacal' (ibid). Mania, that's all there is to these philosophers. After Althusser, often bitten by the yapping sycophant, there is but one slogan: they are all a bunch of maniacs!

I am a 'manic-depressive type' (p. 50). That's it. It's been said. The question is settled.

And I am like Nero, 'that most pitiless of melancholics' (ibid). In

my maxim *Mieux vaut un désastre qu'un désêtre*[35] (a maxim that in my
eyes is evident, minimal), Nero 'has made a return'. (p. 52). So, is
Nero the dialectical synthesis of Mabuse, Tartuffe, a Gallican
priest, and a freemason institutor? Interesting. I'll have to look into
that one more closely.

Nevertheless, psychosis does not suffice. I combine the 'perverse'
(p. 55) with 'logical delirium' (ibid). Psychosis and perversion, and
now we're done with.

8

In sum, and this is the conclusion, I am a 'criminal philosopher'.
Marty's thinking, like that of Frédéric Nef and Roger Pol Droit,[36]
all of whom speak of 'madness', obviously comes down to this: let
the men in white coats take me away. Anybody wanting to retain
a monopoly on a word will unfailingly designate those who define
and use it differently as mad. It seems to me, however, that there
is a Jewish joke which states that there are as many definitions of
Jew as there are Jews. That must have been before our despotic
doctors. No doubt they're all mad, those disparate Jews, those
entirely singular Jews, those Jews for whom the predicate is at
once beyond question and absolutely adrift. Yes, mad, and above
all, those Jews who want the universality of what they create to
exceed the particularity that they also lay claim to, or do not;
those Jews, in sum, for whom the triplet SIT is a fatal attack on
their liberty. So, in opposition to the petty faction, and as in their
despotic eyes I am a mad philosopher, I shall boldly claim: I am
one of those Jews. In this affair, since everything that exists in the
world, and especially names, are only thinkable in situation, then
le juif, c'est moi.

Notes to Part Two

1 This bomb exploded in Paris on October 3 1980, outside the synagogue in rue Copernic, killing four people. *Translator's note.*

2 This collection was published in French as *Circonstances 3: Portées du mot 'juif'*. Éditions Leo Schéer, 2005.

3 Jules Guesde (1845–1922) co-founded the Parti Ouvrier Français with Paul Lafargue in 1882. After a succession of mergers with other socialist groups, it came to form part of the French section of the Second International. Known as having an intransigent, anti-reformist attitude, Jules Guesde had always refused participation with bourgeois governments. In 1914, however, he did an about-face, siding with the national unity government in which he became a Minister without Portfolio. *Translator's note.*

4 Natacha Michel, philosopher, novelist, and playwright, is also a co-founder of the Organisation Politique. *Translator's note.*

5 Alain Badiou, *Ethics: An Essay on the Understanding of Evil*, translated and introduced by Peter Hallward. Verso, 2001.

6 Victor Farias, *Heidegger and Nazism*, Temple UP, 1989 [1985]. In this (fairly anecdotal) book, we see how Heidegger fell prey, for a whole stretch of time, to a simulacrum. He thought he was upholding the event of his own thought.

7 Badiou does not *always* use the term 'réel' in a strict Lacanian sense. *Translator's note.*

8 Alain Badiou. *Saint Paul: The Foundation of Universalism*. Translated by Ray Brassier. Stanford: Stanford UP, 2003.

9 Cécile Winter's argument is illustrated in the text by her discriminating use of upper and lower case for the word 'Jew'/'jew'. Although this is more awkward to do in English than in French, I have decided to follow suit, the reason for which will become clear below. *Translator's note.*

10 The more ink the Nuremberg text and its aftermath have caused to flow, the less the right of the American military to institute themselves as

judges is commented upon today. At the time, certainly, there was some discussion and protest. Half a century later, in the context of the philosophy of human rights, the idea of a tribunal which judges 'crimes' and which is basically ruled by the great powers has re-emerged in a markedly less critical fashion. Perhaps being the only ones to have used the atomic bomb is what confers on them an incontestable moral superiority, and it is true that to this day the American Army remains the only one to have done so.

11 This question is distinct from that of the processing of direct collaboration in the occupied countries.

12 *L'Insurrection du ghetto de Varsovie*, edited by Michel Borwicz, 26 Archives Collection, Julliard, 1967.

13 J. Karski, *Story of a Secret State*, Simon Publications, 2001.

14 See, for example, Tom Segev's book *The Seventh Million: the Israelis and the Holocaust*, trans. Haim Watzman, Owl Books, 2000, pp. 74–75: 'Toward the end of November 1942, the Jewish Agency executive made an official statement asserting that the murders were being carried out in accordance with a master plan to exterminate European Jewry and that a special state apparatus had been established for that purpose. "Multitudes of children up to twelve years of age have been killed with no mercy, and the elderly have been killed as well", the Agency stated, adding that masses of people were also sent off to unknown destinations and all trace of them was lost.

'The statement emerged from a routine meeting. David Ben-Gurion was not present; Moshe Sharett surveyed diplomatic developments and left. The second item on the agenda was "the situation of the Jews in Europe". Three weeks previously, several dozen members of the yishuv had returned from Poland, where they had travelled on business or family visits. They had not been able to get out before the German invasion of September 1939 and had been trapped in the ghettos. Their return was made possible by a deal worked out between Britain and Germany: in exchange for them, Britain released German citizens it held on its territory. Upon arrival in Palestine, they were questioned, and the information they provided indicated that the Nazis were murdering Jews systematically. Among other things, they reported that a locomotive engineer back from the Russian border had told them that Jews were being herded into special buildings, where they were being murdered with poison gas. In a small village called Oswiecim (the Germans called it Auschwitz), there were three furnaces in which Jews were burned, the engineer reported, and another two under construction.

'This testimony confirmed a secret report that the Jewish Agency had received some weeks before. A spy named Eduard Schulte, a German industrialist opposed to the Nazi regime, had told Gerhardt Riegner, representative of the World Jewish Congress in Switzerland, that the Nazis had drawn up a plan to exterminate every Jew in Europe – the "Final Solution". When the information brought by the returnees was reported at the meeting, the members of the Jewish Agency executive were unsure what to do. "Perhaps we should issue a statement on the situation this time", one of them proposed. They decided to establish a committee. Then they talked a bit about the Agency's next budget, and went on to consider the next item on the agenda – a labour dispute at the Assis cannery. On receiving the same information, Rabbi Stephen Wise, president of the World Jewish Congress, immediately announced a press conference. The Jewish Agency's statement was made forty-eight hours before his conference: [footnote p. 95] The Third Reich's "most closely guarded secret" leaked out almost immediately, apparently from Hitler's own staff. The Jewish Agency did not reveal its source. Wise received permission to claim the U.S. State Department as his source. He said that the Nazis were planning to destroy the European Jewry as a whole and that they had begun carrying out their program. His statement was published, and it prompted a few comments from President Franklin Roosevelt and Prime Minister Winston Churchill. But nothing further happened: the extermination of the Jews continued according to plan.'

15 This does not mean they neglected the other benefits. Hence Tom Segev writes (p. 104): 'It is uncertain who was the first to suggest that the Germans would have to pay reparations for the property they had expropriated from the Jews and for the suffering they had caused. The idea seems to have been in the air from the time the war started, apparently sparked by the punitive reparations imposed on Germany at the end of World War I. Ben-Gurion received a memorandum on the subject as early as 1940. Berl Katznelson spoke of it publicly toward the end of that year. By December 1942, there was already a private organisation in Tel Aviv called Justicia that offered to help Nazi victims draft compensation demands.'

16 The book refers to the document: Shenhabi's proposal (September 10 1942) in the Hashomer Hatsaïr – Kibbutz Haartsi Archives (Shenhabi personal archive), VI 1 (4); Shenhabi Plan (May 2 1945) in CZA, S/26 1326, as well as the AYV ('The Old Yad Vashem'), YV/9–YV/10. (cf. *The Seventh Million*, note 29, p. 536).

17 As Heimito von Doderer said about one of his heroines in *The Demons*, 'She knew how to inherit!' And as Kierkegaard said in his *The Sickness Unto Death*, 'to commit a sin is one thing, but to keep doing it is another sin'.

18 *Kedma*, Amos Gitaï's very beautiful film, magnificently shows how at the

beginning there was a lack of rapport between two peoples who, the less they knew about each other, the more ferociously they killed each other; i.e. the ferocity increased the less they had in common geographically or historically, the less their motivations and destinations – those of the surviving Jews fleeing Europe and of the Palestinians fleeing the Jews across the fields of their own country – had strictly any reason to intersect. What threw them together pell-mell in fury was the arbitrariness of a plot, one that the authors – a laughable British regiment shown at the beginning of the film in a manœuvre in fog – can perfectly easily extricate themselves from afterwards: plunged into chaos, the savages, like Lilliputians that the negligent hand of the giant has discarded here and there among the disparate fragments left of their worlds that he has uprooted along the way, have nothing left and so kill each other for the remains like the savages that they are. This is something like a paradigmatic allegory of modern civil wars. When the imperialist ogre has finished helping himself, he can depart, leaving the dregs of the earth pitted against one another, and then deplore the propensity of the miserable to rip out each other's throats.

19 Whence the right of humanitarian intervention! The reader will easily reconstruct the ideological trajectory of today's perfect Gauleiter candidates.

20 What became of the much more undeserved association 'CRS-SS' from May 1968? Nobody has made any complaints. Besides, what against? And we haven't heard that Milosevic is permitted to make any complaints – why not? – before the International Criminal Court for having been assimilated to Hitler. Saddam Hussein hasn't either. Which just shows that transcendental signifiers have owners who reserve the right to use them.

21 M. Warschawski, *Towards an Open Tomb: The Crisis of Israeli Society*, trans. Peter Drucker, Monthly Review Press, 2004.

22 'By presenting the colonial war from August 2000 on as a life-and-death struggle for Israel's survival, Ehud Barak conjured up the demons that haunt the collective memory of the Israeli people. It began with an editorial by journalist Ari Shavit in the daily *Haaretz*, about the first stones that young Palestinians threw in response to Arial Sharon's provocative visit to the Al-Aqsa mosque. Shavit, one of many intellectuals on the Israeli left who renounced all their beliefs about peace within a few weeks, wrote that the problem is not the Israeli–Palestinian conflict and the occupation after all, as he had wrongly believed for too many years. The problem (Shavit wrote) is rather what he called the "Jewish fate": eternal war for survival in a world that has always rejected the existence of Jews and will continue to do so for all eternity. This line of

argument, passed from one media outlet to the next and adopted by the majority of Israeli intellectuals, is rooted in a profound existential angst in post-Auschwitz Jewish consciousness. But the fallacious way that history is taught in Israeli schools lends it credibility. Israeli schools reduce two thousand years of Jewish history to one vast pogrom and a timeless, irrational, and unique anti-Semitism, thus making any attempt at understanding and any effort to fight anti-Semitism futile.

'For the grandchildren of the victims of the Nazi genocide, any existential threat, real or imaginary, is associated with Auschwitz and Treblinka. The Palestinians are Nazis; Arafat equals Hitler; an ambush where soldiers are killed is a massacre; and a bomb in Tel Aviv is Kristallnacht. With associations like these, any possibility of negotiation or compromise evaporates. Nazism in its Palestinian form must be eradicated, and any means are legitimate.

'Yet Israelis do recognize on some level that the equation between Palestinians and Nazis is fallacious. Israel's military power and crushing advantage over the Palestinians make it a bit difficult for Israelis to identify with the wretched Jews of Warsaw and Vilna, or even with the Warsaw Ghetto fighters or the Jewish partisan units in the Belarusian forests. The result is a horrible, perverse mental gymnastic. The continual references to the genocide of the European Jews and the omnipresence of those terrible images lead to a situation where, since the reality of the relationship of forces prevents Israelis from mimicking the behaviour of the Jewish victims, they adopt, in general unconsciously, the behaviour of those who slaughtered the Jewish people. They tattoo Palestinians' arms, make them run naked, confine them behind barbed wire and prison camp watchtowers, and even briefly used German shepherds to control them.

'The house-to-house sweeps in the Deheisheh camp could not help evoking another historical period, even though of course the Palestinians picked up in the raids were not being sent to their deaths but rather to unlimited detention in horrible conditions. The Offer detention camp is not an extermination camp; but it closely resembles the German concentration camps of the 1930s, with its barbed wire, watchtowers, and masses of frightened prisoners deprived of rights and confined in truly inhuman conditions. How can one help seeing that a row of Palestinian civilians with their hands in the air filing past a guard of armed soldiers is a reproduction of the haunting image of Warsaw's Jews on their way to the Umschlagplatz? How could one not be reminded of that same Umschlagplatz when the television broadcasts images of hundreds of men in Jenin, sitting on the ground, their hands tied behind their backs, some of them blindfolded?

'The vocabulary is also a Nazi vocabulary. Consider the article that

Rabbi Israel Rosin wrote for *Haaretz*, in which he said that the families of suicide bombers must be taken hostage and deported to Gaza, and then their houses must be levelled and their villages razed. The journalist B. Michael cited statements identical to Rabbi Rosen's by Nazi officers after the Lidice and Oradur massacres, ending his article: "And if there are people out there who insist on concluding from what they've just read that I'm comparing the Israeli army to the German army – God forbid – then they're making life too easy for themselves. It's the man who proposed [this] to the Israeli army that came up with the equation'. Warschawski, pp. 42–44.

23 B. Michael, 'From the Marked to the Markers', *Yediot Aharonot*, March 15 2002.

24 Cited by Amir Oren, *Haaretz*, January 25 2001.

25 This is the famous story about Goering's response to Fritz Lang. Goering summons Fritz Lang and asks him to stay in Germany. He offers him luxurious conditions. Fritz Lang points out that he is Jewish. 'We', Goering responds, 'are the ones who decide who is Jewish and who isn't.'

26 Cf. http://www.monde-diplomatique.fr/2001/08/HALIMI/15515.

27 'Conversation in the Mountains', in *Paul Celan: Selections*, edited and with an introduction by Pierre Joris, University of California Press, 2005, p. 149.

28 This article was written in response to a rather violent article on Badiou by Eric Marty called 'Alain Badiou: the Future of a Negation (a propos of *Circonstances 3*)', which appeared in Nos 635–636 of *Les Temps Modernes* (Dec. 2005/Jan. 2006). *Translator's note.*

29 Badiou is of course alluding to Arthur Rimbaud's poem 'Adieu' from his *A Season in Hell*. *Translator's note.*

30 Cf. note 24 of Part One.

31 The movement of 1995 was a response to government plans to introduce a series of measures designed to bring France in line with international finance and move it towards an American-style system of pensions. In reaction to this popular movement, the editors of the journal *Esprit* published a petition in *Le Monde* (December 9 1995) supporting the government's 'audacious' plans and condemning the 'corporatist interests' of the workers. Over one hundred intellectuals signed the petition, among whom were all the usual 'court and screen' intellectuals (the phrase is Kristin Ross's), notably Bernard Henry-Lévy, Alain Finkielkraut, Jacques Julliard and André Glucksmann. *Translator's note.*

32 Cf. Frédéric Nef, 'Le "nom des juifs" selon Badiou', in *Le Monde des livres*, December 23 2005. *Translator's note.*

33 Benny Lévy, a long-time secretary of Jean-Paul Sartre, and one-time leader of the Gauche prolétarienne, encountered the philosophy of

Lévinas in the late 1970s, and a few years later became a fervent Talmudist. *Translator's note.*

34 The *baccalauréat* is an examination sat in the final year of the *lycée* (*la terminale*), so usually at age 17 or 18. *Translator's note.*

35 This phrase translates awkwardly into English, but might be rendered as 'better a disaster than a lack of being'. *Translator's note.*

36 Cf. Roger Pol Droit, 'L'universel, avantages et impasses: *CIRCON-STANCES 3 Portées du mot "juif"* d'Alain Badiou', in *Le Monde des Livres*, November 25 2005. See also the response to these attacks on Badiou by Daniel Bensaïd, 'Alain Badiou et les inquisiteurs', *Le Monde des Livres*, January 26 2006. It is also available online at http://multitudes.samiz-dat.net/. *Translator's note.*

Part Three
Historicity of Politics:
Lessons of Two Revolutions

The Paris Commune:
A Political Declaration on Politics[1]

The political parties, groups, unions and factions that have claimed to be representative of the workers and the people long maintained a formal fidelity to the Paris Commune. They adhered to Marx's concluding statement in his admirable text *The Civil War in France*: 'Working men's Paris, with its Commune, will be forever celebrated as the glorious harbinger of a new society.'

They regularly visited the Mur des fédérés, the monument evoking the twenty-thousand shot dead May 1871. Marx again: 'Its martyrs are enshrined in the great heart of the working class.'

Does the working class have a heart? Today, in any case, little is remembered, and badly so. The Paris Commune was recently removed from [French] history syllabuses, in which, however, it had barely occupied a place. The public ranks are swollen with the direct descendants of the *Versaillais*, those for whom communism is a criminal utopia, the worker an outdated Marxist invention, the revolution a bloody orgy, and the idea of a non-parliamentary politics a despotic sacrilege.

As usual, however, the problem is not one of memory but of truth. How are we to concentrate the political truth of the Commune today? Without neglecting textual and factual supports, what is at stake here is to reconstitute, by means that will be largely philosophical, this episode of our history in its irreducibility.

Of course, when I say 'our' history, it has to do with the 'we' of a politics of emancipation, the 'we' whose virtual flag remains red, and not the tri-coloured one flown by the killers of the spring of 1871.

Reference points, 1 – the facts

I shall begin with a selection of dated examples. This will form the first part, after which I shall reorder the account according to new categories (situation, appearing [*apparaître*],[2] site, singularities, event, inexistent aspect [*inexistent*] . . .).

In the very middle of the nineteenth century, in France, Napoleon III is in power. He typifies the racketeering and authoritarian balance-sheet of the Republican Revolution of February 1848. This kind of outcome had been practically guaranteed only a few months after the insurrection that brought down Louis-Philippe in June 1848, when the republican petite bourgeoisie consented to, and even supported, the massacring of Parisian workers by Cavaignac's troops. Just as, in 1919, the German social-democratic petite bourgeoisie were to set up the distant possibility of a Nazi hypothesis by organizing the massacre of the Rosa Luxemburg-led Spartacists.

On July 19 1870, the French government, too self-confident and victim to Bismarck's devious manoeuvres, declares war on Prussia. On September 2, the disaster at Sedan occurs and the Emperor is captured.[3] This danger leads to a partial arming of the Parisian population in the form of a National Guard, the internal framework of which is constituted by workers. But the internal situation is in fact determinant: on September 4, after large demonstrations, the Hôtel-de-Ville is stormed and the empire overthrown. But as was the case in 1830 and 1848, power is at once monopolized behind the scenes by a group of 'Republican' politicians, i.e., the Jules Favres, Simon and Ferry ('the Republic of the Juleses' as Henri Guillemin will say), Emile Picard and Adolphe Thiers, all of whom wish for only one thing: to negotiate with Bismarck in a bid to contain the working-class political insurgency. But they must put people off the scent, so in order to subdue the resolve of the Parisian population they immediately proclaim a Republic, although they fail to specify any constitutional content; and in order to circumvent patriotic sentiment they call themselves 'the Government of National Defence'. Under these conditions the masses leave them to get on with it, and instead join in the resistance, which the long siege on Paris by the Prussians will exacerbate.

In October, in shameful conditions, Bazaine surrenders at Metz with the principal group of French troops. Then, all sorts of little government schemes, recounted in minute detail in the great books Henri Guillemin dedicated to the 1870 war and the origins of the Commune, lead to the surrender of Paris and the armistice of January 28 1871. A majority of Parisians have long been in no doubt that this government is in reality a government of 'National Defection'.

But it is also a government of bourgeois defence against popular movements. Its problem is now to find a way to disarm the Parisian workers of the National Guard. There were at least three reasons why the politicians in power were able to think the situation to their advantage. First, they had managed with great haste to get an Assembly elected that was dominated by rural and provincial reaction, indeed, a sort of *chambre introuvable* of the extreme right that was *legitimist*[4] and socially vengeful. Against revolution nothing beats an election: it is this same maxim that De Gaulle, Pompidou and their allies on the official left will revive in June 1968. Second, the principal and foremost recognized revolutionary leader, Blanqui, is in prison. Third, the clauses of the armistice leave Paris immured by Prussian troops from the North and the East.

Early on the morning of March 18, some military detachments try to seize the cannons held by the National Guard. The attempt comes up against an impressive, spontaneous mobilization in the workers' *quartiers* by the Parisian people, and notably by the Parisian women. The troops withdraw; the government flees to Versailles.

On March 19, the Central Committee of the National Guard, being the worker leadership that had been elected by the units of the Guard, makes a political declaration. This is a fundamental document to which I will return in detail.

On March 26, the new Parisian authorities organize the election of a Commune of 90 members.

On April 3, the Commune attempts a first military sortie to confront the troops that the government, with Prussian authorization, has redirected against Paris. The sortie fails. Those taken prisoner by the troops, including two highly respected members of the Commune, Flourens and Duval, are massacred. A sense of the ferocity of the repression to come fills the air.

On April 9, the Commune's best military leader, the Polish republican Dombrowski, has some success, notably in recapturing Asnières.

On April 16, supplementary elections for the Commune are held in an absolutely above-board manner and in the greatest calm.

Between May 9 and 14, the military situation worsens considerably in the south-west *suburbs*. The forts of Issy and Vanves fall.

All this while (between the end of March and the middle of May), the people of Paris pursue their lives inventively and peacefully. All kinds of social measures concerning work, education, women and the arts are debated and decided upon. For an idea of the prioritization of issues, note, for example, that on May 18 – the government army will enter Paris *en masse* on May 21 – a vote is held on the number of classes to create in primary schools.

In fact Paris is at once peaceful and extraordinarily politicized. Purely descriptive accounts by witnesses to the scene are rare: the non-militant intellectuals generally support Versailles, and most of them (Flaubert, Goncourt, Dumas fils, Leconte de Lisle, Georges Sand . . .) make base remarks. None of the intellectuals are more admirable than Rimbaud and Verlaine, declared partisans of the Commune, and Hugo, who, without understanding anything, will instinctively and nobly oppose the repression.

One chronicle is absolutely extraordinary. Its attribution to Villiers de l'Isle Adam is regularly contested and then reaffirmed. In any case, it makes intensely visible the combination of peace and political vivacity that the Commune had installed in the streets of Paris:

> One enters, one leaves, one circulates, one gathers. The laughter of Parisian children interrupts political discussions. Approach the groups, listen. A whole people entertain profound matters. For the first time workers can be heard exchanging their appreciations on things that hitherto only philosophers had tackled. There is no trace of supervisors; no police agents obstruct the street hindering passers-by. The security is perfect.
>
> Previously, when this same people went out intoxicated for its *bals de barrière*,[5] the bourgeoisie distanced itself, saying quietly: 'If these people were free, what would become of us? What would become of them? They are free and dance no longer. They are free and they work. They are free and they fight.'
>
> When a man of good faith passes close by them today, he understands that a new century has just hatched and even the most sceptical remains wondrous.

Between May 21 and May 28, the troops of Versailles take Paris barricade by barricade, the final combats taking place in the workers' redoubts of the north-east *arrondissements*: the 11th, the 19th, the 20th . . . The massacres succeed each other without interruption, continuing well after the 'blood-soaked week'. At least twenty thousand people are shot dead. Fifty thousand are arrested.

Thus commences the Third Republic, which is still held by some today to be the golden age of 'citizenship'.

Reference points, 2 – the classical interpretation

At this very time, Marx proposed an account of the Commune that is wholly inscribed in the question of the state. For him, it comprises the first historical case in which the proletariat assumes its transitory function of the direction, or administration, of the entire society. From the Commune's initiatives and impasses he is led to the conclusion that the state machine must not be 'taken' or 'occupied', but broken.

Let's note in passing that the chief fault of the analysis probably lies in the notion that between March and May 1871 it was the question of power that was the order of the day. Whence those tenacious 'critiques' that have become commonplaces: what the Commune supposedly lacked was decision-making capacity. *If* it had immediately marched on Versailles, *if* it had seized the gold of the Bank of France . . . To my mind, these 'ifs' lack real content. In truth, the Commune had neither the means to address them properly, nor in all likelihood the means to arrive at them.

Marx's account in fact is ambiguous. On the one hand, he praises everything that appears to lead to a dissolution of the state and, more specifically, of the nation-state. In this vein he notes: the Commune's abolition of a professional army in favour of directly arming the people; all the measures it took concerning the election and revocability of civil servants; the end it put to the separation of powers in favour of a decisive and executive function; and its internationalism (the financial delegate of the Commune was German, the military leaders Polish, etc.). But, on the other hand, he deplores incapacities that are actually statist incapacities [*in-capacités étatiques*]: its weak military centralization; its inability to define financial priorities; and, its shortcomings concerning the national question, its address to other cities, what it did and did not say about the war with Prussia, and its rallying of provincial masses.

It is striking to see that, twenty years later, in his 1891 preface to a new edition of Marx's text, Engels formalizes the Commune's contradictions in the same way. He shows, in effect, that the two dominant political forces of the 1871 movement, the Proudhonians and the Blanquists, ended up doing exactly the opposite of their manifest ideology. The Blanquists were partisans of centralization to excess and of armed plots in which a small number of resolute men would take power, to exercise it authoritatively to the advantage of the working masses. But instead they were led to proclaim a free federation of communes and the destruction of state bureaucracy. Proudhonians were hostile to any collective appropriation of the means of production and promoted small, self-managed enterprises. Yet they ended up supporting the formation of vast worker associations for the purpose of directing large-scale industry. Engels quite logically concludes from this that the Commune's weakness lay in the fact that its ideological forms were inappropriate for making decisions of state. And, moreover, that the result of this opposition is quite simply the end of Blanquism and of Proudhonism, making way for a single 'Marxism'.

But how would the current that Marx and Engels represented in 1871, and even much later, have been more adequate to the situation? With what extra means would its presumed hegemony have endowed the situation?

The fact of the matter is that the ambiguity of Marx's account will be carried [*sera levée*] both by the social-democratic disposition and by its Leninist radicalization, that is, in the fundamental motif of the party, for over a century.

In effect, the 'social-democratic' party, the party of the 'working class' – or the 'proletarian' party – and then later still the 'communist' party, is simultaneously free in relation to the state and ordained to the exercise of power.

It is a purely political organ that is constituted by subjective support – by ideological rupture – and as such is exterior to the state. With respect to domination, it is free; it bears the thematic of revolution or of the destruction of the bourgeois state.

But the party is also the organizer of a centralized, disciplined capacity that is entirely bent on taking state power. It bears the thematic of a new state, the state of the dictatorship of the proletariat.

It can be said, then, that the party *realizes* the ambiguity of the Marxist account of the Commune, gives it body. It becomes the political site of a fundamental tension between the non-state, even anti-state, character of a politics of emancipation, and the statist character of the victory and duration of that politics. Moreover, this is the case irrespective of whether the victory is insurrectional or electoral: the mental schema is the same.

This is why the party will engender (particularly from Stalin onwards) the figure of the party-state. The party-state is endowed with capacities designed to resolve problems the Commune left unresolved: a centralization of the police and of military defence; the complete destruction of bourgeois economic decisions; the rallying and submission of the peasants to workers' hegemony; the creation of a powerful international, etc.

It is not for nothing that, as legend has it, Lenin danced in the snow the day Bolshevik power reached and surpassed the 72 days in which the Paris Commune's entire destiny was brought to a close.

Yet, although it may have provided a solution to the statist problems that the Commune was unable to resolve, it remains to be asked whether in solving them the party-state did not suppress a number of *political* problems that, to its merit, the Commune had been able to discern.

What is in any case striking is that, retroactively thought through the party-state, the Commune is reducible to two parameters: first, to its *social* determination (workers); and second, to a heroic but defective exercise of *power*.

As a result the Commune gets emptied of all properly political content. It is certainly commemorated, celebrated and claimed, but only as a pure point for the articulation of the social nature of state power. But if that is all it consists in, then the Commune is *politically obsolete*. For it is rendered so by – what Sylvain Lazarus has proposed to call – the Stalinist political mode, for which the unique place of politics is the party.

That is why its *commemoration* also happens to proscribe its *reactivation*.

On this point there is an interesting story concerning Brecht. After the war, Brecht returns prudently to 'socialist' Germany, in which Soviet troops lay down the law. He sets out in the year of 1948 by stopping in Switzerland to get news of the situation from abroad. During his stay he writes, with the aid of Ruth Berlau, his lover at the time, a historical play called *The Days of the Commune*. This is a solidly documented work in which historical figures are combined with popular heroes. It is a play that is more lyrical and comical than epic; it is a good play, in my view, although rarely performed. Now, upon arriving in Germany, Brecht suggests staging *The Days of the Commune* to the authorities. Well, in the year 1949, the authorities in question declare such a performance inopportune! As socialism is in the process of being victoriously established in East Germany, there could be no reason to return to a difficult and outmoded episode of proletarian consciousness such as the Commune. Brecht, in sum, had not chosen the good calling-card. He had not understood that, since Stalin had defined Leninism – reduced to the cult of the party – as 'the Marxism of the epoch of victorious revolutions', returning to defeated revolutions was pointless.

That said, what is Brecht's interpretation of the Commune? In order to judge it, let's read the last three stanzas of the song in the play titled *Resolution of the Communards*:

Realizing that we won't persuade you
Into paying us a living wage
We resolve that we will take the factories from you
Realizing that your loss will be our gain

Realizing that we can't depend on
All the promises our rulers make
We've resolved for us the Good Life starts with freedom
Our future must be built by our dictate

Realizing that the roar of cannon
Are the only words that speak to you
We prove to you that we have learned our lesson
In future we will turn the guns on you[6]

Clearly, the general framework here remains that of the classical interpretation. The Commune is cast as a combination of the social and of power, of material satisfaction and of cannons.

Reference points, 3 – a Chinese reactivation

During the Cultural Revolution, and especially between 1966 and 1972, the Paris Commune is reactivated and very often mentioned by Chinese Maoists, as if, caught in the grip of the rigid hierarchy of the party-state, they sought new references outside of the Revolution of October 17 and official Leninism. Thus, in the Sixteen-Point Decision of August 1966, which is a text probably mostly written by Mao himself, a recommendation is given to seek inspiration in the Paris Commune, particularly as concerns the electing and recalling of the leaders of the new organizations emerging from the mass movements. After the overthrow of the municipality of Shanghai by revolutionary workers and students in January 1967, the new organ of power takes 'the Shanghai

Commune' as its name, pointing to the fact that some of the Maoists were trying to link up politically to questions of power and state in a mode other than that which had been canonized by the Stalinist form of the party.

Yet, these attempts are precarious. This can be witnessed in the fact that, as power had been 'seized' and it was imperative to install the new organs of that provincial and municipal power, the name 'Commune' is quickly abandoned, and replaced by the much more indistinct title of 'Revolutionary Committee'. This can also be witnessed in the centennial commemoration of the Commune in China in 1971. That this commemoration involved more than just commemorating, that it still contained the elements of a reactivation, is evident in the magnitude of the demonstrations. Millions of people march all throughout China. But little by little the revolutionary parenthesis is closed, which is evident in the official text published for the occasion, a text that some of us read at the time, and that a far fewer number of us have conserved and can reread (which has probably become very difficult for someone Chinese to do . . .). The text in question is: *Long Live the Victory of the Dictatorship of the Proletariat! In Commemoration of the Centenary of the Paris Commune.*[7]

It is totally ambivalent.

Significantly, it contains in the epigraph a formula written by Marx at the time of the Commune itself:

> If the Commune should be destroyed, the struggle would only be postponed. The principles of the Commune are eternal and indestructible; they will present themselves again and again until the working class is liberated.

This choice confirms that even in 1971 the Chinese consider that the Commune is not simply a glorious (but obsolete) episode of the history of worker insurrections but a historical exposition of principles that are to be reactivated. Hear, also, a statement echoing Marx's statement, possibly one of Mao's: 'If the Cultural

Revolution fails, its principles will remain no less the order of the day.' Which indicates once more that the Cultural Revolution extends a thread that is linked more to the Commune than to October 1917.

The Commune's relevance is likewise made evident by the content of its celebration, in which Chinese communists are opposed to Soviet leaders. For example:

At the time when the proletariat and the revolutionary people of the world are marking the grand centenary of the Paris Commune, the Soviet revisionist renegade clique is putting on an act, talking glibly about 'loyalty to the principles of the Commune' and making itself up as the successor to the Paris Commune. It has no sense of shame at all. What right have the Soviet revisionist renegades to talk about the Paris Commune?

It is within the framework of this ideological opposition between creative revolutionary Marxism and retrograde statism that the text situates both Mao's contribution and, singularly, the Cultural Revolution itself, in continuity with the Commune:

The salvoes of the Great Proletarian Cultural Revolution initiated and led by Chairman Mao himself have destroyed the bourgeois headquarters headed by that renegade, hidden traitor and scab Liu Shao-chi and exploded the imperialists' and modern revisionists' fond dream of restoring capitalism in China.

Chairman Mao has comprehensively summed up the positive and negative aspects of the historical experience of the dictatorship of the proletariat, inherited, defended and developed the Marxist–Leninist theory of the proletarian revolution and the dictatorship of the proletariat and solved, in theory and practice, the most important question of our time – the question of consolidating the dictatorship of the proletariat and preventing the restoration of capitalism.

The capital formula is 'consolidating the dictatorship of the proletariat'. To invoke the Paris Commune here is to understand that the dictatorship of the proletariat cannot be a simple statist formula, and that pursuing the march toward communism necessitates recourse to a revolutionary mobilization of the masses. In other words, just as the Parisian workers of March 18 1871 had done for the first time in history, it was considered necessary to invent within an ongoing revolutionary experience – always a somewhat precarious and unpredictable decision – new forms for a proletarian state. What is more, early on in the piece the Maoists had already declared the Cultural Revolution to be 'the finally discovered form of the dictatorship of the proletariat'.

Nevertheless, the general conception articulating politics and state remains unchanged. The attempted revolutionary reactivation of the Paris Commune remains inscribed in the anterior account and, in particular, is still dominated by the tutelary figure of the party. This is clearly shown in the passage on the Commune's shortcomings:

> The fundamental cause of the failure of the Paris Commune was that, owing to the historical conditions, Marxism had not yet achieved a dominant position in the workers' movement and a proletarian revolutionary Party with Marxism as its guiding thought had not yet come into being. [. . .] Historical experience shows that where a very favourable revolutionary situation and revolutionary enthusiasm on the part of the masses exist, it is still necessary to have a strong core of leadership of the proletariat, that is, 'a revolutionary party . . . built on the Marxist–Leninist revolutionary theory and in the Marxist–Leninist revolutionary style.'

Although the final citation about the Party is by Mao, it could have just as easily been by Stalin. This is why, in spite of its activism and its militancy, the Maoist vision of the Commune ultimately remained prisoner of the party-state framework and, hence, of what I have called the 'first account'.

At the end of this sketch of the classical interpretation, and of that which is in exception to it, we can say, then, that today the political *visibility* of the Paris Commune is not at all evident. At least, that is, if what we mean by 'today' is the moment when we have to take up the challenge of thinking politics outside of its subjection to the state and outside of the framework of parties or of the party.

And yet the Commune was a political sequence that, precisely, did not situate itself in such a subjection or in such a framework.

The method will thus consist in putting to one side the classical interpretation and tackling the political facts and determinations of the Commune using a completely different method.

Preliminaries: what is the 'left'?

To start with, let's note that before the Commune there had been a number of more or less armed popular and workers' movements in France in a dialectic with the question of state power. We can pass over the terrible days of June 1848 when the question of power is thought not to have been posed: the workers, cornered and chased from Paris upon the closing of national workshops, fought silently, without leadership, without perspective. Despair, fury, massacres. But there were the *Trois Glorieuses* of July 1830 and the fall of Charles V; there was February 1848 and the fall of Louis-Philippe; and, lastly, there was September 4 1870 and the fall of Napoleon III. In the space of forty years, young Republicans and armed workers brought about the downfall of two monarchies and an empire. That is exactly why, considering France to be the 'classic land of class struggle', Marx wrote those masterpieces *Workers' Struggles in France, The 18th Brumaire of Louis Napoleon Bonaparte* and *The Civil War in France*.

As regards 1830, 1848 and 1870, we must note that they share a fundamental trait, one that is all the more fundamental as it is still of relevance today. The mass political movement is largely proletarian. But there is general acceptance that the final result of the movement will involve the coming to power of cliques of Republican or Orleanist politicians. The gap between politics and state is tangible here: the parliamentary projection of the political movement attests in effect to a political incapacity *as to the state*. But it is also noticeable that this *incapacity is in the medium term experienced [vécu] as a failing of the movement itself and not as the price of a structural gap between the state and political invention*. At bottom, the thesis prevails, subjectively, within the proletarian movement, that there is or ought to be a continuity between a political mass movement and its statist bottom line. Hence the recurrent theme of 'betrayal' (i.e. the politicians in power betray the political movement. But did they ever have any other intention, indeed, any other *function*?). And each time this hopeless motif of betrayal leads to a liquidation of political movement, often for long periods.

That is of utmost interest. Recall that the final result of the popular movement ('*Ensemble!*') of December 1995[8] and of the *sans-papiers* movement of Saint-Bernard[9] was the election of Jospin, against whom the – empirically justified – cries of 'betrayal' were not long in coming. On a larger scale, May 1968 and its 'leftist' sequence wore themselves out rallying to Mitterrand's aid already well before 1981. Further away still, the radical novelty and political expectancy of the Resistance movements between 1940 and 1945 came to little after the Liberation when the old parties were returned to power under the cover of De Gaulle.

Jospin, Mitterrand and their kind are the Jules Favres, the Jules Simons, the Jules Ferries, the Thiers and the Picards of our conjuncture. And, today, we are still being called upon to 'rebuild the left'. What a farce!

It is true that the memory of the Commune also testifies to the

constant tactics of adjustment that parliamentary swindlers undertake in relation to eruptions of mass politics: the *Mur des fédérés*,
meagre symbol of martyred workers, does it not lie on the side of
the grand avenue Gambetta, that shock parliamentarian and
founder of the Third Republic?[10]

But to all this the Commune stands as an exception.

For *the Commune is what, for the first and to this day only time, broke with
the parliamentary destiny of popular and workers' political movements.* On the
evening of the resistance in the workers' districts, March 18 1871,
when the troops had withdrawn not having been able to take the
cannons, there could have been an appeal to return to order, to
negotiate with the government, and to have a new clique of
opportunists pulled out of history's hat. This time there would
be nothing of the sort.

Everything is concentrated in the declaration by the Central
Committee of the National Guard, which was widely distributed
on March 19:

> The proletarians of Paris, amidst the failures and treasons of the
> ruling classes, have understood that the hour has struck for them
> to save the situation by taking into their own hands the direction
> of public affairs.

This time, this unique time, destiny was not put back in the hands
of competent politicians. This time, this unique time, betrayal is
invoked as a state of things to avoid and not as the simple result of
an unfortunate choice. This time, this unique time, the proposal is
to deal with the situation solely on the basis of the resources of the
proletarian movement.

Herein lies a real *political declaration.* The task is to think its
content.

But first a structural definition is essential: *Let's call 'the Left' the set
of parliamentary political personnel that proclaim that they are the only ones
equipped to bear the general consequences of a singular political movement.* Or,

in more contemporary terms, that they are the only ones able to provide 'social movements' with a 'political perspective'.

Thus we can describe the declaration of March 19 1871 precisely as *a declaration to break with the Left*.

That is obviously what the Communards had to pay for with their own blood. Because, since at least 1830, 'the Left' has been the established order's sole recourse during movements of great magnitude. Again in May 1968, as Pompidou very quickly understood, only the PCF was able to re-establish order in the factories. The Commune is the unique example of a break with the Left on such a scale. This, in passing, is what sheds light on the exceptional virtue, on the paradigmatic contribution – far greater than October 17 – it had for Chinese revolutionaries between 1965 and 1968, and for French Maoists between 1966 and 1976: periods when the task was precisely to break with all subjection to that fundamental emblem, the 'Left', an emblem that – whether they were in power or in opposition (but, in a profound way, a 'great' Communist party is *always* in power) – the Communist parties had turned into.

True, after being crushed, leftist 'memory' absorbed the Commune. The mediation of that paradoxical incorporation took the form of a parliamentary combat for amnesty for exiled or still-imprisoned Communards. Through this combat the Left hoped for a risk-free consolidation of its electoral power. After that came the epoch – about which I've said a word – of commemorations.

Today, the Commune's political visibility must be restored by a process of dis-incorporation: born of rupture with the Left, it must be extracted from the leftist hermeneutics that have overwhelmed it for so long.

In doing this, let's take advantage of the fact that the Left, whose baseness is constitutive, has now fallen so low that it no longer even makes a pretence of remembering the Commune.

But the operation is not easy. It requires that you grant me the patience to put in place some operators and a new *découpage* of events.

The Commune is a site –
ontology of the Commune

Take any situation whatsoever. *A multiple that is an object of this situation – whose elements are indexed by the transcendental of this situation – is a site if it happens to count itself within the referential field of its own indexation.* Or again: a site is a multiple that happens to behave in the situation with regard to itself as with regard to its elements, in such a way as to support the being of its own appearing.

Even if the idea is still obscure, we can begin to see its content: a site is a singularity because it evokes its being in the appearing of its own multiple composition. It makes itself, in the world, the being-there of its being. Among other consequences, this means that the site gives itself an intensity of existence. A site is a being that happens to exist by itself.

The whole point will be to argue that March 18 1871 is a site.

So, at the risk of repeating myself, I shall go over once more, with a view to a singular construction, all the terms of the situation 'Paris at the end of the Franco-Prussian War of 1870'. We are in the month of March 1871. After a semblance of resistance, and shot through with fear of revolutionary and worker Paris, the interim government of bourgeois 'Republicans' capitulates to Bismarck's Prussians. In order to consolidate this political 'victory' – very comparable to Pétain's reactionary revenge in 1940 (where preferring an arrangement with the external enemy to exposure to the internal enemy) – it has an assembly with a royalist majority hastily elected by a frightened rural world, an assembly that sits in Bordeaux.

Led by Thiers, the government hopes to take advantage of the circumstances to annihilate the political capacity of the workers. But on the Parisian front, the proletariat is armed in the form of a National Guard, owing to its having been mobilized during the siege on Paris. In theory, the Parisian proletariat has many hundreds of cannons at its disposal. The 'military' organ of the

Parisians is the Central Committee, at which assemble the delegates of the various battalions of the National Guard, battalions that are in turn linked to the great working-class *quartiers* of Paris – Montmartre, Belleville and so forth.

Thus we have a divided world whose logical organization – what in philosophical jargon could be called its transcendental organization – reconciles intensities of political existence according to two sets of antagonistic criteria. Concerning the representative, electoral and legal dispositions, one cannot but observe the pre-eminence of the Assembly of traditionalist Rurals,[11] Thiers's *capitulard* government, and the officers of the regular army, who, having been licked without much of a fight by Prussian soldiers, dream of doing battle with the Parisian workers. That is where the power is, especially as it is the only power recognized by the occupier. On the side of resistance, political intervention, and French revolutionary history, there is the fecund disorder of Parisian worker organizations, which intermingles with the Central Committee of the twenty *quartiers*, the Federation of the Trade Unions, a few members of the International, and local military committees. In truth, the historical consistency of this world, which had been separated and disbanded [*délié*] owing to the war, is held together only by the majority conviction that no kind of worker capacity for government exists. For the vast majority of people, including often the workers themselves, the politicized workers of Paris are simply incomprehensible. These workers are the non-existent aspect [*l'inexistant propre*] of the term 'political capacity' in the uncertain world of the spring of 1871. But for the bourgeoisie they are still too existent, at least physically. The government receives threats from the stock exchange saying: 'You will never have financial operations if you do not get rid of these reprobates.' First up, then, an imperative task, and a seemingly easy one to carry out: disarm the workers and, in particular, retrieve the cannons distributed throughout working-class Paris by the military committees of the National Guard. It is this initiative that will make of the term 'March 18' (a single day – such as it is exposed in the situation 'Paris in spring 1871') a site, that is, that which *presents itself* in the appearing of a situation.

More precisely, March 18 is the first day of the event calling itself the Paris Commune, that is, the exercise of power by Socialist or Republican political militants and organizations of armed workers in Paris from March 18 to May 28 1871. The balance-sheet of this sequence is the massacring of many tens of thousands of 'rebels' by the troops of the Thiers government and the reactionary Assembly.

What is, exactly, in terms of its manifest content, this beginning called March 18? Our answer is: the appearing of a worker-being – to this very day a social symptom, the brute force of uprisings, and a theoretical threat – in the space of governmental and political capacity.

And what happens? Thiers orders General Aurelles de Paladine to retrieve the cannons held by the National Guard. Close to three in the morning a coup is carried out by some select detachments. A complete success, so it seems. On the walls an announcement by Thiers and his ministers can be read; it bears the paradoxes of a split transcendental evaluation: 'Let the good citizens separate from the bad; let them aid the public force.' Nevertheless, by eleven in the morning the coup has totally failed. The soldiers have been encircled by hundreds of ordinary women, backed up by anonymous workers and members of the National Guard acting on their own behalf. Many of the soldiers fraternize. The cannons are taken back. General Aurelles de Paladine panics, seeing in it the great red peril: 'The Government calls upon you to defend your homes, your families, your property. Some misguided men, obeying only some secret leaders, turn the cannons kept back from the Prussians against Paris.' According to him, it is a matter of 'putting an end to the insurrectional Committee, whose members represent only Communist doctrines, and who would pillage Paris and bury France'. All to no avail.

Despite being without veritable leadership, the rebellion extends, occupying the whole city. The armed workers' organizations make use of the barracks, public buildings, and finally the Hôtel-de-Ville, which, under a red flag, will be the site and symbol of the new power. Thiers saves himself, escaping via a hidden staircase. The minister Jules Favre jumps out of a window. The whole governmental apparatus disappears and sets itself up at Versailles. Paris is delivered to the insurrection.

March 18 is a site because, apart from whatever else appears here under the ambiguous transcendental of the world 'Paris in spring 1871', it appears as the striking, and totally unforeseeable, beginning of a rupture (true, still without concept) with the very thing that had established the norm of its appearing. Note that 'March 18' is the title of a chapter from the militant Lissagaray's magnificent *History of the Paris Commune of 1871*, published in 1876. This chapter is concerned, naturally, with the 'women of March 18', the 'people of March 18', attesting to the fact that 'March 18', now a predicate, has come to be included as an essential element in evaluating the possible outcomes of the day's turn of events. Lissagaray sees clearly that, under the sign of an eruption of being, the fortuities of March 18 have brought about an immanent overturning of the laws of appearing. Indeed, from the fact that the working people of Paris, overcoming the dispersion of their political framework, prevented a governmental act carried out with precision and rapid force (the seizure of the cannons), results the obligation that an unknown capacity appear, an unprecedented power by which 'March 18' comes to appear, under the injunction of being, as an element of the situation that it is.

In fact, from the point of view of well-ordered appearing, the possibility of a popular and worker governmental power purely and simply does not exist. This is the case even for the militant workers themselves, who use the vocabulary of the 'Republic' indistinctly. On the evening of March 18, the members of the Central Committee of the National Guard – the only effective authority of the city whose legal tutors have absconded – remain more or less convinced they should not be sitting at the Hôtel-de-Ville, reiterating that they 'do not have a mandate for government'. In accordance with our conception of 'the Left', this amounts to saying that they balk at breaking with it. It is only with the sword of circumstances hanging over their heads that they end up deciding, as Édouard Moreau – a perfect nobody – will dictate to them the morning of March 19 to 'proceed to elections, to provide for the public services, and to protect the town from a surprise'. With this act *nolens volens*, they directly constitute themselves, against any allegiance to the parliamentary Left, as a political authority. In so doing, they invoke 'March 18' as the beginning of that authority, an authority as a consequence of March 18.

Hence it is essential to understand that March 18 is a site because it imposes itself on all the elements that help to bring about its existence as that which, on the basis of the indistinct content of worker-being, 'forcibly' calls for a wholly new transcendental evaluation of the latter's intensity. The site 'March 18', this empirical 'March 18' in which is dealt out the impossible possibility of worker existence, is, thought as such, a subversion of the rules of political appearing (of the logic of power) by means of its own active support.

The Commune is a singularity – logic of the Commune, 1

As to the thought of its pure being, a site is simply a multiple that happens to be an element of itself. We have just illustrated this by the example of March 18, a complicated set of peripeteia whose result is that 'March 18' gets instituted, in the object 'March 18', as the exigency of a new political appearing, as forcing an unheard-of transcendental evaluation of the political scene.

Yet a site must be thought not simply in terms of the ontological particularity that I have just identified, but also according to the logical unfolding of its consequences.

Indeed, the site is a figure of the instant. It appears only to then disappear. Veritable duration, that is, the time a site opens or founds, pertains only to its consequences. The enthusiasm of March 18 1871 is most certainly the founding of the first worker power in history, but when on May 10 the Central Committee proclaims that to save the 'revolution of March 18, which it had begun so well', it would 'put an end to controversies, put down the malignants, quell rivalry, ignorance, and incapacity', its boastful desperation betrays everything that had appeared, by means of the distribution and enveloping of political intensities, in the city for the past two months.

That said, what is a consequence? This point is crucial for theorizing the historical appearing of a politics. I'll obviously have to skip over the technical details of that theorization for now. The simplest thing to do is to fix a value for the relation of consequence between two terms in a situation by the mediation of their degree of existence. If an element a of a situation is such that the existence of a has a value of p, and if the element b of the same situation exists to the degree of q, we can postulate that b will be a consequence of a in equal measure to the dependency of these intensities, or, if you like, their order. If, for example, on the scale measuring the intensities of existence proper to a certain situation, q is greatly inferior to p, we can validate the dependency of b to a.

We can say, then, that a consequence is a strong or weak relation between existences. The degree to which one thing is the consequence of another is never independent of the intensity of existence they have in the situation under consideration. The aforementioned declaration of the Central Committee of May 10 1871, then, may be read as a thesis on the consequences. It registers:

- The very strong intensity of existence on the day of March 18 1871, the day of that revolution that had 'begun so well'.
- The implicitly disastrous degree of existence of political discipline in the worker camp two months later ('bad will', 'rivalry', 'ignorance,' 'incapacity').
- A desire (though unfortunately abstract) to bring the value of the consequences of the politics in course level with the power of existence of its disappeared origin.

A site is the appearing/disappearing of a multiple whose paradox is self-belonging. The logic of a site involves the distribution of intensities, around the vanishing point, in which the site consists. So, then, we shall begin at the beginning: what is the value of existence of the site itself? After which we can proceed to consider what can be deduced as regards its consequences.

The value of the site's existence cannot be prescribed from anything in its ontology. A sudden appearance can be no more than a barely 'perceptible' local apparition (it is pure image since there is no perception here). And further: its disappearing cannot leave any trace. Indeed, it may well be that ontologically taking on the marks of 'true' change (self-belonging and disappearance in the instant), a site is nevertheless, owing to its existential insignificance, hardly different from a simple continuation of the situation.

For example, on Tuesday May 23 1871, when nearly the whole of Paris is at the hands of the Versaillais soldiery – who shoot workers by the thousands on staircases all over the city – and the Communards, who fight barricade by barricade, no longer have any military or political leadership, the remainder of the Central Committee make their last proclamation, which is hastily stuck up on a few walls and, as Lissagaray said with sombre irony, is a 'proclamation of victors'. The proclamation calls for the conjoint dissolution of the (legal) Assembly of Versailles and the Commune, the retreat of the Parisian army, a provisional government entrusted to the delegates of big cities, and a reciprocal amnesty. How to qualify this sad 'Manifesto'? Owing to its sheer incongruity, it cannot be reduced to the normality of the situation. This Manifesto still expresses, be it in a derisory way, the Commune's self-certitude, its just conviction of having marked the beginning of a new politics. This document is something that, although the wind of the barracks will carry it *aux oubliettes*, can be legitimately held to be one of the site's elements. But in the savage dawn of the worker insurrection, its value of existence is very weak. What is in question here is the site's singular power. This Central Committee manifesto can of course be ontologically situated in that which holds the evental syntagm the 'Paris Commune' together, but as a sign of decomposition or of powerlessness it leads the singularity of this syntagm back to the margins of a pure and simple modification of the situation, or to its simple mechanical development, and is lacking in veritable creation.

On this point, let's cite the terrible passage dedicated to the Commune's last moments by Julien Gracq in *Lettrines*. I included this extract in the preface to my *Théorie du sujet* in 1981 as an indication that all of my philosophical efforts aimed to contribute, however slightly, to preventing us (as the inheritors of the Cultural Revolution and May 1968) from becoming '*dealers in herring vouchers*'.

Gracq had been rereading the third volume of the autobiography of Communard leader Jules Vallès titled *L'insurgé*. Here is a fragment of his commentary:

> Marx was indulgent of the leadership of the Commune, whose shortcomings he had perfectly seen. The revolution also had its Trochu and its Gamelin. Vallès's frankness consternates, and might cause one to take horror at that proclamatory leadership, those chand'vins revolutionaries, on whom the barricaders of Belleville spat as they passed by during the last days of the blood-soaked week. There is no excuse to lead the good fight when one leads it so lightly.

A kind of atrocious nausea arises while following the *Ubuesque* masquerade, the pathetic disorder, of the last pages, wherein the unfortunate Commune delegate – no longer daring to show his sash which he clasped under his arms in a newspaper – a sort of incompetent district official, of petroleur Charlot leaping between shell blasts, incapable of doing anything at all, treated harshly by the rebels who bare their teeth, wanders like a lost dog from one barricade to another distributing in disorderly fashion vouchers for herrings, bullets, and fire, and imploring the spiteful crowd – which was hard on his heels because of the fix into which he had plunged it – pitifully, lamentably, 'Leave me alone, I ask you. I need to think alone.'

In his exile as a courageous incompetent, he must have sometimes awoken at night, still hearing the voices of all the same series of people who were to be massacred in a few minutes, and who cried so furiously at him from the barricade: 'Where are the orders? Where is the plan?'[12]

So that this kind of disaster doesn't arise, the appearing of the site must have a force of appearing that compensates for its evanescence. Nothing has potential for an event [*est en puissance d'événement*] but a site whose value of existence is maximal. This was the case in all certainty on March 18 1871, when, women at the front, the working people of Paris forbade the army from disarming the National Guard. But it is no longer the case concerning the Commune's political leadership as of the end of April.

We will call a site whose intensity of existence is not maximal a *fact*.

We will call a site whose intensity of existence is maximal a *singularity*.

You will notice that the repressive force of the Versaillais is accompanied by a propaganda that systematically desingularizes the Commune, presenting it as a monstrous set of facts to be (forcibly) returned to the normal order of things. This results in some extraordinary statements, such as the one published in the conservative journal *Le Siècle* on May 21 1871, right in the middle of the massacre of workers: 'The social difficulties have been resolved or are in the process of being resolved.' It could not have been better put. On the other hand, as early as March 21, only three days after the insurrection, Jules Favre was given to proclaiming that Paris was at the mercy of 'a handful of villains, holding above the rights of the Assembly I don't know what kind of rapacious and bloody ideal'. In the appearing of a situation, strategic and tactical choices oscillate between fact and singularity, because it is, as always, a question of relating to a logical order of circumstances.

When a world finally comes to be situated – from what becomes of the site in it – and is placed between singularity and fact, then it is down to the network of consequences that it comes to decide.

March 18 and its consequences – logic of the Commune, 2

A singularity diverges further from simple continuity than a fact because it is attached to an intensity of maximal existence. If, now, we are further compelled to make a distinction between weak and strong singularities, it is so that we can establish the consequences woven by an evanescent site with the elements of the situation that presented it in the world.

To be brief, we shall say that *existing* maximally for the time of its appearing/disappearing accords a site the power [*puissance*] of a singularity. And further, that to *make (something) exist* maximally is all the force such a singularity has.

We shall reserve the name of event for a strong singularity.

A few remarks are in order about the predicative distinction strength/weakness as it applies to singularities (that is, to sites whose transcendental intensity of existence is maximal).

Now, it can be seen that in work of the nature of the appearing of truth, the Paris Commune, crushed in blood in two months, is nonetheless much more significant than September 4 1870, the date when the political regime of the Second Empire collapsed and the Third Republic – which lasted seventy years – began. This in no way relates to the actors: on September 4 it was also the working people who, under a red flag, invaded the square of the Hôtel-de-Ville and, as Lissagaray recounted so vividly, caused the officials to go to pieces: 'Important dignitaries, fat functionaries, ferocious Mamelukes, imperious ministers, solemn chamberlains, moustached generals, shake pitifully on September 4, like a bunch of weak hams.' On one hand, then, we have an insurrection that establishes nothing of duration; on the other, a day that changes the state. But September 4 was to be confiscated by bourgeois politicians primarily concerned to re-establish the order of property, while the Commune, Lenin's ideal referent, will inspire a century of revolutionary thought, thus meriting the famous evaluation Marx gave of it before its bloody end:

> The Commune was . . . the initiation of the Social Revolution of the 19th century. Whatever therefore its fate at Paris, it will make *le tour du monde*. It was at once acclaimed by the working class of Europe and the United States as the magic word of delivery.[13]

Let's posit then that September 4 is a weak singularity, because it is aligned on the general development of European states, which converge on the parliamentary form. Moreover, let's say that the Commune is a strong singularity because it proposes to thought a rule of emancipation, and is relayed – perhaps against the grain – by October 1917 and, more specifically, by the summer of 1967 in China, and May 1968 in France. For is it not only the exceptional intensity of its sudden appearing that counts (i.e. the fact that they have to do with violent and creative episodes within the domain of appearance) but what, over time, such evanescent emergences set up by way of uncertain and glorious consequences.

Beginnings can, then, be measured by the re-beginnings they authorize.

It is in that aspect of a singularity which continues by means of the concentration, external to it, of its intensity that we can judge whether an aleatory adjunction to the world warrants being considered – beyond facts and continuities – not just as a singularity but as an event.

The Commune is an event –
logic of the Commune, 3

Everything, then, depends on the consequences. And note that there exists no stronger a transcendental consequence than that of making something appear in a world which had not existed in it previously. This was the case on March 18 1871, when a collection of unknown workers were thrust to the centre of the political scene, workers unknown even to specialists of the revolution – those old surviving 'quarante-huitards' – whose inefficient logomachy unfortunately did much to encumber the Commune. Let's return to March 19, and to the first declarations made by the Central Committee, the only accountable organ to emerge from the March 18 insurrection: 'Let Paris and France put together the bases of an acclaimed Republic with all its consequences, the only government that will close forever the era of invasion and civil wars.' By whom is this unprecedented political decision signed? Twenty people, three-quarters of whom are proletarians that the circumstances alone constitute and identify. Right on cue with the well-worn theme of 'foreign agents', the governmental *Officiel* complacently asks: 'Who are the members of the Committee? Are they communists, Bonapartists, or Prussians?' Instead, they were yesterday's inexistent workers, brought into a provisionally maximal political existence as the consequence of an event.

Hence, we can identify a strong singularity by the fact that, for a given situation, it has the consequence of making an inexistent term exist in it.

In more abstract fashion, we will posit the following definition: *given a site (a multiple affected with self-belonging) which is a singularity (its intensity of existence, as instantaneous and as 'evanescent' as it may be, is nevertheless maximal), we will say that this site is a strong singularity, or an event, if, in consequence of the (maximal) intensity of the site, something whose value of existence was nil in the situation takes on a positive value of existence.*

So, what I'm basically saying is that an event *has, as a maximally true consequence of its (maximal) intensity of existence, the existence of an inexistent.*

This obviously implies a violent paradox. Because if an implication is maximally true and so also is its antecedent, then its consequent must be; we thus come to the seemingly untenable conclusion whereby, under the effect of an event, the inexistent aspect of a site comes to exist absolutely.

And indeed: the unknown members of the Central Committee, who were politically inexistent in the world the day before, come to exist absolutely the same day as their appearing. The Parisian people obey their proclamations, encourage them to occupy the public buildings, and turn out for the elections they organize.

The paradox can be analysed under three headings. In the first place, the principle of this overturning of worldly appearing from inexistence to absolute existence is a vanishing principle. All the event's power is consumed in the existential transfiguration. As evental multiplicity, March 18 1871 has not the least stability.

Secondly, if the inexistent aspect of a site must ultimately capture, in the order of appearing, a maximal intensity, it is only to the extent that this intensity henceforth take the place of what has disappeared; its maximality is the subsisting mark, in the world, of the event itself. The 'eternal' existence of an inexistent consists in the trace [*tracé*] or statement, in the world, of the evanescent event. The proclamations of the Commune, the first worker power in universal history, comprise a historic existent whose absoluteness manifests the coming to pass in the world of a wholly new ordering of its appearing, a mutation of its logic. The existence of an inexistent aspect is that by which, in the domain of appearing, the subversion of worldly appearing by subjacent being is played out. It is the logical marking of a paradox of being, an ontological chimera.

Destruction – logic of the Commune, 4

Lastly, an inexistent aspect must come again within the space in which existence is henceforth held together. Worldly order cannot be subverted to the point of being able to require the abolition of a logical law of situations. Every situation has at least one proper inexistent aspect, and if this aspect happens to be sublimated into absolute existence, another element of the site must cease to exist, thereby keeping the law intact and ultimately preserving the coherence of appearing.

In 1896, adding another conclusion to his *History of the Commune of 1871*, Lissagaray makes two observations. The first is that the band of reactionaries and workers' assassins of 1871 is still in place. Parliamentarism playing its part, it has even been augmented with 'some bourgeois fiefs who, under the mask of democrats, facilitate its advances'. The second is that the people henceforth constitutes its own force: 'Three times [in 1792, in 1848 and in 1870] the French proletariat made the Republic for others; now it is ripe for its own.' In other words, the Commune event, begun on March 18 1871, did not have the effect of destroying the dominant group and its politicians. But something more important was destroyed: the political subordination of workers and the people. What was destroyed was of the order of subjective incapacity: 'Oh!,' exclaims Lissagaray, 'they are not uncertain of their capacities, these workers of the country and the towns.'[14] The absolutization of worker political existence (the existence of the inexistent), convulsive and crushed, had all the same destroyed the necessity of a basic form of subjection; that is, the subjection of a possible proletarian politics to the scheming of (leftist) bourgeois politicians. Like every veritable event, the Commune had not *realized* a possible, it had created one. This possible is simply that of an independent proletarian politics.

That a century later the necessity of subjection to the Left has been reconstituted, or rather reinvented under the very name of 'democracy', is another story, another sequence in the often tormented history of truths. It remains the case that where an inexistent aspect (worker political capacity) was held in place, the destruction of what legitimated this inexistence (subjective incapacity) came to pass. At the beginning of the twentieth century, what occupies the place of death is no longer worker political awareness [*conscience*], but – even if it was not yet realized – the prejudice that classes are natural in character, and that it is the millenary vocation of proprietors and the wealthy to conserve social and state power. The Paris Commune accomplished this destruction for the future, even in the apparent putting to death of its own super-existence [*surexistence*].

Here we have a transcendental maxim: if, in the form of an evental consequence, what was worth nothing comes to equal the whole, then an established given within the domain of appearing is destroyed. What had sustained the cohesion of a world is struck with non-existence; such that, if the transcendental indexation of beings is the (logical) base of the world, then it is with good reason that it must be said: 'the world shall rise on new foundations'.

When the world is violently enchanted by the absolute consequences of a paradox of being, the whole of the domain of appearing, threatened with the local destruction of a customary evaluation, must come again to constitute a different distribution of what exists and what does not.

Under the eruption being exerts on its own appearing, nothing in a world can come to pass except the possibility – mingling existence and destruction – of another world.

Conclusion

I believe this other world resides for us in the Commune, yet altogether elsewhere than in its subsequent existence, what I have called its *first* existence, that is, in the party-state and its social worker referent. Instead, it exists in the observation that a political rupture is always a combination of a subjective capacity and an organization – totally independent of state – of the consequences of that capacity.

Further, it is important to argue that such a rupture is always a rupture with the Left, in the formal sense I have given to that term. Today, this amounts to saying a rupture with the representative form of politics, or, if one wants to go further in the way of founded provocation, a rupture with 'democracy'.

The notion that the consequences of a political capacity are obligatorily of the order of power and state administration belongs to the first account of the Commune, not to the one that interests us. Instead, our problem is rather to return – prior to this first account (prior to Lenin, if you will) – to what was alive but defeated in the Commune: to the fact that a politics appears when a *declaration* is at one and the same time a *decision as to the consequences*, and, thus, when a decision is active in the form of a previously unknown collective discipline. Because we must never stop recalling that those who are nothing can only stick to a wager on the consequences of their appearing in the element of a new discipline, a discipline that is a practical discipline of thought. The Party in Lenin's sense certainly comprised the creation of such a discipline, but one that was ultimately subordinated to constraints of State. Today's task, being undertaken notably by the Organisation Politique, is to support the creation of such a discipline subtracted from the grip of the state, the creation of a thoroughly political discipline.

The Cultural Revolution:
The Last Revolution?[15]

Why?

Why discuss the 'Cultural Revolution', the official name for a long period of serious disturbances in Communist China between 1965 and 1976? For at least three reasons:

1. The Cultural Revolution has been a constant and lively reference of militant activity throughout the world, and particularly in France, at least between 1967 and 1976. It is part of our political history and the basis for the existence of the Maoist current, the only true political creation of the sixties and seventies. I can say 'our', for I was part of it, and in a certain sense, to quote Rimbaud, 'I am there, I am still there.' In the untiring inventiveness of the Chinese revolutionaries, all sorts of subjective and practical trajectories have found their justification – to change subjectivity, to live otherwise, to think otherwise: the Chinese – and then we – called that 'revolutionization'. Their aim: 'To change the human being in what is most profound.' They taught that in political practice, we must be both 'the arrow and the bull's eye', because the old worldview is also still present within us. By the end of the sixties, we were present everywhere: in the factories, in the suburbs, in the countryside. Tens of thousands of students became proletarian or went to live among the workers. For this too we had the phrases of the Cultural Revolution: the 'great exchanges of

experience', 'to serve the people', and, always the essential slogan: the 'mass alliance'. We fought against the brutal inertia of the PCF (Parti communiste français), against its violent conservatism. In China too the party bureaucracy was attacked; that was called 'the struggle against revisionism'. Even the splits, the confrontations between revolutionaries from different orientations, were referred to in the Chinese manner: 'to hunt down the black gangsters', ending with those who are 'leftist in appearance and rightist in reality'. When we came across a popular political situation, a factory strike or a confrontation with the fascistic landlords, we knew that we had 'to excel in the discovery of the proletarian left, to rally the centre, to isolate and crush the right'. Mao's *Little Red Book* has been our guide, not, as the puppets say, in the service of a dogmatic catechism, but on the contrary, so that we can clarify and invent new behaviours in all sorts of disparate situations that were unfamiliar to us. With regard to all this, since I am not one of those who justify their abandonment and their rallying to the established reaction with references to the psychology of illusions or to blind morality, we can only quote our sources, and pay homage to the Chinese revolutionaries.

2. The Cultural Revolution is the typical example (yet another notion from Maoism, the typical example: a revolutionary discovery that must be generalized) of a political experience that saturates the form of the party-state. I use the term 'saturation' in the sense given to it by Sylvain Lazarus;[16] I will attempt to show that the Cultural Revolution is the last significant political sequence that is still internal to the party-state (in this case, the Chinese Communist Party), and fails as such. But May 1968 and its aftermath, that is slightly different. The Polish movement or Chiapas, that is very different. The Organisation Politique, that is absolutely different. But without the saturation of the sixties and seventies, nothing would as yet be thinkable, outside the spectre of the party-state, or the parties-state.[17]

3. The Cultural Revolution is a great lesson in history and

politics, in history as thought from within politics (and not the other way around). Indeed, depending on whether we examine this 'revolution' (the word itself lies at the heart of the saturation) according to the dominant historiography or according to a real political question, we arrive at striking disagreements. What matters is for us to see clearly that the nature of this discord is not of the order of empirical or positivist precision or lack thereof. We can be in agreement as to the facts, and end up with judgments that are perfectly opposed to one another. It is precisely this paradox that will serve as our point of entry into the subject matter.

Narratives

The dominant historiographical version was compiled by various specialists, especially by Sinologists, as early as 1968, and it has not changed since then. It was consolidated by the fact that covertly it became the official version of a Chinese state dominated after 1976 by people who escaped from and sought revenge for the Cultural Revolution, headed by Deng Xiaoping.

What does this version say?[18] It says that, in terms of revolution, it was a matter of a power struggle at the top echelons of the bureaucracy of the party-state. That Mao's economic voluntarism, incarnated in the call for 'the Great Leap Forward', was a complete failure, leading to the return of famine to the countryside. That following this failure, Mao finds himself in the minority among the leading party authorities, and that a 'pragmatic' group imposes its law, the dominant personalities of which are Liu Shaoqi (then named president of the Republic), Deng Xiaoping (general secretary of the Party) and Peng Zhen (mayor of Beijing). That, as early as 1963, Mao attempted to lead some counter-attacks, but that he failed among the regular party authorities. That he then had recourse to forces foreign to the party, whether external (the student Red Guards) or external/internal, particularly the army, over which he took control again after the elimination of Peng Dehuai and his replacement by Lin Biao.[19] That then, solely because of Mao's will to regain power, there ensued a bloody and chaotic situation, which persisted until the death of the culprit (in 1976).

It is totally feasible to accept that nothing in this version is properly speaking incorrect. But its real meaning can emerge only from a political understanding of the events, that is, their concentration in a form of thinking still active today.

1. No stabilization? True. But that is because it turned out to be impossible to develop the political innovation within the framework of the party-state. Neither the most extensive creative freedom of the student and working masses (between 1966 and 1968) nor the ideological and state control of the army (between 1968 and 1971), nor the *ad hoc* solutions to the problems isssued in a Politburo dominated by the confrontation among antagonistic tendencies (between 1972 and 1976) allowed the revolutionary ideas to take root so that an entirely new political situation, completely detached from the Soviet model, could finally see the light of day on the scale of society as a whole.

2. Recourse to external forces? True. But this was intended, and it actually had the effect, both on a short-term and on a long-term basis, perhaps even until today, of partly disentangling party and state. It was a matter of destroying bureaucratic formalism, at least for the duration of a massive movement. The fact that this provoked the anarchy of factions at the same time signals an essential political question for times to come: what gives unity to a politics, if it is not directly guaranteed by the formal unity of the state?

3. A struggle for power? Of course. It is rather ridiculous to oppose 'power struggle' and 'revolution' since by 'revolution' we can only understand the articulation of antagonistic political forces over the question of power. Besides, the Maoists constantly quoted Lenin, for whom the question of the revolution in the final instance

is explicitly that of power. Rather, the real problem, which is very complex, would be to know whether the Cultural Revolution does not in fact put an end to the revolutionary conception of the articulation between politics and the state. Indeed, this was its great question, its central and violent debate.

4. The 'Great Leap Forward' – a cruel failure? Yes, in many respects. But this failure is the result of a critical examination of Stalin's economic doctrine. It can certainly not be attributed to a uniform treatment of questions related to the development of the countryside by 'totalitarianism'. Mao severely examined (as witnessed by numerous written notes) the Stalinist conception of collectivization and its absolute disdain for the peasants. His idea was certainly not to collectivize through force and violence in order to ensure accumulation at all costs in the cities. It was, quite the contrary, to industrialize the countryside locally, to give it a relative economic autonomy, in order to avoid the savage proletarianization and urbanization that had taken a catastrophic shape in the USSR. In truth, Mao followed the communist idea of an effective resolution of the contradiction between city and countryside, and not that of a violent destruction of the countryside in favour of the cities. If there is a failure, it is of a political nature, and it is a completely different failure from Stalin's. Ultimately, we should affirm that the same abstract description of facts by no means leads to the same mode of thinking when it operates under different political axioms.

Dates

The quarrel is equally clear when it comes to dates. The dominant point of view, which is also that of the Chinese State, is that the Cultural Revolution lasted for ten years, from 1966 to 1976, from the Red Guards to Mao's death. Ten years of troubles, ten years lost for a rational development.

In fact, this dating can be defended, if one reasons from the strict point of view of the history of the Chinese State, with the following criteria: civil stability, production, a certain unity at the head of the administration, cohesion in the army, etc. But this is not my axiom and these are not my criteria. If one examines the question of dates from the point of view of politics, of political invention, the principal criteria become the following: when can we say that there is a situation of collective creations of thought of the political type? When does practice with its directives stand in a verifiable excess over the tradition and function of the Chinese party-state? When do statements of universal value emerge? Then, we proceed in a completely different way to determine the boundaries of the process named the 'Great Proletarian Cultural Revolution', which we among ourselves called 'the GPCR'.

As far as I am concerned, I propose that the Cultural Revolution, in this conception, forms a sequence that runs from November 1965 to July 1968. I can even accept (this is a matter of political technique) a drastic reduction, which would situate the revolutionary moment properly speaking between May 1966 and September 1967. The criterion is the existence of a political activity of the masses, its slogans, its new organizations, its own places. Through all of this an ambivalent but undeniable reference is constituted for all contemporary political thought worthy of the name. In this sense, there is 'revolution' because there are the Red Guards, the revolutionary rebel workers, innumerable organizations and 'general headquarters', totally unpredictable situations, new political statements, texts without precedent, etc.

Hypothesis

How to proceed so that this gigantic upheaval is exposed to thought and makes sense today? I will formulate a hypothesis and experiment on several levels, both factual and textual, of the sequence I am referring to (that is, China between November 1965 and July 1968).

The hypothesis is the following: We are in the conditions of an essential division of the party-state (the Chinese Communist Party, in power since 1949). This division is essential in that it entails crucial questions regarding the future of the country: the economy and the relation between city and countryside; the eventual transformation of the army; the assessment of the Korean War; the intellectuals, universities, art and literature; and, finally, the value of the Soviet, or Stalinist, model. But it is also and above all essential because the minority trend among the party cadres is at the same time led, or represented, by the person whose historical and popular legitimacy is the greatest, that is, Mao Zedong. There is a formidable phenomenon of non-coincidence between the historicity of the party (the long period of the popular war, first against the Japanese, then against Chiang Kai-shek) and the present state of its activity as the framework of state power. Moreover, the Yanan period will be constantly invoked during the Cultural Revolution, particularly in the army, as a model of communist political subjectivity.

This phenomenon has the following consequences: the confrontation between positions cannot be ruled by bureaucratic formalism, but neither can it be ruled by the methods of terrorist purging that Stalin used in the thirties. In the space of the party-state, though, there is only formalism or terror. Mao and his group will have to invent a third recourse, a recourse to political mass mobilization, to try to break with the representatives of the majority trend and, in particular, their leaders at the upper echelons of the party and the state. This recourse assumes that one admit uncontrolled forms of revolt and organization. Mao's group, after a great deal of hesitation, will in fact impose that these be admitted, first in the universities and then in the factories. But, in a contradictory move, it will also try to bring together all organizational innovations of the revolution in the general space of the party-state.

Here we are at the heart of the hypothesis: the Cultural Revolution is the historical development of a contradiction. On one hand, the issue is to arouse mass revolutionary action in the margins of the state of the dictatorship of the proletariat, or to acknowledge, in the theoretical jargon of the time, that even though the state is formally a 'proletarian' state, the class struggle continues, including forms of mass revolt. Mao and his followers will go so far as to say that under socialism, the bourgeoisie reconstitutes itself and organizes itself *within the Communist Party itself.* On the other hand, with actual civil war still being excluded, the general form of the relation between the party and the state, in particular concerning the use of repressive forces, must remain unchanged at least in so far as it is not really a question of *destroying* the party. Mao will make this known by noting that 'the over-whelming majority of cadres are good'.

This contradiction will at the same time produce a succession of instances of local revolt that exceed the party's authority, the violent anarchy of these excesses, the inevitability of a call to order of extraordinary brutality, and, in the end, the decisive entrance on to the stage of the popular army.

These successive excesses establish the chronology (the stages) of the Cultural Revolution. The leading revolutionary group will first try to keep the revolt within the context of the educational institutions. This attempt began to fail in August 1966, when the Red Guards spread throughout the cities. Afterwards, it will be a question of containing the revolt within the framework of youth in school and university. But from the end of 1966 and particularly from January 1967 onward, workers become the principal force of the movement. Then the quest is on to keep the party and state administrations at a distance, but they will be in the midst of the turmoil starting in 1967 through a series of power struggles. Finally, the aim will be to keep the army in check at any cost as a power in reserve, a last resource. But this will turn out to be almost impossible with the unleashing of violence in August 1967 in Wuhan and Canton. It is precisely with an eye on the real risk of a schism among the armed forces that the slow movement of repressive inversion will set in, beginning in September 1967.

Let us put it like this: the political innovations which gave the sequence its unquestionable revolutionary appeal could not be deployed except in so far as they exceeded the aim assigned to them by those whom the actors of the revolution themselves (the youth and its innumerable groups, the rebel workers . . .) considered to be their natural leaders: Mao and his minority group. By the same token, these innovations have always been localized and particular; they could not really turn into strategic and reproducible propositions. In the end, the strategic meaning (or the universal range) of these innovations was negative. Because what they themselves meant, and what they strongly impressed upon the militant minds of the entire world, was nothing but the end of the party-state as the central product of revolutionary political activity. More generally, the Cultural Revolution showed that it was no longer possible to submit either the revolutionary mass actions or the organizational phenomena to the strict logic of class representation. That is why it remains a political episode of the highest importance.

Experimental fields

I would like to experiment with the above hypothesis by testing it according to seven referents, taken in chronological order:

1. The 'Sixteen Points' decision of August 1966, which is probably for the most part from the hand of Mao himself, and which in any case is the most innovative central document, the one that breaks most abruptly with the bureaucratic formalism of parties-state.

2. The Red Guards and Chinese society (in the period from August 1966 to at least August 1967). Without a doubt, this

involves an exploration of the limits of the political capacity of high-school and university students left more or less to themselves, whatever the circumstances.

3. The 'revolutionary rebel workers' and the Shanghai Commune (January/February 1967), a major and unfinished episode, because it proposes an alternative form of power to the centralism of the party.

4. The power seizures: the 'great alliance', 'triple combination', and 'revolutionary committees', from January 1967 to the spring of 1968. Here the question is whether the movement really creates new organizations, or whether it amounts only to a regeneration of the party.

5. The Wuhan incident (July 1967). Here we are at the peak of the movement: the army risks division, and the far left pushes its advantage, but only to succumb.

6. The workers' entry into the universities (end of July 1968), which is in reality the final episode of the existence of independent student organizations.

7. Mao's cult of personality. This feature has so often been the object of sarcasm in the West that in the end we have forgotten to ask ourselves what meaning it might well have had, and in particular, what its meaning is within the Cultural Revolution, where the 'cult' functioned as a flag, not for the party conservatives, but for worker and student rebels.

The Decision in Sixteen Points

This text was adopted at a session of the Central Committee on August 8 1966. With a certain genius it presents the fundamental contradiction of the endeavour called the 'Cultural Revolution'. One sign of this presentation is of course the fact that the text does not explain, or barely explains, the name ('cultural') relating to the ongoing political sequence, except for the enigmatic and metaphysical first sentence: 'The Cultural Revolution seeks to change people in what is most profound.'[20] Here, 'cultural' is equivalent to 'ideological', in a particularly radical sense.

A whole portion of the text is a pure and simple call for free revolt, in the great tradition of revolutionary legitimizations.

The text is quite probably illegal, as the composition of the Central Committee was 'corrected' by Mao's group with the support of the army (or certain units loyal to Lin Biao). Revolutionary militants from the university are present, while conservative bureaucrats have been prevented from taking part. In reality, and this is very important, this decision begins a long period of non-existence both of the Central Committee and of the party's secretariat. The important central texts from now on will be signed conjointly by four institutions: the Central Committee, certainly, but which is now only a phantom; the 'Cultural Revolution Group', a highly restricted *ad hoc* group,[21] which nonetheless dispenses of the real political power properly speaking in so far as it is recognized by the rebels; the State Council, presided over by Zhou Enlai; and, finally, as the guarantee of a minimum of administrative continuity, the formidable Military Commission of the Central Committee, restructured by Lin Biao.

Certain passages of the circular are particularly virulent, concerning both the immediate revolutionary requirement and the need to oppose the party with new forms of organization.

Concerning popular mobilization, we will cite in particular points 3 and 4, entitled 'Put Daring Above Everything Else and Boldly Arouse the Masses' and 'Let the Masses Educate Themselves in the Movement'. For example:

> What the Central Committee of the Party demands of the Party committees at all levels is that they persevere in giving correct leadership, put daring above everything else, boldly arouse the masses, change the state of weakness and incompetence where it

exists, encourage those comrades who have made mistakes but are willing to correct them to cast off their mental burdens and join in the struggle, and dismiss from their leading posts all those in authority who are taking the capitalist road and so make possible the recapture of the leadership for the proletarian revolutionaries.

Or, again:

Trust the masses, rely on them and respect their initiative. Cast out fear. Don't be afraid of disturbances. Chairman Mao has often told us that revolution cannot be so very refined, so gentle, so temperate, kind, courteous, restrained and magnanimous. Let the masses educate themselves in this great revolutionary movement and learn to distinguish between right and wrong and between correct and incorrect ways of doing things.

One detail of point 7 is particularly important and will have immense practical consequences. Here it is:

no measure should be taken against students at universities, colleges, middle schools, and primary schools because of problems that arise in the movement.

Everybody in China understands that, at least for the period that is now beginning, the revolutionary youth in the cities is guaranteed a form of impunity. It is evident that this is what will allow the youth to spread through the country, parading the revolutionary spirit, in any case until September 1967.

Concerning the forms of organization, point 9, entitled 'Cultural Revolutionary Groups, Committees, and Congresses', sanctions the invention, within and by the movement, of multiple political regroupings outside the party:

Many new things have begun to emerge in the great Proletarian Cultural Revolution. The cultural revolutionary groups, committees, and other organizational forms created by the masses in many schools and units are something new and of great historic importance.

These new organizations are not considered temporary, which proves that the Maoist group, in August of 1966, envisions the destruction of the political monopoly of the party:

Therefore, the cultural revolutionary groups, committees and congresses should not be temporary organizations but permanent, standing mass organizations.

In the end, we are clearly dealing with organizations that are subject to mass democracy, and not to party authority, as shown by the reference to the Paris Commune, that is, to a proletarian situation previous to the Leninist theory of the party:

It is necessary to institute a system of general elections, like that of the Paris Commune, for electing the members to the cultural revolutionary groups and committees and delegates to the cultural revolutionary congresses. The lists of candidates should be put forward by the revolutionary masses after full discussion, and the elections should be held after the masses have discussed the lists over and over again.

If these members or delegates prove incompetent, they can be replaced through election or recalled by the masses after discussion.

However, if we read the text carefully, knowing what it means 'to read a text' when it comes from the leadership of a communist party, we observe that, through crucial restrictions on the freedom of criticism, some kind of lock is put on the revolutionary impulse to which the text constantly appeals.

First of all, it is held, as if axiomatically, that in essence the party is good. Point 8 ('The Question of Cadres') distinguishes four types of cadres, as put to the test of the Cultural Revolution (let us remember that in China, a 'cadre' is anyone who dispenses authority, even if minimal): good, comparatively good, those who have made serious mistakes that can be fixed, and lastly 'the small number of anti-Party and anti-socialist Rightists'. The thesis is then that 'the first two categories (good and comparatively good) are the great majority'. That is, the state apparatus and its internal leadership (the party) are essentially in good hands, which renders paradoxical the recourse to such large-scale revolutionary methods.

Secondly, even if it is said that the masses must take the initiative, the explicit criticism by name of those responsible for the state or the party is in fact severely controlled 'from above'. On this point, the hierarchical structure of the party makes a sudden come-back (point 11, 'The Question of Criticizing by Name in the Press'):

> Criticism of anyone by name in the press should be decided after discussion by the Party committee at the same level, and in some cases submitted to the Party committee at a higher level for approval.

The result of this directive will be that innumerable cadres of the party, to begin with the president of the Republic, Liu Shaoqi, will be violently criticized for months, even years, by mass revolutionary organizations in the 'small journals', cartoons, mural posters, before their name appears in the central press. But, at the same time, these criticisms will keep a local character, or be open to annulment. They will leave in the air what *decisions* correspond to them.

Point 15, 'The Armed Forces', finally, which is extremely succinct, raises a decisive question as if in a void: Who has authority over the repressive apparatus? Classically, Marxism indicates that a revolution must break down the repressive apparatus of the state it aims to transform from top to bottom. That is certainly not what is understood in this case:

> In the armed forces, the Cultural Revolution and the socialist education movement should be carried out in accordance with the instructions of the Military Commission of the Central Committee of the Party and the General Political Department of the People's Liberation Army. Here again, we come back to the centralized authority of the party.

Ultimately, the Decision in Sixteen Points combines approaches that are still heterogeneous, and, because of its war-like appeal, it prepares the successive impasses of the movement in its relation to the party-state. Of course, there is always the question of how to define, on the basis of the mass movement, a political path that would be different from the one imposed during previous years by the principal current among the party leadership. But two essential questions remain unsolved: who designates the enemies, who sets the targets of revolutionary criticism? And what is, in this sombre affair, the role of the considerable repressive apparatus: public security, militias and army?

Red Guards and Chinese society

Following on the heels of the August circular, the phenomenon of the 'Red Guards', organizations of high-school students, will take on extraordinary significance. We know of the gigantic meetings at Tiananmen, which carry on until the end of 1966, where Mao shows himself, mute, to hundreds of thousands of young men and women. But the most important point is that revolutionary organizations storm the cities, using trucks lent by the army, and then the rest of the country, taking advantage of the free train transportation according to the programme of 'exchange of experiences'.

It is clear that what we have here is the strike force behind the movement's extension to the whole of China. Within this movement an absolutely amazing freedom reigns; groups openly confront each other, the journals, tracts, banners and never-ending mural posters reproduce revelations of all kinds along with the political declarations. Fierce caricatures spare almost no one (in August of 1967, the questioning of Zhou Enlai in one of the great mural posters put up overnight will be one of the reasons for the fall of the so-called 'ultra-leftist' tendency). Processions with gongs, drums and loud proclamations take place until late at night.

On the other hand, the tendency toward militarization and uncontrolled action by shock groups soon makes its appearance. The general slogan speaks of a revolutionary struggle against old ideas and old customs (that is what gives content to the adjective 'cultural', which in Chinese means rather 'civilizational' and, in old Marxist jargon, 'superstructural'. Many groups gave this slogan a destructive and violent, even persecutory, interpretation. The hunting-down of women wearing braids, of formally educated intellectuals, of hesitant professors, of all the 'cadres' who do not use the same phraseology as such-and-such a splinter group, the raiding of libraries or museums, the unbearable arrogance of small revolutionary chiefs with regard to the mass of the undecided – all that will soon provoke a genuine revulsion among ordinary people against the extremist wing of the Red Guards.

At bottom, the problem had already been raised in the communiqué of May 16 1966, Mao's first public act of rebellion against the majority of the Central Committee. This communiqué bluntly declares the need to contend that 'without destruction, there is no construction'. It stigmatizes the conservatives, who preach the 'constructive' spirit to oppose any destruction of the basis of their power. But the balance is hard to find between the evidence of destruction and the slow and tortuous character of construction.

The truth is that, armed only with the slogan of 'the fight of the new against the old', many Red Guards gave in to a well-known (negative) tendency in revolutions: iconoclasm, the persecution of people for futile motives, a sort of assumed barbarism. This is also an inclination of youth left to its own devices. From this we will draw the conclusion that every political organization must be transgenerational, and that it is a bad idea to organize the political separation of youth.

For sure, the Red Guards in no way invent the anti-intellectual radicalism of the revolutionary spirit. At the moment of pronouncing the death sentence of the chemist Lavoisier during the French Revolution, the public accuser Fouquier-Tinville offered this remarkable statement: 'The Republic has no need for scientists.' What happens is that a true revolution considers that it has itself created everything it needs, and we should respect this creative absolutism. In this regard the Cultural Revolution was a true revolution. On the question of science and technology, the fundamental slogan was that what matters is to be 'red', not to be an 'expert'. Or, in the 'moderate' version, which would become the official one: one must be 'red and an expert', but red above all.

However, what made the barbarism of certain revolutionary shock groups considerably worse was the fact that there was never, in the sphere of youth action, a global political space for political affirmation, for the positive creation of the new. The tasks of criticism and of destruction had a self-evidence to them that was lacking in the tasks of invention, and all the more so as the latter remained tied to the relentless struggles going on at the top levels of the state.

The Shanghai Commune

The end of 1966 and the beginning of 1967 represent an important moment of the Cultural Revolution with the massive and decisive appearance on the scene by the factory workers. Shanghai plays a pilot role during this important time.

We should consider the paradox inherent in this appearance on the scene of those who officially constitute the 'leading class' of the Chinese State. This comes about, if I may say so, from the Right. In December 1966, indeed, it is the local bureaucrats, the conservative leadership of the party and the municipality who use a working-class contingent – most notably the trade unionists – against the Maoist movement of the Red Guards. Not unlike the way, I might add, in which in France, in May 1968 and the years to follow, the PCF attempted to use the old guard of the CGT (Conseil Générale du Travail) against the revolutionary students who were allied with young workers. Taking advantage of a changing situation, the bosses of the party and municipality of Shanghai launch the workers on the path of all kinds of sectoral demands of a purely economic nature, and in so doing set them up against any intervention coming from the young revolutionaries in the factories and in the administrations (just as in May 1968, the PCF put up a barricade around the factories with picket-lines drawn from its employees, and everywhere hunted down the 'leftists'). Using violent tactics, these unionized movements become quite sizeable, especially the strikes of the transportation and energy sectors, which seek to foster an atmosphere of chaos so that the party bosses can present themselves as the saviours of order. For all these reasons, the revolutionary minority will be forced to intervene against the bureaucratized strikes and to oppose the 'economism' and the demand for 'material incentives' with an austere campaign in favour of communist work and, above all, for the primacy of global political consciousness over and above particular demands. This will be the backdrop for the great slogan supported in particular by Lin Biao: 'Fight against egoism and criticize revisionism' (we know that 'revisionist' for the Maoists designates abandoning all revolutionary dynamics followed by the USSR, by the communist parties that depend on it, and by a large number of cadres from the Chinese Party).

In the beginning, the Maoist workers' group is rather weak. There is talk of 4,000 workers by the end of 1966. It is true that this group will link itself to the Red Guards and constitute an activist minority. But this does not take away the fact that its field of action in the factories properly speaking is not very large, except in certain machine-tool factories where it will be the glory and serve as an example invoked by revolutionaries for several years to come. In my opinion, it is indeed because the direct action of the workers in the factories comes up against very lively resistance (the bureaucracy has its stronghold there) that the Maoist activists will begin to deploy themselves on the scale of an urban power. With aid from a segment of the cadres who have been loyal to Mao for a long time, as well as from a fraction of the army, they will purge the municipality and the local party committee. Hence what will be called the 'seizure of power ', which under the name of the 'Shanghai Commune' will mark a turning point in the Cultural Revolution.

This power struggle is immediately paradoxical. On the one hand, like the Decision in Sixteen Points above, it finds inspiration in a complete counter-model of the party-state: the coalition of the most disparate organizations that constituted the Paris Commune and whose ineffective anarchy had already been criticized by Marx. On the other hand, this counter-model has no possibility of national development in so far as on the national level the figure of the party remains the only one allowed, even if a number of its traditional elements are in crisis. Throughout the tumultuous episodes of the revolution, Zhou Enlai has remained the guarantee of the unity of the state and of a minimal level of functionality of the administration. As far as we know, he was never disavowed by Mao in this task, which forced him to navigate as closely as possible, including as closely as possible to the right-wing elements (it is he who will put Deng Xiaoping back in the saddle, 'the second highest in power of those who, despite being in the party, are taking the capitalist road', to use the revolutionary phrase, and this from the middle of the 1970s onward). Zhou Enlai, however, made it very clear to the Red Guards that if the 'exchanges of experience' in the entire country were admissible, no revolutionary organization of national importance could be allowed.

Thus the Shanghai Commune, drawn after endless discussions from local student and worker organizations, can attain only a fragile unity. Here again, if the gesture is fundamental (the 'power struggle' by the revolutionaries), its political space is too narrow. As a result, the workers' entry on to the scene marks both and at the same time a spectacular broadening of the revolutionary mass base, a gigantic and sometimes violent test of bureaucratized forms of power, and the short-lived outline of a new articulation between the popular political initiative and the power of the state.

The power seizures

During the first months of 1967, following the lesson of the events in Shanghai where the revolutionaries have overthrown the anti-Maoist municipality, we will see 'seizures of power' proliferate throughout the country. There is a striking material aspect to this movement: the revolutionaries, organized in small splinter and battle groups essentially made up of students and workers, invade all kinds of administrative offices, including those of the municipalities or the party, and, generally in a Dionysian confusion that is not without violence and destruction, they install a new 'power' in them. Frequently, the old guards who resist are 'shown to the masses', which is not a peaceful ceremony. The bureaucrat, or the presumed bureaucrat, carries a dunce's cap and a sign describing his crimes; he must lower his head, and receive some kicks, or worse. These exorcisms are otherwise well-known revolutionary practices. It is a matter of letting the gathering of ordinary people know that the old untouchables, those whose insolence was silently accepted, are themselves from now on given over to public humiliation. After their victory in 1949, the Chinese communists organized ceremonies of this kind everywhere in the countryside, in order morally to criticize the old large landowners, the 'local despots and evil tyrants', making it known to the smallest Chinese peasants, who for centuries counted for nothing, that the world had 'risen on new foundations' and that from now on they were to be the true masters of the country.

However, we should note that, from February onwards, the 'commune' disappears as the term by which to designate the new local powers, only to be replaced by the expression 'revolutionary committee'. This change is by no means insignificant, because 'committee' has always been the name for the provincial or municipal party organs. We will thus see a vast movement to install new 'revolutionary committees' in all the provinces. And it is not at all clear if these reduplicate, or purely and simply replace, the old and dreaded 'party committees'.

In fact, the ambiguity of the name designates the committee as the impure product of the political conflict. For the local revolutionaries, it is a matter of substituting a different political power for the party, after the nearly complete elimination of the old leading cadres. For the conservatives, who defend themselves at every step, it is a matter of putting back in place the local cadres after the mere fiction of a critique. They are encouraged along this path by the repeated declarations from the Central Committee about the good nature of the vast majority of party cadres. For the Maoist national leadership, concentrated in the very small 'Central Committee's Cultural Revolution Group', a dozen persons, it is a matter of defining the stakes for the revolutionary organizations (the 'seizing of power') and of inspiring a lasting fear in their adversaries, all the while preserving the general framework for the exercise of power, which remains in their eyes the party and the party alone.

The formulas that are gradually put forward will privilege unity. There will be talk of a 'triple combination', which means: to unify in the committees one-third of newly arrived revolutionaries, one-third of old cadres having accomplished their self-criticism, and one-third of military personnel. There will be talk of a 'great alliance', meaning that locally the revolutionary organizations are asked to unite among themselves and to stop the confrontations (sometimes armed ones). This unity in fact implies a growing amount of coercion, including with regard to the content of the discussions, as well as an increasingly severe limitation of the right to organize freely around one initiative or conviction or another. But how could it be otherwise, except by letting the situation drift into civil war, and by leaving the outcome in the hands of the repressive apparatus? This debate will occupy almost the entire year of 1967, which in all regards is clearly a decisive year.

The Wuhan incident

This episode from the summer of 1967 is particularly interesting, because it presents all the contradictions of a revolutionary situation at its culminating point, which of course coincides with the moment that announces its involution.

In July 1967, with the support of the conservative military, the counter-revolution of the bureaucrats dominates the enormous industrial city of Wuhan, numbering no less than 500,000 workers. The effective power is held by an army officer, Chen Zaidao. True, there are still two workers' organizations, which confront each other, causing dozens of casualties during the months of May and June. The first organization, with *de facto* support from the army, is called the 'One Million Heroes' and is linked to the local cadres and to the old unionists. The second, a tiny minority, is called 'Steel', and embodies the line of Maoism.

The central leadership, worried about the reactionary control over the city, sends its minister for Public Security to go on site together with a very famous member of the 'Central Committee's

Cultural Revolution Group', named Wang Li. The latter is extremely popular among the Red Guards, because he is known for his outspoken 'leftist' tendencies. He has already claimed that there was a need to purge the army. The envoy carries a message from Zhou Enlai, ordering the support for the 'Steel' rebel group, in conformity with the directive addressed to the cadres in general and to the military in particular: 'Excel in identifying and supporting the proletarian left within the movement.' Let us add in passing that Zhou Enlai has taken upon himself the excruciating task of serving as arbiter between the factions, between the rivalling revolutionary organizations, and that, in order to do so, he receives day and night visits from delegates from the province. He is thus largely responsible for the progress made by the 'great alliance', for the unification of the 'revolutionary committees', as well as for the discernment of what constitutes 'the proletarian left' in these concrete situations, which are becoming more and more confused and violent.

The day of their arrival, the delegates from the Centre hold a big meeting with the rebel organizations in a city stadium. The revolutionary exaltation is reaching its high point.

We can see how all the actors from the active stage of the Revolution are well in place: the conservative cadres and their capacity for mobilization which is not to be underestimated, first in the countryside (the militias coming from the rural suburbs will participate in the repression against the Red Guards and the rebels after the turning point of 1968), but also among the workers, and of course within the administration; the rebel organizations, formed by students and workers, who count on their activism, their courage, and the support of the central Maoist group in order to gain the upper hand, even though they are often in the minority; the army, forced to choose sides; and the central power, trying hard to adjust its politics to the situation at hand.

In some cities, the situation that binds these actors together is extremely violent. In Canton, in particular, no day goes by without

confrontations between the armed shock groups from rival organizations. The army decides locally to wash its hands of the affair.
Hiding behind the pretext that the Decision in Sixteen Points says
that one should not intervene in problems that come up during the
course of the movement, the local military chief merely demands
that before engaging in a street battle, one signs before him a
'declaration of revolutionary brawl'. Only the use of backup troops
is prohibited. The result is that, in Canton as well, there are dozens
of deaths every day throughout the summer.

In this context, the situation is about to turn sour in Wuhan. On
the morning of July 20, the shock troops of 'One Million Heroes',
supported by units from the army, occupy the strategic points and
launch a witch-hunt for the rebels throughout the city. An attack
hits the hotel where the delegates from the central power reside.
One group of military catches hold of Wang Li together with a few
Red Guards and brutally beats them up. The irony of the situation:
now it is the turn of the 'leftist' to be 'shown to the masses', with a
sign around his neck stigmatizing him as 'revisionist', he who had
seen revisionists everywhere! The minister for Public Security is
locked up in his room. The university and the steel foundries,
which had been the epicentre of the rebellious tendency, are taken
by force by armed groups protected with tanks. However, when
the news begins to spread, other units of the army take sides against
the conservatives and their leader, Chen Zaidao. The 'Steel'
organization mounts a counter-attack. The revolutionary committee is put under arrest. A few military manage to free Wang Li,
who will leave the city by running through the woods and waste-
lands.

We are clearly on the verge of civil war. It will take the cold-
bloodedness of the central power, as well as the firm declarations
coming from numerous army units in all the provinces, to change
the course of the events.

What lessons for the future can we draw from this kind of
episode? In a first moment, Wang Li, his face all swollen up, is

welcomed as a hero in Beijing. Jiang Qing, Mao's wife and a great rebel leader, greets him with warm accolades. On July 25, one million people show him their support in the presence of Lin Biao. The ultra-left tendency, which believes in its good fortune, demands a radical purging of the army. This is also the moment when, in August, posters everywhere denounce Zhou Enlai as rightist.

But all this has only the appearance of an instant. True, in Wuhan, support for the rebel groups becomes mandatory, and Chen Zaidao will be replaced. But, two months later, it is Wang Li who will be brutally eliminated from the leaders' group, there will be no significant purging of the army, the importance of Zhou Enlai will only continue to grow, and the return to order will begin to make itself felt against the Red Guards and certain rebellious worker organizations.

What now becomes evident is the fundamental role of the popular army as a pillar in the Chinese party-state. The army has been given a stabilizing role in the Revolution, having been asked to support the rebel left, but there is no expectation or any tolerance for its division, which would set the scene for civil war on a large scale. Those who desire to go to such lengths will all, little by little, be eliminated. And the fact of having made a pact with these elements will cast a stubborn suspicion upon Jiang Qing herself, including, it seems, on the part of Mao.

What happens is that, at this stage of the Cultural Revolution, Mao wishes that unity should prevail among the ranks of the rebels, particularly among the workers, and he begins to fear the enormous damage done by the spirit of factionalism and arrogance among the Red Guards. In September of 1967, after a tour in the province, he launches the slogan 'nothing essential divides the working class', which, for those who know how to read, means first of all that there are violent troubles between the rebellious and conservative organizations, and, secondly, that it is imperative to put an end to these disturbances, to disarm the organizations, and to return the legal monopoly of violence, as well as its political stability, to the repressive apparatus. Starting in July, all the while giving proof of his usual fighter's spirit and rebelliousness (he still says, with visible delight, that 'the whole country is up in riots' and that 'to fight, even violently, is a good thing; once the contradictions appear in plain daylight, it is easier to solve them'), Mao worries about the war of factions, and declares that 'when the revolutionary committees are formed, the petit-bourgeois revolutionaries must be given the correct leadership', he stigmatizes leftism, which 'in fact is a form of rightism', and above all, he shows his impatience with the fact that, since January with the takeover of power in Shanghai 'the bourgeois and petit-bourgeois ideology that was rampant among the intellectuals and the young students has ruined the situation'.

The workers enter the universities

By February 1968, after the movement's involution at the end of the summer of 1967, the conservatives think that their time for revenge has come. Mao and his gang, however, are still on the alert. They launch a campaign stigmatizing the 'February countercurrent' and they renew their support for the revolutionary groups and the construction of new organs of power.

In the meantime, the universities can no longer be kept under the yoke of rivalling splinter groups, given the general logic of a return to order and the perspective of an upcoming party congress charged with drawing up a balance sheet of the revolution (in fact, this congress will be held at the beginning of 1969, confirming the power of Lin Biao and the military). An example must be set, all the while avoiding the crushing pure and simple of the last Red Guards, concentrated in the buildings of the University of Beijing. The adopted solution is totally extraordinary: thousands of organized workers are called upon, without any weapons, to occupy the university, to disarm the factions and directly to ensure their authority. As the leaders' group would say later on: 'The working class must lead in every aspect', and 'the workers will stay for a long time, and even forever, in the universities'. This episode is one of the most astonishing ones of the entire period, because it renders visible the need for the violent and anarchic youth force to recognize a 'mass-based' authority higher than itself, and not only, nor even principally, the institutional authority of the recognized leaders. The moment is all the more surprising and dramatic in that certain students open fire against the workers, there will be deaths, and in the end Mao and all the leaders of the Maoist group will gather with the best-known student leaders, most notably Kuai Dafu, the venerated head of the Red Guards in the university of Beijing, and renowned nationwide. There exists a retranscription of this head-to-head meeting between the stubborn revolutionary youths and the old guard.[22] We can see Mao expressing his profound disappointment caused by the spirit of factionalism among the youth, together with a remnant of political friendship for them, and the will to find a way out. We can clearly see that Mao, by bringing in the workers, wanted to prevent the situation from turning into one of 'military control'. He wanted to protect those who had been his initial allies and had been the bearers of enthusiasm and political innovation. But Mao is also a man of the party-state. He wants its renovation, even a violent one, but not its destruction. In the end he knows full well that by subjugating the last outpost of young rebellious 'leftists', he eliminates the last margin left to anything that is not in line (in 1968) with the recognized leadership of the Cultural Revolution: the line of party reconstruction. He knows it, but he is resigned. Because he holds no alternative hypothesis – nobody does – as to the existence of the state, and because the large majority of people, after two exalted but very trying years, want the state to exist and to make its existence known, if necessary with brute force.

The cult of personality

We know that the cult of Mao has taken truly extraordinary forms during the Cultural Revolution. There were not only the giant statues, the *Little Red Book*, the constant invocation, in any circumstances, of the Chairman, the hymns for the 'Great Helmsman', but there was also a widespread and unprecedented one-sidedness to the references, as though Mao's writings and speeches could suffice for all occasions, even when it is a question of growing tomatoes or deciding on the use (or not) of the piano in symphonic orchestras.[23] It is striking to see that the most violent rebel groups, those who break most decisively with the bureaucratic order, are also those who push this aspect of the situation the furthest. In particular, they are the ones who launched the formula of 'the absolute authority of Mao-Zedong thought', and who declare the need to submit oneself to this thought even without understanding it. Such statements, we must confess, are purely and simply obscurantist.

We should add that, since all the factions and organizations that are at loggerheads with each other claim Mao's thought for their own, the expression, which is capable of designating orientations that are completely contradictory, ends up losing all meaning, except for an overly abundant use of citations whose interpretation is in a state of constant flux.

I would nonetheless like to make a few remarks in passing. On the one hand, this kind of devotion, as well as the conflict of interpretations, is totally commonplace in established religions, and among us, without being considered a pathology. Quite the contrary – the great monotheisms remain sacred cows in this regard. In comparison with the services rendered to our countries by any of the characters, whether fictive or ecclesiastical, in the recent history of these monotheisms, however, Mao has certainly been of an infinitely greater service to his people, whom he liberated simultaneously from the Japanese invasion, from the rampant colonialism of 'Western' powers, from the feudalism in the countryside and from precapitalist looting. On the other hand, the sacralization, even in terms of the biography, of great artists is also a recurring feature of our 'cultural' practice. We give importance to the dry-cleaning bills of this or that poet. If politics is, as I think, a procedure of truth, just as poetry indeed can be, then it is neither more nor less inappropriate to sacralize political creators than it is to sacralize artistic creators. Perhaps less so, all things considered, because political creation is probably rarer, certainly more risky, and it is more immediately addressed to all, and in a singular way to all those – like the Chinese peasants and workers before 1949 – whom the powers-that-be generally consider to be inexistent.

All this by no means frees us from the obligation to illuminate the peculiar phenomenon of the political cult, which is an invariant feature of communist states and parties, brought to the point of paroxysm in the Cultural Revolution.

From a general point of view, the 'cult of personality' is tied to the thesis according to which the party, as representative of the working class, is the hegemonic source of politics, the mandatory guardian of the correct line. As was said in the thirties, 'the Party is always right'. The problem is that nothing can guarantee such a representation, nor such a hyperbolic certainty as to the source of rationality. By way of a substitute for such a guarantee, it thus becomes crucial for there to be a *representation of the representation*, one that would be a singularity, legitimated precisely by its singularity alone. Finally, one person, a single body, comes to stand for this superior guarantee, in the classical aesthetic form of genius. It is also curious, by the way, to see that, trained as we are in the theory of genius in the realm of art, we should take such strong offence to it when it emerges in the order of politics. For the communist parties, between the twenties and sixties, personal genius is only the incarnation, the fixed point, of the doubtful representative capacity of the party; it is easier to believe in the rectitude and the intellectual force of a distant and solitary man than in the truth and purity of an apparatus whose local petty chiefs are well known.

In China, the question is even more complicated. Indeed, during the Cultural Revolution, Mao incarnates not so much the party's representative capacity so much as that which discerns and struggles against the threatening 'revisionism' within the party itself. He is the one who says, or lets it be said in his name, that the bourgeoisie is politically active within the Communist Party. He is also the one who encourages the rebels, who spreads the slogan 'it is right to revolt', and encourages troubles, at the very moment when he is being canonized as the party's chairman. In this regard, there are moments when for the revolutionary masses he is less the guarantee of the really existing party than the incarnation, all by himself, of a proletarian party that is still to come. He is somewhat like a revenge of singularity upon representation.

Ultimately, we should maintain that 'Mao' is a name that is intrinsically contradictory in the field of revolutionary politics. On the one hand, it is the supreme name of the party-state, its undeniable chairman, he who, as military leader and founder of the regime, holds the historical legitimacy of the Communist Party. On the other hand, 'Mao' is the name of that which, in the party, cannot be reduced to the state's bureaucracy. This is obviously the case in terms of the calls to revolt sent out to youth and the workers. But it is also true within the structure of legitimacy of the party itself. Indeed, it is often by way of decisions that are temporarily minoritarian, or even dissident, that Mao has ensured the continuation of this utterly unique political experience of the Chinese Communists between 1920 and the moment of victory in the forties (suspicion with regard to the Soviet counsellors, abandonment of the model of insurrection, 'surrounding of the cities by countryside', absolute priority to the mass line, etc.). In all aspects, 'Mao' is the name of a paradox: the rebel in power, the dialectician put to the test by the continuing needs of 'development', the emblem of the party-state in search of its overcoming, the military chief preaching disobedience to the authorities . . .[24] This is what has given to his 'cult' a frenetic appearance, because subjectively he accumulated the accord given to the stately pomp of the Stalinist type, together with the enthusiasm of the entire revolutionary youth for the old rebel who cannot be satisfied with the existing state of affairs, and who wants to move on in the march to real communism. 'Mao' was the name for the 'construction of socialism', but also for its destruction.

In the end, the Cultural Revolution, even in its very impasse, bears witness to the impossibility truly and globally to free politics from the framework of the party-state that imprisons it. It marks an irreplaceable experience of saturation, because a violent will to find a new political path, to relaunch the revolution, and to find new forms of the workers' struggle under the formal conditions of socialism ended up in failure when confronted with the necessary maintenance, for reasons of public order and the refusal of civil war, of the general frame of the party-state.

We know today that all emancipatory politics must put an end to the model of the party, or of multiple parties, in order to affirm a politics 'without party', and yet at the same time without lapsing into the figure of anarchism, which has never been anything else than the vain critique, or the double, or the shadow, of the communist parties, just as the black flag is only the double or the shadow of the red flag.

However, our debt toward the Cultural Revolution remains enormous. Because, tied to this grandiose and courageous saturation of the motif of the party, as the contemporary of what clearly appears today as the last revolution that was still attached to the motif of classes and of the class struggle, our Maoism will have been the experience and the name of a capital transition. And without this transition, whenever there isn't anybody loyal to it, there is nothing.

A Brief Chronology of the Cultural Revolution

Translated by Bruno Bosteels

1. Recent prehistory
(from 'One Hundred Flowers' to 'the Black Gang')

(a) Campaign 'Let a hundred flowers blossom' (1956). In June 1957, the campaign becomes a violent denunciation and persecution of 'rightist intellectuals', often qualified later on as 'evil geniuses'. The launching of the 'Great Leap Forward' in May 1958, and in August 1958 of the 'popular communes'. In August 1959, purging of Peng Dehuai (Defence Minister), who criticizes the movement of collectivization. Lin Biao replaces him.

(b) Starting in 1961, the recognition of a disastrous outcome of economic voluntarism. The Central Committee decides to 're-adjust' the objectives. Liu Shaoqi replaces Mao Zedong as president of the Republic. Between 1962 and 1966, fifteen million copies are sold in China of Liu's works, against six million of Mao's. Publication of the historical piece by Wu Han (deputy mayor of Peking), *The Purging of Hai Rui* (an indirect criticism of this event). In September 1965, at a conference of the Politburo, Mao demands but does not obtain the condemnation of Wu Han. He retires to Shanghai.

2. The opening (from the article by
Yao Wenyuan to the Decision in Sixteen Points)

(a) In collaboration with Jiang Qing, Mao's wife, Yao Wenyuan publishes a violent article in Shanghai against Wu Han. It is aimed at the mayor of Beijing, Peng Zhen, held to be the chief of the 'black gang'. In January and February 1966, a first 'Group of the Central Committee for the Cultural Revolution' is formed to judge the case, paradoxically put under the authority of Peng Zhen. This group (called 'the Group of Five') disseminates the 'February Theses', which are quite insignificant, and which tend to limit criticism.

(b) Meanwhile another group is constituted in Shanghai, under the aegis of Lin Biao and Jiang Qing, which holds a 'discussion on the literary and artistic activities in the army'. The texts are transmitted to the Military Commission of the Central Committee (organ of the highest importance). The division of the party seems consummated.

(c) In May 1966, 'enlarged' meeting of the Politburo. Nomination of a new 'Central Committee's Cultural Revolution Group', and vehement condemnation of the group of Peng Zhen in a fundamental document for all subsequent events, known as the 'May 16 Circular'. It is necessary, the text says, 'to criticize the representatives of the bourgeoisie infiltrated in the party, the government, the army and the cultural milieu'. By May 25, seven students of Beida University attack the president of the university in a large-character poster. True beginning of the student mobilization.

(d) Mao leaves Beijing. The authorities send 'work groups' to the universities in order to control the movement. Between the end of May and the end of July, the so-called 'fifty days' period, in which the brutal containment by these 'work groups' is predominant.

(e) On July 18 Mao returns to Beijing. Abolition of the work groups. From August 1 until August 12, a session of the 'enlarged' Central Committee is held. It is not according to the rules. Lin Biao uses the army to prohibit the presence of regular members and to allow the presence of revolutionaries who come from the student world. The Maoist line in these conditions obtains a brief majority. Mao publicly supports the Beida University poster. He appears before the crowd on July 9. Political charter of the revolution: the 'Decision in Sixteen Points'. It reads in particular: 'In the great Proletarian Cultural Revolution, the only method is for the masses to liberate themselves, and any method of doing things in their stead must not be used.' That is to say, there will be no repression of the initiatives coming from the student groups.

3. The 'Red Guards' period

(a) By August 20, arriving from high-school and university institutions, activist groups of 'Red Guards' spread out in the city, in order to 'destroy completely the old thought, culture, customs and habits'. In particular, a very harsh persecution of intellectuals and professors, once more considered, according to Mao himself, as 'evil geniuses'. Succession of immense gatherings of Red Guards in Beijing, following in particular the right given to them to circulate freely on the trains, for the sake of 'large exchanges of experience'. Criticism of Liu Shaoqi and Deng Xiaoping in posters, tracts, cartoons, small newspapers . . .

(b) Starting in November, first political incidents linked to the intervention of the Red Guards in factories. The anti-Maoists use the official unions and certain peasant militias against the revolutionaries, who themselves begin to be divided into splinter groups ('factionalism'). Violence here and there.

4. The entry of the workers and the 'power struggles'

(a) The authorities in place in Shanghai provoke disturbances by encouraging all kinds of 'economist' demands in the workers' milieux. Particularly acute problem: the salary of temporary peasant workers, and the question of bonuses. Transportation strike, and hunting-down of student groups. In January 1967, a set of Red Guards and of 'rebel revolutionaries' have formed 'factory committees' by occupying the administrative offices, the means of communication, etc. They overthrow the party committee, and decide to form the 'Shanghai Commune'. Endless negotiations among the groups. Domination of the workers' groups and still a very limited presence of the old cadres of the army and State.

(b) The 'power struggles' become generalized in the entire country, starting in February 1967. Great disorder in the state and the economy. The very unequal politicization explains why the putting into place of new organs of power is anarchic and precarious. Tendency to purge and 'judge' all the old cadres, or conversely, manipulation by the cadres of 'revolutionary' groups that are more or less fake. Settling of accounts mixed in with revolutionary zeal.

(c) The central authority is then concentrated in the Central Committee's Cultural Revolution Group, the State Council, led by Zhou Enlai, and finally the Military Commission, controlled by Lin Biao. It is this authority that decides on a formula for the new powers, called the 'triple combination': one-third of representatives from the 'revolutionary masses', one-third of party cadres who have withstood the test or 'corrected' themselves, and one-third of military personnel. The revolutionary 'mass' organization must first unite among them (the 'great alliance'). The name of the new organ is 'the Revolutionary Three-in-One Combination Committee'. The first provincial committee of this kind is formed on February 13 (in the province of Kweichow).

5. Disturbances, violence and splits of all kinds

(a) At the same time that the critique of Liu Shaoqi begins in the official press (still without mentioning his name), disorder spreads everywhere. Numerous incidents of violence, including armed ones, oppose either the Maoists to the conservatives, the security and armed forces alternately to the former and to the latter, or else, finally, the Maoist groups among themselves. The mass organizations split up very frequently. The revolutionary leadership also divides itself. One tendency aims to unify the revolutionary organizations as quickly as possible, and everywhere to put into place committees that will give due space to the old cadres. In fact, this tendency quickly seeks to reconstruct the party. Zhou Enlai, who, it is true, is in charge of the maintenance of the elementary functions of the state, is the most active figure in this direction. Another tendency wants to eliminate a very large number of cadres, and to expand the purge to the administration, including the army. Its best-known representatives are Wang Li and Qi Benyu.

(b) In July, the Wuhan incident puts the region and, finally, the whole country, in a climate of civil war. The army in this city openly protects the traditional cadres and the workers' organizations that are tied to them. Wang Li, sent on an envoy by the central authority, which seeks to support the 'rebels', is locked up and beaten. It is necessary for external military forces to intervene. The unity of the army is thus threatened.

(c) Appearance of the posters against Zhou Enlai. During all of August, moments of anarchic violence, particularly in Canton. Weapon depots are sacked. Dozens of people die every day. The British Embassy is set on fire in Beijing.

6. The beginning of the return to order and the end of the revolution properly speaking

(a) In September 1967, Mao, after a tour in the province, decides in favour of the 'reconstructive' line. Fundamentally, he supports Zhou Enlai and gives the army an extended role (where the factions do not manage to reach an agreement, there will be 'military control'). The extreme-left group (Wang Li) is eliminated from the central organs of power. 'Study sessions of Mao Zedong Thought' are organized for everyone, often under the aegis of the military. Slogans: 'Support the left, and not the factions', based on a statement included in Mao's report: 'Nothing essential divides the working class.'

(b) In many places, this rectification is practised by way of a violent repression of the Red Guards, and even of the rebel workers, and as an occasion for political revenge (this is the 'February Counter-Current'). As a result, Mao calls once again for action by the end of March 1968: it is necessary to defend the revolutionary committees and to fear neither disturbances nor factionalism.

(c) However, this is the last 'mass' brawl. The central authority decides to put an end to the last bastions of the student revolt, which are abandoned to the often bloody wars among splinter groups, all the while avoiding, at least in Beijing, direct military control. Detachments of workers are sent into the universities. The central group of the Cultural Revolution receives the most famous 'leftist' students, who have physically resisted the entry of these workers. It turns out to be a dialogue of the deaf (the most notorious 'rebel' student, Kuai Dafu, will be arrested).

(d) The directive 'the working class must be in command in everything' seals the end of the Red Guards and of the revolutionary rebels, and in the name of 'struggle, criticism, reform', opens a phase devoted to the reconstruction of the party. A huge number of young revolutionaries is sent to the countryside, or to faraway camps.

7. Marking the aftermath

(a) The Ninth Congress of the Party, in April 1969, ratifies an authoritarian return to order, largely structured by the army (45 per cent of the members of the Central Committee) under the direction of Lin Biao.

(b) This militarist period, which is terribly oppressive, leads to new violent confrontations in the midst of the party. Lin Biao is eliminated (probably assassinated) in 1971.

(c) Until Mao's death, a long and complex period, marked by the endless conflict between Deng Xiaoping and many old cadres who have returned to business under the protection of Zhou Enlai, on one hand, and, on the other, the 'Gang of Four', which embodies the memory of the Cultural Revolution (Yao Wenyuan, Zhang Chunqiao, Jiang King and Wang Hongwen).

(d) Right after the death of Mao, in 1976, the four are arrested. Deng takes over power for a long period, which is indeed largely defined by the implantation of capitalist methods (during the Cultural Revolution, he was called 'the second highest among the officials who, despite being of the party, have taken the capitalist road'), with the maintenance of the party-state.

Notes to Part Three

1 Conference paper delivered by Alain Badiou at the Maison des écrivains in Paris in January 2003. This was the third in the series of Rouge-Gorge conferences. The second half of the essay, beginning with the section on the ontology of the site, also comprises a small section of *Logiques des mondes*, the much-awaited follow-up to Badiou's major work *L'être et l'événement* (*Being and Event*, originally published in 1988 and in English translation in 2005). The principal change in perspective between these two works, really the only knowledge needed to follow the argument here, consists in the move from ontology, as the science of being, to logic, redefined as the science of appearing, or of being-there. Thus, whereas in *L'être et l'événement* Badiou defines being as a multiple of multiples, so that everything that is must be seen as a pure multiple, in *Logiques des mondes* he makes the cohesion of appearing, or the 'there' of a world, depend on what he calls its transcendental, that is, the structure of order that measures the identities and differences in this world by assigning varying degrees of greater or lesser intensity to the existence of its objects. The following extract studies the possibility of real change within a given regime of appearing, with specific references to a well-known sequence in revolutionary politics, namely, the Paris Commune of 1871. The result is a complete rearticulation of the conditions in which a given space can become the site of a radically transformative event.

The programmatic blurb for this series of conferences, included at the back of each booklet, reads as follows: 'This conference cycle, proposed by the Political Organization, is meant to clarify the links between history and politics at the moment when a new century begins. Here, in light of this question, a variety of fundamental episodes in the historicity of politics will be examined. For example, the Russian Revolution, the Resistance, the Cultural Revolution, May 1968 . . . In each case it will be a matter of doing justice to the singularity of the events, all the while retaining, in thought, whatever light they shed on politics, on the history of its forms, its creations, and thus on what it is that we have to do and think, now.' *Translator's note.*

2 The French verb *apparaître* (to appear) is usually better translated as a noun (appearing, appearance). The phrase 'dans l'apparaître' I have most often rendered as 'in the domain of appearing'.

3 The battle of Sedan, September 1870, ended when Napoleon III capitulated to the Prussians, who then proceeded to march on Paris. *Translator's note.*

4 The French adjective 'legitimist' derives from the Legitimists, who were French adherents to the 'legitimate' Bourbon dynasty overthrown in 1830. *Translator's note.*

5 A tradition of dance-halls created under Louis XIV, *bals de barrière* were located on the outskirts of town and frequented by the lower classes. *Translator's note.*

6 Bertolt Brecht, *The Days of the Commune*, trans. by Clive Barker and Arno Reinfrank, Eyre Methuen, 1978.

7 *Long Live the Victory of the Dictatorship of the Proletariat! In Commemoration of the Centenary of the Paris Commune*, Foreign Language Press, 1971.

8 'Tous Ensemble!' was a directive of the 1995 winter strikes in France that brought two million workers and their supporters to the streets. They were sparked, among other things, by plans by the Juppé government to attack the national health system and introduce a shaky pension scheme. *Translator's note.*

9 The *sans-papiers* (undocumented workers) movement is associated with the Saint-Bernard church, which was occupied by hundreds of African workers in 1996 protesting the persecutory effects of French government laws. *Translator's note.*

10 Léon Michel Gambetta (1838–82) was a French statesman and prime minister (1881–82). A parliamentary opponent of Napoleon III, he was Minister of the Interior in the Government of National Defence, and helped form the Third Republic. *Translator's note.*

11 The Assembly of 'Rurals' was the nickname of the National Assembly of 1871, so called because it comprised mainly reactionary monarchists – provincial landlords, officials, rentiers and traders – elected in rural districts. The were about 430 monarchists among the Assembly's 630 deputies. *Translator's note.*

12 Cf. Julian Gracq, *Lettrines: Œuvres complètes*. Gallimard, 1989, pp. 205–206; and Alain Badiou, *Théorie du sujet*, Seuil, 1982, pp. 14–15.

13 Karl Marx, *Civil War in France*, First Draft, Archives of Marx and Engels, 1934, p. 173. Available online at www.marx2mac.com/M&E/CWFdrf71.html#s0

14 Proper-Olivier Lissagaray, 'The Eighteenth of March', *History of the*

Commune of 1871, trans. Eleanor Marx Aveling, International Publishing, 1898, pp. 78–87. Trans. of 'Le 18 mars', *Histoire de la commune de 1871*, La Découverte, 2000, pp. 111–119.

15 From the second conference in the Rouge Gorge series, delivered by Alain Badiou in February 2002 at the Maison des écrivains in Paris. *Translator's note.*

16 Sylvain Lazarus, *Anthropologie du nom*, Seuil, 1996, p. 37.

17 On the party-state or parties-state as central figures of politics in the twentieth century, see the previous conference in the series of Rouge Gorge, *Les trois régimes du siècle*, presented by Sylvain Lazarus (2001).

18 A book that gives an idea of the general style of the official and 'critical' versions (for once, these strangely agree) of the Cultural Revolution is that by Simon Leys [i.e. Pierre Ryckmans], *The Chairman's New Clothes: Mao and the Cultural Revolution*, trans. Carol Appleyard and Patrick Goode, Schocken Books, 1981.

19 With regard to these episodes, and more generally the principal facts of the period, see the chronology included at the end of this chapter.

20 Badiou, as is often the case, does not give textual references here, but elsewhere in his work, when dealing with the Cultural Revolution, he tends to quote from the French translations included in another 'little red book' that also seems to be his source here: *La Grande Révolution Culturelle Prolétarienne: Recueil de documents importants*, Beijing: Editions en langues étrangères, 1970. In English, the corresponding line of the 'Sixteen Points' sounds even more metaphysical: 'The great Proletarian Cultural Revolution now unfolding is a great revolution that touches people to their very souls', in *The Chinese Cultural Revolution*, ed. K. H. Fan, Monthly Review Press, 1968, p. 162. All subsequent quotations in the text are from this edition. *Translator's note.*

21 Until September 1967, the leading Maoist group comprises a dozen persons: Mao, Lin Biao, Chen Boda, Jiang Qing, Yao Wenyuan, Zhou Enlai, Kang Sheng, Zhang Chunqiao, Wang Li, Guan Feng, Lin Jie, Qi Benyu. Chen Yi, an old centre-right veteran and courageous humorist, is said to have asked: 'Is that it, the great Chinese Communist Party? Twelve persons?' We could nonetheless note that the leading group of the Committee of Public Safety between 1792 and 1794 was far more restricted. Revolutions combine gigantic mass movements with an often very restricted political leadership.

22 The account has been translated and amply commented upon (in Italian) by Sandro Russo, without a doubt the most competent and loyal analyst today of everything to do with the Cultural Revolution.

23 The examples are real, and have given rise to articles translated into French in the magazine *Pekin Informations*. There we learn how the

Maoist dialectic allows one to grow tomatoes, or how to find the right line in terms of the use of the piano in symphonic music in China. Besides, these texts are extremely interesting, and even convincing, not because of their explicit content, but in terms of what it means to attempt to create *another thinking* entirely.

24 On Mao as paradox, see the wonderful book by Henry Bauchau, *Essai sur la vie de Mao Tsé-toung*, Flammarion, 1982.

Index